SOTHIS PRESS

Sothis Press aims to completely reimagine the public domain book with an emphasis on universal access to captivatingly designed print editions. We believe that technology will enable every single book ever published to be perpetually accessible in beautiful print form. Sothis is beauty in ubiquity.

www.sothis.press
1 Waterhouse Square, London, EC1N 2ST

Notes on the Settlement and Indian Wars, 1763-1783

Society and Manners of the Western Settlers

Joseph Doddridge

SOTHIS PRESS

ISBN 978-1-0368-4738-8

Notes on the Settlement and Indian Wars of the Western Parts of Virginia and Pennsylvania, From 1763 to 1783, Inclusive
is in the public domain.

This edition is published by
Sothis Press © 2023. The company
is registered in England and Wales.
The Company Number is 14900389.

Notes on the Settlement and Indian Wars

Of the Western Parts of Virginia and Pennsylvania from 1763 to 1783, inclusive, together with a Review of the State of Society and Manners of the First Settlers of the Western Country.

By JOSEPH DODDRIDGE

With a Memoir of the Author by
His Daughter
NARCISSA DODDRIDGE.

Republished with the addition of new and valuable material.

By JOHN S. RITENOUR and WM. T. LINDSEY.

PITTSBURGH, PA.
1912

THE NEW WERNER COMPANY, AKRON, OHIO

TABLE OF CONTENTS

APPENDIX

PREFACE.

This is the third printing of "Doddridge's Notes." The first was in 1824, by Mr. Doddridge himself, at the office of the Wellsburg, Va., Gazette. It consisted exclusively of the "Notes." Hon. S. W. Pennypacker, former governor of Pennsylvania, well-known as a lover of old books, says, in a few lines inscribed on the margin of a first copy which he owned, that Dr. Doddridge "folded the paper on which it was printed and tanned the leather with which it was bound."

The second edition, edited by Alfred Williams, of Circleville, O., was printed at Albany, N. Y., in 1876, by Joel Munsell. Miss Narcissa Doddridge had designed personally undertaking this enterprise herself, but death prevented. Her family then took it up, and at their request it was completed under the supervision of Mr. Williams.

Miss Doddridge's memoir of her father embodies much important historical information respecting the foundation of the Episcopal church in Western Virginia and Ohio. The liberty has been exercised of somewhat abridging its unessential fullness for this edition, but it has not been thus deprived in any degree of either interest or value. The elisions have been confined to prolixities in the correspondence of Dr. Doddridge and his friends. The text of Miss Doddridge is practically untouched.

The reminiscences of Rev. Thomas Scott in the second edition are omitted from this edition because all the information they contain has been written into the memoir by Miss Doddridge.

In addition to the memoir, the 1876 edition contained an appendix comprising a number of sketches bearing on the pioneer life of this region in the closing years of the eighteenth century. These are all preserved in the present publication, excepting three which are of comparative unimportance. Fresh contributions, however, are numerous valuable and enlightening footnotes by the late James Simpson, of Cross Creek, Washington county, and others; a list of the frontier forts of Washington county; a compilation reciting the story of the origin of Logan's "Lament," and detailing concisely the later unhappy career and tragic death of that celebrated Indian; a sketch of the short life and early death of Michael Cresap, and the final enforced withdrawal of Simon Girty, the renegade, from American soil, to die in his old age in poverty, intemperance and obscurity, on the Canadian farm near Detroit with which he had been rewarded by British gratitude for his countless bloody crimes against the white settlers of the western frontier; an account of the noted frontiersman, Capt. Samuel Teter, and his descendants, together with a brief description of the notable brick mansion raised on the site of Fort Teter by Isaac Manchester a hundred years ago on the skirts of civilization, and still preserved near West Middletown in as good condition as when built.

There is also a pertinent statistical table from E. Dana Durand, Director of the Census, showing the estimated Indian population of the United States at various periods from 1789 to 1910, inclusive, and how this population is now distributed among the several states. The elegy by Dr. Doddridge in the appendix is preserved merely as an example of early western frontier poetry.

The footnotes in this 1912 edition are all original with it excepting the eleven which Dr. Doddridge himself prepared to accompany the first printing. These eleven are indicated with a bracketed capital D (D). The second edition contained no other footnotes.

J. S. R. W. T. L.

EARLY SETTLEMENT AND INDIAN WARS.

TO THE READER.

After considerable delay I have fulfilled my engagement to the public with respect to the history of the settlement and wars of the western parts of Virginia and Pennsylvania. The causes of the delay of the work were unavoidable, and a recital of them can be of no service.

Whether the Notes are well executed, or otherwise, must be left to the candid decision of my country, and I am well aware the decision will speedily be made. It will be the opinion of some readers that I have bestowed too great a portion of the book on the primitive aspect of the country, and the history of the state of society and manners of its early inhabitants. My reason for having bestowed so much attention on these subjects is this: these matters of our early history, which, if faithfully preserved, will hereafter be highly interesting, are fast hastening into oblivion, and in a few more years would be totally lost. On the contrary, the events of the war are much longer remembered.

Had we a similar history of the early state of any of the European countries, to that which is here presented to the world, of our own, with how much interest would this record be read by all classes of people. For instance, had we the memorials of the people who erected those rude monuments which are scattered over our country, the record would give a classic character to every section of the new world; but in every region of the world, except our own, the commencement of the period of their history was long posterior to that of their settlement; their early history is therefore buried in impenetrable oblivion, and its place is occupied by immense regions of fable and conjecture.

To the two first parts of this history, it is presumed, no great additions will hereafter be necessary. Future generations will be competent to mark any changes which may take place in the physical condition, and in the scientific and moral state of our country, from the data here given, and unquestionably the changes which are to take place in all those departments, in the progress of time, will be great indeed.

The history of our Indian wars is, in every respect, quite imperfect. The very limited range of the war, which I had in view, in this work, is not fully executed. The want of health, and in some instances the want of proper information, have prevented the relation of several events which took place in this section of the country in the course of our conflicts with the sons of the forest, and which, although of minor importance in their final results, would nevertheless form an interesting portion of the history of those conflicts.

The various attacks on Wheeling fort, and the fatal ambuscade near Grave creek, have been omitted for want of a correct account of those occurrences. These omissions are the less to be regretted as Noah Zane, Esq., has professed a determination to give the public the biography of his father, Col. Ebenezer Zane, the first proprietor and defender of the important station at Wheeling. This work will be no more than a measure of justice to the memory of a man who held such an important and perilous station as that which fell to the lot of Col. Zane, and who filled that station with so much honor to himself and advantage to our infant country, as he did. This biography will contain an accurate account of all the attacks on Wheeling, as well as all other events of the war which took place in its immediate neighborhood.

A well written history of the whole of our wars with the Indians in the western regions would certainly be a valuable acquisition to our literature. It would, however, be a work of time and considerable labor, as its materials are scattered over a large tract of country, and in point of time extend through half a century.

The whole amount of our present memorials of this widely extended warfare consists merely of detached narrations, and these are for the most part but badly written. In many instances they are destitute of historical precision with regard to the order of time, and the succession of facts, so that they are read only as anecdotes, and of course with but little advantage to science.

This work is desirable, on many accounts. The bravery, victories and sufferings of our forefathers, ought to be correctly and indelibly recorded. Those who have lived and died for posterity ought to be rewarded with imperishable fame in the grateful remembrance of their descendants. The monuments conferred on moral worth, by the pen of the historian, are more durable than those erected by the chisel of the sculptor.

A measure of justice is certainly due to our barbarian enemies themselves. For whatever of system, prudent foresight and arrangement, they observed in their wars with us, they ought to have full credit. For the full amount of all the patriotic motives by which these unfortunate people were actuated in their bloody conflicts, they deserve our sincerest commiseration.

The wars of these people are not to be regarded as wholly the offspring of a savage thirst for blood. They fought for their native country. They engaged in the terrible war of 1763 with a view to recover from the possession of the white people the whole of the western settlements. Their continuance of the war, after the conclusion of our revolutionary contest, had for its object the preservation of as much of their country as they then had in possession. On the part of the most intelligent of the Indian chiefs, they fought from a motive of revenge and with a valor inspired by desperation. They foresaw the loss of their country and the downfall of their people, and therefore resolved on vengeance for the past, and the future wrongs to be inflicted on them.

There is yet another reason for the work under consideration. The present generation are witnesses of both the savage and civilized state of mankind. Both extremes are under our inspection. To future generations the former will exist only in history. The Indian nations are now a subjugated people, and every feature of their former state of society must soon pass away. They will exist only through the medium of their admixtures with the white people. Such has been the fate of many nations. Where are now the Assyrians, Chaldeans and Romans? They no longer exist; and yet the English, French and Italians are, in part, descendants of the ancient Romans. Such will be the fate of the aborigines of our country. They will perish, or lose their national character and existence by admixtures with their conquerors. To posterity therefore their history will be highly acceptable. Indeed it may be said of all history, that like good wine it grows better by age.

In the execution of this work I have aimed at truth and nothing but truth. Impartiality imposes no restraint on my pen; for independently of the circumstance that the contents of this history, in general, interfere with no party, I am incumbered with but few individual obligations of gratitude. To political party, religious and other communities, I owe no obligations of any kind for any benefits conferred on me, so that I have felt fully at liberty to speak the truth concerning all classes of our people, and I trust I have done so.

If any material facts in the historical parts of this work have been omitted, the omission has happened from want of information. Incorrect statements, if there be any, have taken place in consequence of improper information. In either case I am not blamable, as I have done the best my circumstances allowed in collecting materials for the work.

Should my humble attempts at writing the history of my country meet with good acceptance among my fellow citizens I shall continue to collect, from all quarters, the materials for the work herein recommended, as a desideratum in the literature of our country.

As aids in this work I earnestly invite communication from all those gentlemen who possess a knowledge of occurrences which took place during our Indian war, and not narrated in this work. I am particularly anxious to obtain the history of the settlement of the Dunkards, on Dunkard creek, and the Dunkard bottom of Cheat river.

JOSEPH DODDRIDGE.

Wellsburg, June 17, 1824.

PREFACE TO FIRST EDITION.

For some years past I have had it in view to write the Notes on the Settlement and Indian Wars of the western parts of Virginia and Pennsylvania, which are now presented to the public. At times I was deterred from commencing the work by an apprehension of my inability to execute a task of so much labor and difficulty: a labor, not of compilation, as most histories are, but consisting mainly of original composition from memory of events which took place when I was quite young.

Encouraged, however, by the often repeated solicitations of those whose friendship I esteem, and whose good opinion I respect, I concluded that, as with my forefathers I had toiled amongst the pioneers of our country in "turning the wilderness into fruitful fields," I would venture to act in the same character, as an historian of that part of the western country with which I am best acquainted, and whose early history has never yet, to any extent, been committed to record, in hopes that having saved the principal materials of this history from oblivion, some abler hand may hereafter improve upon the work, by giving it any enlargement, different arrangement, or embellishment of style, which it may be thought to require.

Many considerations present themselves to the generous and enlightened mind of the native of the west, to induce him to regard a work of this kind as a sacred duty to his country and his ancestors, on the part of him who undertakes to execute it, rather than a trial of literary skill, a toil for literary fame, or a means of procuring gain.

Something is certainly due to the memory of our brave forefathers, who, with but little aid from the colonial governments before the revolutionary war, and with still less assistance from the confederation, after the declaration of independence, subdued the forest by their persevering labor, and defended their infant country by their voluntary and unrequited military service against the murderous warfare of their savage enemies.

The extensive catacombs of ancient Greece and Palestine, the pyramids of Egypt, and even the rude sepulchral monuments of our own country, serve to show the sacred regard of generations of remote antiquity for the remains of the illustrious dead. This pious regard for the ashes of ancestors is not without its useful influence on the morals and piety of their descendants. The lettered stone and sculptured monument contain the most impressive lessons of biography, because the mournful remains of the subjects of those lessons are so near at hand, when they are presented to us on the sepulchres where their ashes repose.

Is the memory of our forefathers unworthy of historic or sepulchral commemoration? No people on earth, in similar circumstances, ever acted more nobly or more bravely than they did. No people of any country, or age, ever made greater sacrifices for the benefit of posterity than those which were made by the first settlers of the western regions. What people ever left such noble legacies to posterity as those transmitted by our forefathers to their descendants? A wilderness changed into a fruitful country, and a government the best on earth. They have borne the burden and heat of the day of trial. They have removed every obstacle from our path, and left every laudable object of ambition within our reach.

Where shall we now find the remains of the valiant pioneers of our country, so deserving the grateful remembrance of their descendants? Alas! many of them, for want of public burying grounds, were buried on their own farms, which their labor had ravished from the desert. The land has passed to other hands, and the fragile wooden enclosures which once surrounded their graves have fallen to decay, and never to be replaced. The swells which once designated the precise spot of their interment have sunk to the common level of the earth. In many instances the earthy covering of their narrow houses will, if they have not already, be violated with the plow-share, and the grain growing over them will fill the reaper's sickle, or the grass the mower's scythe. Ungrateful descendants of a brave and worthy people to whom you owe your existence, your country and your liberty, is it thus you treat with utter neglect the poor remains of your ancestors?

In how many instances has the memory of far less moral worth than the amount possessed by many of the fathers of our western country, occupied the chisel of the sculptor, the song of the poet, and the pen of the historian; while the gloomy shade of impenetrable oblivion is rapidly settling over the whole history, as well as the remains, of the fathers of our country.

Should any one say "no matter what becomes of the names, or remains of these people," it is answered, if such be your insensibility to the calls of duty, with regard to the memory of your ancestors, it is not likely that your name will, or ought to, live beyond the grave. You may die rich; but wealth will be your all. Those worthy deeds which spring from the better, the generous feelings of our nature, can never be yours; but must the well earned fame of the benefactors of our country perish as quickly as a prodigal offspring may dissipate your ill gotten estates? No! This would be an act of injustice to the world. They lived, toiled and suffered for others; you, on the contrary, live for yourself alone. Their example ought to live, because it is worthy of imitation; yours, on the contrary, as an example of sordid avarice, ought to perish forever.

The history of nation origin has been held sacred among all enlightened nations, and indeed has often been pursued beyond the period of the commencement of history far into the regions of fable. Among the Greeks the founders of their nation and the inventors of useful arts were ranked among the gods, and honored with anniversary rites of a divine character. The Romans, whose origin was more recent and better known, were not slow in recording the illustrious deeds of the founders of their empire, and bestowing anniversary honors upon their memory. The benefits of the histories of those illustrious nations were not confined to themselves alone. They gave light to the world. Had they never existed what an immense deduction would have been made from the literary world. The fabulous era would have been drawn nearer to us by at least two thousand years.

National history is all important to national patriotism, as it places before us the best examples of our forefathers. We see the wisdom of their councils, their perseverance in action, their sufferings, their bravery in war, and the great and useful results of their united wisdom and labors. We see in succession every act of the great drama which led us from infancy to maturity, from war to peace, and from poverty to wealth, and in proportion as we are interested in the results of this drama we value the examples which it furnishes. Even the faults which it exhibits are not without their use.

History gives a classic character to the places to which it relates, and confers upon them a romantic value as scenes of national achievements. What would be the value of the famous city of Jerusalem were it not for the sacred history of the place? It is a place of no local importance in any respect whatever. Palestine itself, so famous in history, is but a small tract of country, and for the most part poor and hilly. The classic character of Greece and Rome has given more or less importance to almost every mountain, hill and valley, lake and island, which they contain, on account of their having been the places of some great achievements, or of their having given birth to illustrious personages. Classic scenes, as well as classic monuments and persons, constitute an impressive part of national history, and they contribute much to the patriotism of the nation to which they belong.

If the Greeks should succeed in their present contest with the Turks, their liberty will be justly attributable, in a great degree, to the potent efficacy of the history of their ancestors. This history may produce another Leonidas, Epaminondas, Lycurgus, Sophocles, Timon and Demosthenes, to rival the mighty deeds of their forefathers, and establish a second time the independence of their native country.

The history of our own country ought to furnish the first lessons of reading for our children, but unfortunately most of them are too large for school books. The selections in common use for schools are mostly foreign productions. They are good in themselves; but better adapted to mature age than youth, because the historical facts to which they allude have reference to times, places and persons of which they have no knowledge, and therefore must be read by our children without an understanding of their contents. This circumstance retards the progress of the pupil. This practice ought to be discontinued; our youth ought first to be presented with the history of their own country, and taught to believe it to be of greater importance to their future welfare than that of any other nation or country whatever.

The notes now presented to the public embrace no very great extent of our country, nor do they detail the events of many years, yet the labor of collecting and arranging them was considerable, as there never existed any printed records of the greater number of events herein related; or if such did exist, they never were within the reach of the author.

The truth is, from the commencement of the revolutionary war until its conclusion, this country and its wars were little thought of by the people of the Atlantic states, as they had their hands full of their own share of the war, without attending to ours. Far the greater number of our campaigns, scouts, buildings, and defenses of forts were effected without the aid of a man, a gun, a bullet, or charge of powder from the general government. The greater number of our men were many years in succession engaged in military service along our frontiers, a considerable part of their time from spring till winter, without an enlistment by government or a cent of pay. Their officers were of their own election. Their services were wholly voluntary, and their supplies while in service were furnished by themselves. Thus owing to our distant situation, and the heavy pressure of the revolutionary war upon the general government, the report of the small but severe and destructive conflicts which very frequently took place in this country was lost in the thunder of the great battles which occurred along our Atlantic border; campaigns begun and ended without even a newspaper notice; as a printing press was then unknown in the country.

It was not until after the conclusion of the revolutionary war that the general government undertook to finish the Indian war, first by placing a cordon of spies, and rangers, and forts, along the frontiers, and afterwards by the campaigns of Harmar, St. Clair, and Wayne. These latter campaigns are matters of history, and need not be repeated here.

The want of printed documents was not the only difficulty the author had to contend with; when he traveled beyond the bounds of his own memory he found it extremely difficult to procure information from the living concerning the events which he wished to relate; in personal interviews with several gentlemen extensively concerned in the events of the war, they promised to furnish the documents required, but they have not been furnished, and he soon found that he had no chance of obtaining them but that of writing them from their verbal narrations.

I do not intend this observation as a reflection on the integrity of the gentlemen to whom I allude. They are men who are not liberal scholars, and therefore not in the habit of writing on historical subjects, so that however vivid their remembrance of the transaction in question, when they undertake its narration on paper, they never can please themselves, and therefore give up the task for fear of public exposure; not knowing that the historian will give the facts narrated by incompetent scribes his own dress and arrangement.

In delineating the manners and customs of the early inhabitants of our country, the author presents to his readers a state of society with every advantage afforded by experience to aid him in giving its faithful portrait, for it was the state of society in which he himself was raised, and passed his early years.

In this department of history every reader wishes to be told not only the truth, but the whole truth. Let the picture of human manners be ever so rude, barbarous or even savage, he wishes to see it in its full dimensions, and in all its parts. The reader, it is hoped, will not complain if the author has introduced him to the interior of the cabins, the little forts and camps with their coarse furniture, which were tenanted by our forefathers. The rude accommodations presented to his inspection, in the homely visit, will form an agreeable and even a romantic contrast to the present state of society in our country. This contrast will show him what mighty changes may be effected under an enlightened and free government in the course of a few years; while the worst states of society in other regions of the world have remained the same from time immemorial, owing to the influence of that despotism which regards any change of the manners or the conditions of society as criminal, and therefore prevents them by the severest penalties, because *ignorance* and *poverty* are favorable to the perpetuity of that slavery, on the part of the common people, which is essential to its existence.

In the whole of these Notes the author has given the English names, alone, to our plants, birds and beasts. Men of science may apply the Linnean names if they choose; the mere English reader can do better without them.

Thus, reader, the author has brought his work to a conclusion. He has faithfully endeavored to fill up the little chasm which existed in the history of our country. He can only answer for a good intention, and a strict regard to truth in all his narrations; for all its results to his country, and himself personally, he most willingly submits to the imperial court of public opinion, from whose awful decisions there is no appeal; without invoking that justice which, whether asked or unasked, the work will be sure to receive.

THE EARLY SETTLEMENT AND INDIAN WARS

OF

WESTERN VIRGINIA AND PENNSYLVANIA.

CHAPTER I.

STATE OF THE WILDERNESS.

To a person who has witnessed all the changes which have taken place in the western country, since its first settlement, its former appearance is like a dream, or romance. He will find it difficult to realize the features of that wilderness which was the abode of his infant days. The little cabin of his father no longer exists: the little field and truck patch, which gave him a scanty supply of coarse bread and vegetables, have been swallowed up in the extended meadow, orchard, or grain field. The rude fort, in which his people had resided so many painful summers, has vanished, and " Like the baseless fabric of a vision left not a wreck behind." Large farms, with splendid mansion houses and well filled barns, hamlets, villages, and even cities, now occupy the scenes of his youthful sports, hunting or military excursions. In the place of forest trees or hawthorn bushes he sees the awful forum of justice, or the sacred temple with its glittering spire pointing to the heavens; and instead of the war whoop of savages or the howling of wolves he hears the swelling anthem or pealing organ.

Every where surrounded by the busy hum of men, and the splendor, arts, refinements and comforts of civilized life, his former state and that of his country have vanished from his memory; or, if sometimes he bestows a reflection on its original aspect, the mind seems to be carried back to a period of time much more remote than it really is. The immense changes which have taken place in the physical and moral state of the country have been gradual, and, therefore, scarcely perceived from year to year; but the view, from one extreme to the other, is like the prospect of the opposite shore, over a vast expanse of water, whose hills, valleys, mountains and forests present a confused and romantic scenery, which loses itself in the distant horizon.

One advantage, at least, results from having lived in a state of society ever on the change, and always for the better, it doubles the retrospect of life. With me, at any rate, it has had that effect. Did not the definite number of my years teach me the contrary, I should think myself at least one hundred years old, instead of fifty. The case is said to be widely different with those who have passed their lives in cities, or ancient settlements, where, from year to year, the same unchanging aspect of things presents itself. There life passes away as an illusion, or dream, having been presented with no striking events, or great and important changes, to mark its different periods, and give them an imaginary distance from each other, and it ends with a bitter complaint of its shortness. It must be my own fault if I shall ever have occasion to make this complaint. I do not recollect to have ever heard it made by any of my contemporary countrymen, whose deaths I have witnessed.

A wilderness of great extent, presenting the virgin face of nature, unchanged by human cultivation or art, is certainly one of the most sublime terrestrial objects which the Creator ever presented to the view of man; but those portions of the earth which bear this character derive their features of sublimity from very different aspects. The great deserts of Africa wear an imposing aspect, even on account of their utter barrenness of vegetation, where no tree affords fruit, or shelter from the burning heat of the day, no bird is heard to sing, and no flower expands its leaves to the sun, as well as from their immense extent.

In the steppes of Russia, the oriental plain of Tartary, the traveler, did not his reason correct the illusion of his senses, at the rising and setting of the sun, would imagine himself in the midst of a boundless ocean, so vast, so level and monotonous is the prospect around him.

What must be the awful sublimity of the immense regions of polar solitude, where the distant sun reflects his dazzling rays from plains of snow, and mountains of ice, but without warming.

The valley of the Mississippi, whose eastern and western boundaries are the Alleghany and Rocky Mountains, the northern chain of lakes which separate us from Canada, and the southern, the gulf of Florida, in addition to the imposing grandeur of its vast extent, is an immense region of animal and vegetable life, in all their endless varieties. In all this vast extent of country no mountain rears its towering head to vary the scenery, and afford a resting place for the clouds, no volcano vomits forth its smoke, flame and lava in sublime but destructive grandeur. Even those portions of this valley which in ages past were the beds of lakes, but have been drained by the sinking of the rivers, present a rich vegetable mould.[1]

This great country seems to have been designed by Divine Providence for the last resort of oppressed humanity. A fruitful soil, under a variety of climates, supplies abundantly all the wants of life, while our geographical situation renders us unconquerable. From this place of refuge we may hear, as harmless thunder, the military convulsions of other quarters of the globe, without feeling their concussions. Vice and folly may conquer us: the world never can. Happy region! large and fertile enough for the abode of many millions. Here the hungry may find bread, and conscience the full possession of its native rights.

---

[1] There is every evidence that those tracts of our country which consist of beds of rounded gravel and stones have formerly been lakes, which have been drained by the lowering of the beds of the rivers. These tracts of country have been covered with a vegetable mould, from the decay of vegetable matters on their surface, so as to have become good land for cultivation. Such are the Pickaway and Sandusky plains, and indeed the greater part of the Scioto country, as well as many other tracts of land along other rivers. The Ohio river has lowered its bed from fifty to eighty feet. Steubenville, Beavertown and Cincinnati stand on the first alluvion of the river; this alluvion is at least seventy feet above the present bed of the river. This phenomenon of the lowering of the waters is not confined to our own country. The former bed of the Red sea is from thirty to forty feet above the present surface of its waters. The Black sea is sinking by the wearing down of the canal of Constantinople; and it seems every way probable that a considerable portion of the deserts of Africa, next the sea. were once covered with the waters of the Atlantic. Large tracts of our southern sea coasts are evidently alluvial. The causes of the sinking of the beds of rivers, and the recession of the sea form its shores, must be left to the investigation of geologists. (D).

With the geography and geology of this country I have no concern. I leave these subjects to the geographer and natural historian. The aspect which it bore at the time of its discovery and settlement must alone be presented to the reader.

One prominent feature of a wilderness is its solitude. Those who plunged into the bosom of this forest left behind them not only the busy hum of men, but domestic animal life generally. The departing rays of the setting sun did not receive the requiem of the feathered songsters of the grove, nor was the blushing aurora ushered in by the shrill clarion of the domestic fowls. The solitude of the night was interrupted only by the howl of the wolf, the melancholy moan of the ill-boding owl, or the shriek of the frightful panther. Even the faithful dog, the only steadfast companion of man among the brute creation, partook of the silence of the desert; the discipline of his master forbid him to bark, or move, but in obedience to his command, and his native sagacity soon taught him the propriety of obedience to this severe government. The day was, if possible, more solitary than the night. The noise of the wild turkey, the croaking of the raven, or " the woodpecker tapping the hollow beech tree," did not much enliven the dreary scene.

The various tribes of singing birds are not inhabitants of the desert; they are not carnivorous and therefore must be fed from the labors of man. At any rate they did not exist in this country at its first settlement.

Let the imagination of the reader pursue the track of the adventurer into this solitary wilderness. Bending his course towards the setting sun, over undulating hills, under the shade of large forest trees, and wading through the rank weeds and grass which then covered the earth. Now viewing from the top of a hill the winding course of the creek whose stream he wishes to explore, doubtful of its course, and of his own, he ascertains the cardinal points of north and south by the thickness of the moss and bark on the north side of the ancient trees. Now descending into a valley and presaging his approach to a river by seeing large ash, bass-wood and sugar trees, beautifully festooned with wild grape vines. Watchful as Argus, his restless eye catches every thing around him. In an unknown region, and surrounded with dangers, he is the sentinel of his own safety, and relies on himself alone for protection. The toilsome march of the day being ended, at the fall of night he seeks for safety some narrow, sequestered hollow, and by the side of a large log builds a fire, and, after eating his coarse and scanty meal, wraps himself up in his blanket, and lays him down on his bed of leaves, with his feet to the little fire, for repose, hoping for favorable dreams ominous of future good luck, while his faithful dog and gun repose by his side.

But let not the reader suppose that the pilgrim of the wilderness could feast his imagination with the romantic beauties of nature without any drawback from conflicting passions. His situation did not afford him much time for contemplation. He was an exile from the warm clothing and plentiful mansions of society. His homely woodsman's dress soon became old and ragged; the cravings of hunger compelled him to sustain from day to day the fatigues of the chase. Often had he to eat his venison, bear meat, or wild turkey, without bread or salt. Nor was this all; at every step the strong passions of hope and fear were in full exercise. Eager in the pursuit of his game, his too much excited imagination sometimes presented him with the phantom of the object of his chase in a bush, a log, or mossy bank, and occasioned him to waste a load of his ammunition, more precious than gold, on a creature of his own brain, and he repaid himself the expense by making a joke of his mistake. His situation was not without its dangers. He did not know at what tread his foot might be stung by a serpent, at what moment he might meet with the formidable bear,[1] or, if in the evening, he

[1] It is said, that for some time after Braddock's defeat, the bears, having feasted on the slain, thought that they had a right to kill and eat every human being with whom they met. An uncle of mine, of the name of Teter, had like to have lost his life by one of them. It was in the summer time, when bears were poor, and not worth killing; being in the woods, he saw an old male bear winding along after him; with a view to have the sport of seeing the bear run, he hid himself behind a tree; when the bear approached him, he sprang out and hallooed at him; but cuffee, instead of running off as he expected, jumped at him with mouth wide open; my uncle stopped him by applying the muzzle of his gun to his neck, and firing it off; this killed him in an instant. If his gun had snapped, the hunter would have been torn to pieces on the spot. After this, he says he never undertook to play with a bear. (D).

knew not on what limb of a tree, over his head, the murderous panther might be perched, in a squatting attitude, to drop down upon and tear him to pieces in a moment. When watching a deer lick from his blind at night the formidable panther was often his rival in the same business, and if, by his growl, or otherwise, the man discovered the presence of his rival, the lord of the world always retired as speedily and secretly as possible, leaving him the undisturbed possession of the chance of game for the night.

The wilderness was a region of superstition. The adventurous hunter sought for ominous presages of his future good or bad luck in every thing about him. Much of his success depended on the state of the weather; snow and rain were favorable, because in the former he could track his game, and the latter prevented them from hearing the rustling of the leaves beneath his feet. The appearance of the sky, morning and evening, gave him the signs of the times with regard to the weather. So far he was a philosopher. Perhaps he was aided in his prognostics on this subject by some old rheumatic pain, which he called his *weather clock*. Say what you please about this, doctors, the first settlers of this country were seldom mistaken in this latter indication of the weather. The croaking of a raven, the howling of a dog, and the screech of an owl, were as prophetic of future misfortunes among the first adventurers into this country. as they were amongst the ancient pagans; but above all, their dreams were regarded as ominous of good or ill success. Often when a boy I heard them relate their dreams, and the events which fulfilled their indications. With some of the woodsmen there were two girls of their acquaintance, who were regarded as the goddesses of their good or bad luck. If they dreamed of the one, they were sure of good fortune; if of the other, they were equally sure of bad. How much love or aversion might have had to do in this case I cannot say, but such was the fact.

Let not the reader be surprised at the superstition which existed among the first adventurers into the western wilderness. Superstition is universally associated with ignorance, in all those who occupy perilous situations in life. The comets used to be considered harbingers of war. The sea captain nails an old horse shoe to the foot of the mast of his ship to prevent storms. The Germans used to nail the horse shoe on the door-sill to prevent the intrusion of witches. The German soldier recites a charm, at the rising of the sun, when in the course of the day he expects to be engaged in battle, by the means of which he fancies that he fortifies himself against the contact of balls of every description.[1] Charms, incantations, and amulets, have constituted a part of the superstition of all ages and nations. Philosophy alone can banish their use.

The passion of fear excited by danger, the parent of superstition. operated powerfully on the first adventurers into this country. Exiled from society, and the comforts of life, their situation was perilous in the extreme. The bite of a serpent, a broken limb, a wound of any kind, or a fit of sickness in the wilderness, without those accommodations which wounds and sickness require, was a dreadful calamity. The bed of sickness without medical aid, and, above all, to be destitute of the kind attention of a mother, sister, wife, or other female friends, those ministering angels in the wants and afflictions of man, was a situation which could not be anticipated by the tenant of the forest with other sentiments than those of the deepest horror.

Many circumstances concurred to awaken in the mind of the early adventurer into this country the most serious and even melancholy reflections. He saw everywhere around him indubitable evidences of the former existence of a large population of barbarians, which had long ago perished from the earth. Their arrow heads furnished him with gun flints; stone hatchets, pipes, and fragments of earthen ware, were found in every place. The remains of their rude fortifications were met with in many places, and some of them of considerable extent and magnitude. Seated on the summit of some sepulchral mound containing the ashes of tens of thousands of the dead, he said to himself: "This is the grave, and this, no doubt, the temple of worship of

---

[1] Many years ago I saw a manuscript of this wonderful charm, but have so forgotten its contents that I cannot now undertake to give a translation of it. (D)

a long succession of generations long since mouldered into dust; these surrounding valleys were once animated by their labors, hunting and wars, their songs and dances; but oblivion has drawn her impenetrable veil over their whole history; no lettered page, no sculptured monument informs who they were, from whence they came, the period of their existence, or by what dreadful catastrophe the iron hand of death has given them so complete an overthrow, and made the whole of this country an immense Golgotha."

Such, reader, was the aspect of this country at its first discovery, and such the poor and hazardous lot of the first adventurers into the bosoms of its forests. How widely different is the aspect of things now, and how changed for the better the condition of its inhabitants! If such important changes have taken place in so few years, and with such slender means, what immense improvements may we not reasonably anticipate for the future!

CHAPTER II.

Remains of an Extinct People.

The western country, in common with almost every other region of the earth, exhibits evidences of a numerous population which must have existed and perished long anterior to the period of history. The evidences of the most remote population of our country are found only in the few and rude remains of their works which have escaped the ravages of time. Such of these antiquities as have come under the notice of the author shall be described with some remarks upon them.

Arrow heads, at the first settlement of the country, were found everywhere. These were made of flint stone of various sizes and colors, and shaped with great art and neatness. Their fabrication required more skill and labor than that of making our ordinary gun flints. From the great numbers of these arrow points, found all over the country, it is presumable that they must have been in general use, by a large population, and for a great length of time. The author has never been informed whether, at the discovery and settlement of America by the Europeans, the Indians were in the habit of using them. Some of these arrow points were of great size and weight, so that those who used them must have been gigantic fellows, and of great muscular strength. For a long time after the settlement of the country the Indian arrow heads furnished the main supply of gun-flints for our hunters and warriors, many of whom preferred them to the imported flints. The arrow points have nearly vanished from the country. I have not seen one for many years.

Stone pipes and hatchets were frequently found here in early times. The pipes were rudely made, but many of them of very fanciful shapes. The existence of these pipes shows very clearly that the practice of smoking acrid substances is of great antiquity. Before the use of tobacco, the Indians smoked the inner bark of the red willow mixed with sumac leaves. They do so still, when they cannot procure tobacco.

Some fragments of a rude kind of earthen ware were found in some places. It was made of potter's-earth mixed with calcined shells, and burnt to a proper hardness. This ware was no doubt used for cooking.

Some rude trinkets of copper have been found in some of the Indian graves. These, however, were but few in number, and exhibited no skill in the art of working metals. Many years ago I procured ten copper beads, which were found in one of the smaller graves on Grave-creek flat. The whole number found at the time was about sixty. They appeared to have been made of hammered wire, cut off at unequal lengths, and in some of them the ends were not more than half their surface in contact, and so soldered.

The ancient forts, as they are called, are generally formed in the neighborhood of the large graves along the river, and mostly on the first alluvion of their bottoms. They are of all shapes and various dimensions. They have been so often described by different authors that a description of them is not necessary here. Whether they were really fortifications, or ordinary inclosures of their towns, is not so certain. It is said to be a common practice among the Indians of Missouri to inclose a piece of ground, which they intend for a town, with stockades, on each side of which they throw up a mound of earth, and that, when one of their towns has been so long deserted that the stockading has rotted down, the remaining mound of earth has precisely the same appearance as one of the ancient forts. If this was their origin, and most probably it was, they were fortifications in the same degree that the walls of all ancient towns and cities were, and not otherwise. The circular mounds at Circleville, in Ohio, are the only ones I have ever seen, which appear to have been exclusively intended for a fortress.

The sepulchral mounds make by far the greatest figure among the antiquities of our country. In point of magnitude some of them are truly sublime and imposing monuments of human labor for the burial of the dead.

The large grave, on Grave-creek flat, is the only large one in this section of the country.[1] The diameter of its base is said to be one hundred yards, its altitude at least seventy-five feet, some give it at ninety feet. The diameter at the top is fifteen yards. The sides and top of the mound are covered with trees, of all sizes and ages, intermingled with fallen and decaying timber, like the surrounding woods. Supposing this august pyramid to contain human bones, in equal proportion with the lesser mounds which have been opened from time to time, what myriads of human beings must repose in its vast dimensions.[2]

The present owner of this mound, the author has been informed, has expressed his determination to preserve it in its original state during his life. He will not suffer the axe to violate its timber, nor the mattocks its earth. May his successors to the

---

[1] Mr. A. B. Tomlinson opened this Grave Creek mound in 1888. (See "Foster's Prehistoric Races," page 190.)

[2] President Jefferson mentions having made a perpendicular cut through an Indian grave on the river Rivanna, near Monticello, with a view to examine its internal structure and contents. The base of the grave was forty feet in diameter, its height seven feet and a half. After a careful examination of the bones contained in the sepulchre, he concluded that it might contain one thousand skeletons. Supposing this estimate correct, what must be the number of skeletons contained in the great pyramid of Grave creek? Those who are curious enough to make the calculation are requested to do so, and give the result.—*Notes on Virginia*, p. 131. (D)

title of the estate forever feel the same pious regard for this august mansion of the dead, and preserve the venerable monument of antiquity from that destruction which has already annihilated, or defaced, a large number of the lesser depositories of the dead.

Most of the writers on the antiquities of our country represent the sepulchral mounds under consideration as peculiar to America. Were such the fact, they would be objects of great curiosity indeed; as their belonging exclusively to this quarter of the globe would go to show that the aborigines of America were different from all other nations of the earth, at least in their manner of disposing of their dead.

But the fact is not so. The history of these ancient sepulchres of the dead embraces Europe, Asia and Africa, as well as North and South America. Large groups of those mounds are met with in many places between St. Petersburgh and Moscow in Russia. When the people of that country are asked if they have any tradition concerning them they answer in the negative. They suppose that they are the graves of men slain in battle; but when, or by whom constructed, they have no knowledge. Near the mouth of the river Don there is a group of five mounds which from time immemorial have been denominated *The Five Brothers.* Similar mounds are very numerous along the shores of the Black sea, and those of the sea of Azof, and throughout the whole country of the Crimea. They are found throughout ancient Greece. In the neighborhood of ancient Troy there are several of them nearly as large as any in America. The mound described by Robbins, in the vicinity of Wadinoon in Africa, is certainly an ancient sepulchral mound although he calls it a natural one.[1]

This is more probable as the remains of fortifications or town-walls, similar to those in our country, exist in abundance in the neighborhood of Wadinoon. On the hills near Cambridge in England are shown two large barrows as the tombs of Gog and Magog. The cairns of Scotland are structures of the same

---

[1] For description see "Robbins' Journal," page 220.

kind, but made wholly of stone. Peru and Mexico contain a vast number of those mounds of all shapes and of the largest dimensions. Lastly, the famous pyramids of Egypt have been ascertained to be sepulchral edifices. In all probability they are coeval with the sepulchral monuments of other quarters of the globe already mentioned. They were designed for the last and permanent exhibition of the regal grandeur of those monarchs by whom they were successively erected.

The great number and magnitude of the sepulchral monuments of antiquity serve to show that during the time of their erection, over so large a portion of the earth, mankind generally must have been actuated by a strong desire to preserve the remains of the dead from dissolution, and their names and renown, as far as possible, from oblivion. The extensive catacombs of Egypt, Syracuse and Palestine, are fully illustrative of the general wish for the preservation of the body after death, and posthumous fame. What must have been the labor and expense of excavating limestone or marble rocks to such vast extent and with such exquisite workmanship for the purpose of furnishing elegant and imperishable recesses for the dead.

The ancient Egyptians held the first rank, among the nations of antiquity, in their care and skill for preserving the remains of their dead.[1] To the most splendid and extensive catacombs they added the practice of embalming their bodies; many of which have so far escaped the ravages of time. These embalmed bodies, preserved from putrefaction by serates and bandages of linen, are still found, sometimes in solitary cells, and sometimes in large numbers, in newly discovered catacombs; but for want of letters, their early history has vanished forever.

---

[1] Upwards of twenty years ago the author saw a hand and part of the arm of an Egyptian mummy in the Franklin library of Philadelphia. It was covered with two bandages of what is called six hundred linen. Between the skin and the first bandage there was a layer of plaster of some kind of gum, and the same between the first and outer bandage. The thumb and fingers were separately, and very neatly, bandaged. It was, in size and appearance, the left hand of a small woman. This relic of antiquity is no doubt several thousand years old. (D)

While the ancient Egyptians skillfully preserved the individual bodies of their dead, other nations were in the practice of collecting the bones of their people and depositing them in sepulchral monuments of a national character.

Nearly all the sepulchral mounds which have been thoroughly opened, in Asia and America, contain, about the center of the bottom, a coffin, or vault of stone, containing but one skeleton. This, we may reasonably suppose, was the sarcophagus of the patriarch, or first monarch of the tribe or nation to which the sepulchre belonged. Thenceforward all his people were deposited in the grave of the founder of the nation. In process of time, the daily increasing mound became the national history. Its age was the age of the nation, and its magnitude gave the census of their relative numbers, and military force, with regard to other nations about them. What a sublime spectacle to the people to whom it belonged must one of those large sepulchres have been! The remains of the first chief of the nation, with his people, and their successors, through many generations, reposing together in the same tomb!

It is a well known fact that some nations of Indians, ever since the settlement of America by the Europeans, have been in the habit of collecting the bones of their dead, from every quarter, for the purpose of depositing them, with those of their people, at their chief towns. This must have been the general practice during the time of the erection of the large ancient graves of our country; for the bones found in those of them which have been opened have been thrown promiscuously together in large collections, as if emptied out of baskets or bags.

Besides the large graves, smaller ones are found in many places, remote from the large mounds and all traces of the ancient forts. Most of these are made wholly of stone, and for the most part contain but a single skeleton. Were these solitary mounds erected to the memory of the individual whose remains they cover? Such appears to have been the fact. That a similar custom prevailed among the ancient Hebrews, we have an evidence in the burial of Absalom, the rebellious son of David, who, although unworthy of a place in the royal sepulchre, was nevertheless honored with such a rude monument of stones as we often meet with in our country. After he was slain by Joab, the commander-in-chief of his father's army, "They took Absalom and cast him into a great pit in the wood, and cast a *very great* heap of stones upon him."

From all these facts it appears that the strong desire of posthumous fame induced those nations, amongst whom the art of writing was unknown, to preserve the remembrances of their chiefs, or friends, by erecting over their dead bodies a heap of earth, or a pile of stones, as well as to make the congregated dead of many generations a national monument and a national record.

Nearly all the sepulchral mounds which have been opened in Asia and America have been found to contain more or less charcoal and calcined bones. From this fact it appears that those ancient tombs were altars for sacrifice. The early histories of the Greeks and Romans inform us that it was customary to offer sacrifices on the tombs of heroes slain in battle, with the revolting fact that the victims offered on those sepulchral altars were often the prisoners taken in war.

Islanders, surrounded by a great extent of ocean, and thereby precluded from emigrations, are less liable to change their languages, manners and customs, than the inhabitants of continents. Hence those of the Society islands of the South sea, and those of the Sandwich islands of the Pacific, still continue the ancient practice of depositing the bones of their dead in mounds, or as they call them morai; and these morai are their temples, on the tops of which their idols are placed for worship. The truth is, these mounds were the high places of the pagan nations, mentioned in the Old Testament, and among these we may safely reckon the famous tower of Babel.

It was on the top of one those mounds, in the island of Owhyhee, that Capt. Cook, wrapped up in three hundred ells of Indian cloth, and mounted on a scaffold of rotten railing, was worshipped as a god, under the name of Oranoo; but while receiving the devotions of the islanders he was every moment afraid of tumbling down and breaking his neck.[1]

Having given the history of the ancient sepulchral mounds, as they exist in every quarter of the globe, two questions only remain for discussion: At what period of the world were they erected, and whether by a barbarous or civilized people?

The great antiquity of the monuments in question may be ascertained by many facts which cannot fail to strike the notice of an attentive observer of the relics of antiquity. In America, as far as the author knows, none of the large mounds are found on the first or lower bottoms of our rivers, but always on the second or highest alluvion; and such is their situation in Asia and Europe. None of them are to be seen on those tracts of country which were the beds of lakes or inland seas, such as the great oriental plain of Tartary, a great part of which was formerly covered by the waters of the Black and Caspian seas, and those of the sea of Azof, but which have been drained off by the breaking down of the Thracian Bosphorus, which formed the canal of Constantinople; but they are found in abundance along the higher grounds of the southern and western shores of those seas, and in the neighboring country of Crim Tartary. The gain of the land upon the waters of our globe has been immensely great; but this gain has been but slowly made. The very sites of our ancient tombs give a very remote antiquity for the period of their erection. Their situations, mainly along the large rivers and on the shores of lakes, announce the primeval state of nations. As the spoils of the water are more easily obtained than those of the forest, and these last more easily than the productions of the earth, the first employment of man must have been that of fishing, and his first food the productions of the waters.

These mounds and forts are not found in any great numbers along the shores of the main oceans. This circumstance goes to show that those by whom they were made were not in the prac-

[1] For a particular description of the antiquities of our country, the reader is referred to the ingenious notes of Caleb Atwater, Esq., of Circleville, lately published in the *Archaeological Americana.* (D)

tice of navigating the great seas. That their existence is of higher antiquity than the commencement of the period of history is evident from the fact that none of them contain a single inscription of any kind. Even the famous pyramids of Egypt do not contain a single letter or hieroglyphic to announce the time when, or the persons by whom, they were erected. If letters had been in use at the time of the building of those stupendous repositories of departed grandeur they would doubtless have been used to announce the names and honor of those who erected them for sepulchral and imperishable monuments of their own power, wealth and majesty.

Another evidence of the great age of these rude remains of antiquity is this; there exists nowhere even a traditionary account of their origin. At the earliest period of the Grecian history they were supposed, but only supposed, to be the graves of giants. After what lapse of time does tradition degenerate into fable? At what period of time does fable itself wear out, and consign all antiquity to a total and acknowledged oblivion? All this has happened with regard to the antiquities under consideration.

From all these considerations, it appears that any inquiry concerning the history of the antiquities of our country would be a fruitless research. "Close shut those graves, nor tell a single tale," concerning the numerous population whose relics they enclose.

The antiquities of our country do not present to the mind of the author the slightest evidences that this quarter of the world was ever inhabited by a civilized people before it was discovered by the Europeans. They present no traces of the art of building, sculpture or painting; not a stone marked with a hammer is anywhere to be found. It is supposed, by some, that the aborigines of this country were in the habit of using iron tools and implements of war; that such was the fact appears to me very doubtful. There can exist no specimens of iron coeval with the antiquities of this country, as iron, in almost any situation, is liable to rust and pass to its primitive state of ore. At the discovery of America the Indians knew nothing of the use of iron.

Any people who have ever been in the habit of using iron will be sure to leave some indelible traces of its use behind them; but the aborigines of this country have left none.

Barbarians, in many instances, have possessed, and do still possess, the art of writing; but it is not to be presumed that a civilized people ever were destitute of that art. The original inhabitants of this country possessed it not, or they would certainly have left some traces of it behind them.

If they possessed some trinkets of copper, silver, gold, or even tools and military weapons of iron, they nevertheless furnish no evidences of civilization, as all history goes to show that the ornamental or military use of these metals is consistent with the grossest barbarism. The Calmuc Tartars have their gold and silversmiths; and yet what people on earth are more barbarous than the Calmucs. The same may be said of the Circassians; they have an abundance of gold and silver ornaments; yet they are savages. Copper may have found its way to this country from Peru, a country in which that metal is abundant; a few gold and silver coins, if such have been found in our country, may have come from Asia, or even Europe; but they certainly were never manufactured here.

If at the period of time herein alluded to there was anything like civilization in the world, it was exclusively confined to Egypt, and the islands in the neighborhood of that country. The pyramids of Egypt, and the queen's palace in the island of Cyprus, are built of hewn stone; but piling up huge stones, in useless edifices, by the hands of slaves, is no great evidence of civilization. In fact the edifices themselves, although they manifest a degree of mechanical skill, and the use of iron tools, are evidences of the grossest barbarism on the part of those by whose orders they were built. It was exhausting the lives and resources of a nation in useless monuments, not of national grandeur, but solely for that of the individual monarch.

It is not worth while to amuse ourselves with the fanciful creations of a vivid imagination unsupported by facts. The evidences of science and civilization are not furnished by the antiquities of our country, and in vain, beyond the period of history, do we look for them in any other region of the earth. By what events could the monuments of arts, sciences and civilization, have been utterly destroyed? Storms, earthquakes, volcanoes, and war, destructive as they are, are not sufficiently so to efface them. The shores of our rivers and lakes have been inhabited by a race of barbarians, who have subsisted by hunting and fishing. They have left us their forts or town walls, and their graves, and but little else. If they had left behind them any monuments of arts and sciences, they in like manner would have descended to us; but nothing of the kind has come to our hands. They were not, therefore, possessed of those arts and sciences which are essential to a civilized state of society. It is often asked whether those people, who have left behind them the antiquities of our country, were the ancestors of the present Indians? Unquestionably they were; and, reader, their cotemporaries of Europe and Asia were your ancestors and they were mine. Humiliating as this statement may seem, it must be true; otherwise there must have been two creations of the human race, and this we have no reason to suppose.

Perhaps the moral philosopher might say with truth, that the intellectual faculties of man, on a general scale, like those of the individual, have been doomed to pass through a tedious infancy, nonage and youth, before they shall reach the zenith of manhood. However rude, and indicative of barbarism, the antiquities which those remote generations have left behind them, their relation to us, as ancestors, is no way dishonorable to us. It is only saying that theirs was the infant state of the intellectual faculties of man. What were the intellectual faculties of Sir Isaac Newton in his infancy, and nonage, in comparison to the state of their full development, when he not only grasped the dimensions of our globe, but, in the science of astronomy, whirled in triumph through the signs of heaven? Yet it is no way dishonorable to this prince of philosophers that he was once an infant and a boy.

It may be asked, by what events has all remembrance of those remote generations been so far effaced that even the fabulous era of the world has left them in total and acknowledged oblivion? Here we are truly in the dark. One-third of the period of time assigned for the duration of the world passed away before the dreadful catastrophe of the flood, "When all fountains of the great deep were broken up, and the windows of heaven were opened, and rain was upon the earth forty days and forty nights."

To this it may be objected, even by the believer, that in all probability this flood did not extend to every region of the globe, but might have been confined to that part of it which was known to the writer of the sacred history. This point cannot be easily settled; but admitting that such was the fact; and admitting for the moment all the objections of that too fashionable philosophy which rejects the authenticity of Divine revelation altogether, what would be the result? Would the limitation of the extent of the history of this destruction, on the one hand, or the total denial of its authenticity on the other hand, have any bearing on the physical evidences of the mighty revolutions which have taken place on our globe? The natural history of those revolutions is exhibited, and its awful import cannot be mistaken. The philosopher sees all over the surface of the earth, and even within its bowels, the spoils of the ocean. All fossil coal, he says, was vegetable matter. If so, by what tremendous convulsions have such immense quantities of vegetable matters been buried, over so great a portion of the globe, and at such depths below its surface? All limestone, marble and selenite, he says, have been formed from the shells of the numerous tribes of shell fish, because, like those shells, they are carbonates of lime; and yet there is no description of stone more abundant than the carbonates of lime. If this be correct, what must be the age of the world, and what destructive revolutions must have rent and changed the position of its component parts in every quarter!

Yet it seems every way probable that those destructive convulsions which have been occasioned by floods, earthquakes and subterranean fires, never took place over the whole extent of the globe at any time; but have affected different regions in succession so that, however great the destruction of animated nature at any one of those tremendous revolutions, the greater amount of it still remained in other regions.

After having passed in review the antiquities of our country, particularly the melancholy monuments of the ancient dead, what have we gained? Simply this, that the generations of remote antiquity were everywhere the same, at least in their reverence for the dead, whose monuments constitute almost the only history which they have left behind them; and that, for want of letters, and other testimonials of arts and sciences, we are warranted in saying that their state of society must have been that which we denominate the barbarous; yet their history, rude as it is, is entitled to respect. They were no doubt the antediluvian race: they were the primeval fathers of mankind, the immediate progenitors of our race, to whom the munificent creator gave dominion over the "fish of the sea, the fowl of the air, and every living thing that moveth upon the earth." From them we have inherited our existence and our charter to this possession of the world. Even the barbarous state of society is entitled to respect; for barbarism has its virtues.

Much as the physical happiness of man has been augmented by civilization, how far has his moral state received improvement from the augmentation of his science and civilization? Have they made his heart the better? Have they taught him the noble philanthropy of the good Samaritan? Or has he only exchanged the ferocity of the savage for the cunning of the sharper? Are the vices of our nature diminished in force, or are they only varnished like a whited sepulchre and placed under concealment, so as to obtain their objects with greater effect and on a broader scale? Have the political institutions of the world become sources of freedom, peace and good will to the people? Let the boasted region of our forefathers, enlightened Europe, answer the inquiry. There legal contributions, insupportable in their amount, induce all the miseries of pauperism; royal ambition presents its millions of subjects to the deadly machinery of modern warfare; but are the valiant dead honored with a monument of their existence and bravery? No! that insatiable avarice which knows nothing sacred makes a traffic of their bones, while the groaning engine converts them to powder to furnish manure for an unfriendly soil. If this is civilization, pray what is barbarism?

A veneration for antiquity seems to be natural to man; hence we consider as barbarians those who demolish the relics of antiquity. We justly blame the Turks for burning the fine marble columns of ancient Greece into lime; but do we display a juster taste, with regard to the only relics with which our country is honored? When those relics shall have disappeared, and nothing but their history shall remain, will not future generations pronounce us barbarians for having demolished them? Those venerable sepulchral mounds ought to be religiously preserved, and even planted with evergreens. They would figure well in our grave yards, public squares and public walks; but what is likely to be their fate? If in fields, for the sake of a few additional ears of corn, or sheaves of wheat, they are plowed down. If within the limits of a town, demolished to afford a site for a house, or garden, or to fill up some sunken spot, while the walls which inclosed the town or fort of the ancients are made into brick. Such is man! Such are the enlightened Americans!

CHAPTER III.

Origin of the American Indians.

Whether the Indians of North and South America, and the Tartars of the north-eastern coasts of the Pacific ocean, have had a common origin, is an inquiry which has long exercised the ingenuity of the statesmen and historians of our country, some of whom have derived our aboriginal population from Asia, while others of them confer the honor of having given population to Asiatic Tartary, to America.

Resemblance of languages, manners and customs, mode of life, religious ceremonies, and color, are regarded as evidences of a community of origin.

Of these tests the first, namely, that of a similarity of languages, is considered the most important and conclusive, and has therefore received the greatest amount of attention from the learned.

Dr. Barton, a former professor of medicine in the University of Pennsylvania, has given a vocabulary of about fifty corresponding words, of about eighty different languages of the North and South American Indians, and about thirty of those of the Asiatic Tartars, for the purpose of showing the identity of their origin by the resemblance of their languages.

To the mind of the author of this work, this laborious research has resulted in nothing very conclusive; as from the specimens given in those vocabularies the resemblance between these numerous languages appears as small as can well be imagined. This want of success in the learned author is not to be wondered at: as nothing is more permanent than a written language, so nothing can be more fleeting and changeable than an unwritten one.

The languages in question are all of the latter class, that is to say, they are all unwritten languages and, of course, constantly on the change, so that if they had all originally sprung even from the same language, in the lapse of some thousands of years, they would no doubt have been as wide of the original, and as different from each other, as the various languages of these wandering tribes are at present.

What is the Hebrew language at present? A mere written language, and nothing else. Its pronunciation has gone with the breath of those who spoke it. Had it not been a written language what traces of it would now remain? Most likely all traces of it, by this time, would have been wholly obliterated. Many words of it might have remained among the Arabs, Copts and Syrians, while the original would have been buried in utter oblivion.

The present languages of Europe exhibit clearly what immense changes take place in languages in the lapse of a few centuries. The English, French, Italian, Spanish and Portuguese languages, have all sprung from the downfall of the Roman empire, and all these languages are composed mainly of the languages of the Roman empire, and the German, that of their conquerors; and yet how different are their languages from each other. A man of science can readily trace out their resemblance to each other. Not so with the illiterate, to whom they are all distinct languages, as much so as they would have been if they had no common origin. Had these languages never been written, the community of their originals would, in all human probability, have been lost sight of long before this time.

For proof that such would have been the case, let it be understood that the English language is made up of Latin and German. Take all the words which have been derived from those two languages from a page of English, and you will have but a few shreds from other languages behind; yet when an Englishman hears the German spoken, his ear scarcely recognizes a single word which bears any resemblance to his own language; so widely different are the pronunciations of these languages although so nearly allied to each other. The same observations would hold good with regard to the Latin language, did we use the pronunciation of Cicero and Virgil in reading and speaking it. On this subject we may go farther, and suppose all the languages above enumerated to have been unwritten from their first formation till this date, and now for the first time to be committed to writing; out of a dozen scribes, scarcely any two of them would spell the same words with the same letters. This difference of orthography would still further obliterate the traces of the community of the originals of those kindred languages, so far as the mere sound is concerned in perpetuating the remembrance of their common origins.

The present German language is cleft into a great variety of dialects, so widely different from each other that the peasantry of different districts of the German empire do not well understand each other. Yet a scholar in that language readily discovers that all of those dialects have had a common origin, and by strict attention to the varied pronunciation of the diphthongs and triphthongs which in that language are very numerous he can understand them all. Not so were the language unwritten.

The present Saxon language is common German. How widely different must it have been among our forefathers, several centuries ago, from what it is now!

It seems every way probable that the Gaelic of the highlands of Scotland, the Welsh of England, and the Irish, were originally the same language; but for a long time past they have been three distinct languages.

The reader by this time I trust must see that among wandering barbarians, constantly forming new tribes, and seeking new habitations, languages, so far as the mere sound of words is concerned, furnish, after the lapse of several thousand years, but a poor test of community of origin. With reference to the test of a common origin, furnished by similarity of languages, Mr. Jefferson has ventured the probability of there being twenty radical languages among the American Indians for one amongst the Asiatic Tartars, and hence he gives America the honor of having given population to Tartary. His words are these:

"But imperfect as is our knowledge of the languages spoken in America, it suffices to discover the following remarkable fact; arranging them under the radical ones to which they may be palpably traced, and doing the same by those of the red men of Asia, there will be found probably twenty in America for one in Asia of those radical languages, so called, because if they were ever the same they have lost all resemblance to each other." *Notes on Virginia*, p. 137.

A gigantic conclusion! A conclusion which an accurate knowledge of one hundred of the languages of America and Asia would scarcely have warranted. With all deference to the usual accuracy of this illustrious philosopher, it may be said that a zeal for the honor of the aborigines of his native country must have led him to confer upon them the priority of claim to individual and national existence.

There is one feature of language much more permanent than its sound, and that is the arrangement of its sentences, with regard to the nominative case, with its verb, and objective case. On this test, it seems to me, some reliance may be placed with safety, as it does not appear likely that any people ever made any change in their mode of expression: because it is the arrangement of the members of a sentence which fixes the regular succession of ideas. If the agent is first in the sentence, then the action, and lastly the subject of the action, the ideas of those who speak a language so arranged, follow each other in the same order; should the members of the sentence be differently disposed, a corresponding difference will take place in the thoughts of those who speak the language in question. From all this it is reasonable to infer that the arrangement of sentences, especially among barbarians who have no written languages, is the most unvarying feature of all their dialects. In this respect at least, "words and things."

In the Hebrew the verb stands almost uniformly at the beginning of the sentence, next the nominative, and then the objective case. It would be of some importance to know whether this arrangement is that of Asiatic languages generally, and whether our Indian languages have the same arrangement of sentences.

In the German, which is probably one of the oldest languages of the world, the nominative case is at the beginning of the sentence, then the objective case, and last of all the verb.

In the English the nominative is the beginning of the sentence, next the verb, and lastly the objective case, so that the cases in our language are determined by the position of the nouns and not by their terminations.

In the Latin and Greek languages there seems to have been no definite arrangement of the members of a sentence, nor was it requisite there should, as their concord and government were determined by the termination of their verbs and substantives.

The test of a sameness in the arrangement of the members of sentences has, as far as I know, never been attended to, in any attempt to discover a resemblance between the Asiatic and American languages. A likeness in the sounds of words alone has been regarded as furnishing the evidences of their affinity. But who shall determine the point in question? Where shall we find a philologist sufficiently versed in the languages of Asiatic Tartary, and those of the Indians of America, to determine the question of their resemblance to each other? As these languages contain no science, and are therefore not worth learning, it is not likely that such a person will be found before the Indian languages shall have vanished from the earth.

With the religious rites and ceremonies of the Tartars, and American Indians, we are too little acquainted to justify any conclusion concerning the identity of their origin from them. The most that we know on this subject is that their pawaws or priests are professed sorcerers, who are supposed capable of inflicting misfortunes, disease and death, by charms and incantations. The angikoks of Greenland, and Esquimaux, were men of the same profession. Most likely the Tartar priesthood is of the same cast.

The next thing to be considered is the sameness of color as having relation to the question under discussion. Here, it is hoped, a little prolixity in stating the physical causes of all the varieties of human colors will be excused. On this subject two questions present themselves. First, what is color; and, secondly, what are the natural causes of the various colors of the human skin?

Color is a certain arrangement of particles on the surface of bodies, so constituted as to reflect, or absorb, the rays of light in such a manner as to make a specific impression on the organs of vision denominated color. That arrangement of particles on the surface of bodies which absorbs all the rays of light is denominated black; on the contrary, that which reflects them at their angle of incidence produces the white color. The various angles of reflection of the rays of light constitute the ground work of all colors between the extremes of black and white. Color is therefore a mere modification of particles on the surface of bodies.

There are four cardinal varieties of human color. First, the clear white of the hyperborean, such as that of the Swedes, Danes, and Poles, and others in the same parallels of latitude. Secondly, the swarthy color of the inhabitants of the south of Europe, and the northern parts of Africa and Asia. Thirdly, the jet black of the negroes, and Abyssinians of Africa, but with this difference, that the latter have the features of Europeans, and long straight hair: and lastly, the red, or copper color of the Asiatic Tartars, and American Indians. Varying with the parallels of latitude from that of Sweden to the torrid zone, the human skin exhibits every possible shade of difference between the white and the deepest black.

Concerning the physical cause of the various colors of mankind, a great variety of opinions has been entertained. I shall however take no notice of any of them, but give that theory on this subject which appears to be founded in truth, and which now generally prevails. It is that which attributes all the varieties of human color to the influence of climate, and different modes of living. Every phenomena of the subject in question evidently coincides with this opinion.

The sciences of anatomy and physiology have clearly decided that the *rete mucosum* of the skin is the basis of its color. This, however, requires some explanation. The skin consists of three membranes. The outer one is the epidermis, or scarf skin, the second is the rete mucosum, or, as the expression imports, a mucous membrane, or net work, which lies immediately under the scarf skin, and lastly the true skin. This latter, or true skin, is perfectly white in all people; the epidermis, or scarf skin, is universally transparent. Through this transparent scarf skin, the color of the rete mucosum, underneath, is discovered. That the state of the rete mucosum, with regard to color, is varied by the influence of climate, and modes of life, there can be no doubt. The zones of the earth are scarcely better marked out by their parallels of latitude, than are the inhabitants of their respective latitudes, designated by their shades of color, from the white of the north, to the black of the tropical regions. Those latter regions alone exhibit considerable variety of color. Their inhabitants are not all black. It may be said, however, that none of them are white. There must be something peculiar in the air, and certain portions of Africa, which gives the sooty color of the negro and Abyssinian. Physiology will in time discover this phenomenon.

Whatever may have been the original color of mankind, a change once induced by removals from one region to others would be augmented through successive generations until the influence of climate would have exerted its full effect. Even the influence of mothers to have their offspring of that color esteemed most beautiful would have considerable effect in hastening on the change from the original color. The shining black, among the Africans, is equal in point of beauty to the lily and the rose among the whites. The sight of a white person, among those of the Africans who have not been in the habit of seeing Europeans, never fails to excite the deepest horror. At first sight they ascribe the whiteness of the skin to some loathsome and incurable disease.

Evidences of the influence of climate on the human color present themselves constantly to our observation. The descendants of the Africans in our country are far from having the sooty black color of their forefathers, the natives of Africa. The latter are distinguished from the former at first sight. In America there are many full blooded negroes scarcely a shade nearer the black than many of our mulattoes. These are denominated *white negroes*. Africa exhibits none of this description. These people exhibit one presumptive evidence that the original color of mankind was white. The skin of a full blooded negro infant, for some time after birth, is nearly white. It is not until the skin of the child has been exposed to the air for some time that the rete mucosum becomes of such a texture as to exhibit the black color.

Many of our young men of a fair complexion, after performing several voyages down the river, and among the West India islands, return swarthy men, and remain so for life. Every mother is aware of the influence of the sun in tanning their children, especially during the prevalence of the equinoctial wind in the spring of the year, and therefore take every pains to prevent their blasting influence on the lily and the rose of their little progeny during that season.

It may be asked, why the Indian color in America among the white people? Why this difference of color in the same region? All circumstances alike, the red color of the Indian is the color which is natural to our country. Many of those of the white people who have been brought up among the Indians from their infancy differ from them but little in point of color, and are to be distinguished from them only by the differences in their features. There are many of our white people of a darker hue than many of the Indians. We do not so readily perceive this, because a white man, let his color be ever so dark, is still a white man, while an Indian with a whiter skin is still an Indian. We lose sight of the color of both in the national character of each, of which we never lose sight. Were any number of white people to adopt the Indian mode of living in its full extent, in a few generations the difference of color between them and the Indian would not be great. How much whiter is a French Canadian boatman than an Indian? Scarcely a single shade. Thus physiology has ascertained beyond a shadow of doubt that the rete mucosum is the basis of the human color, and innumerable facts go to show that the various states of this membrane, which exhibit all the varieties of the human color, are occasioned by the influence of different climates and modes of living.

But from the varieties of this membrane, so slight in themselves that physiology can scarcely discover them, except in their effects, what mighty consequences have arisen! What important conclusions have been drawn!

An African is black, has a woolly head, and a flat nose; he is therefore not entitled to the rights of human nature! But he is a docile being, possessed of but little pride of independence, and a subject of the softer passions, who rather than risk his life in the defense of his liberty will "Take the pittance and the lash." He is, therefore, a proper subject for slavery.

The Indian has a copper colored skin, and therefore the rights of human nature do not belong to him! But he will not work, and his high sense of independence, and strong desire of revenge, would place in danger the property and life of the oppressor who should attempt to force him to labor. He is, therefore, to be exterminated; or at least despoiled of his country, and driven to some remote region where he must perish! Such has been, and such is still to a certain extent, the logic of nations possessed of all the science of the world!—of Christian nations. How horrid the features of that slavery to which this logic has given birth! The benevolent heart bleeds at the thought of the cruelties which have always accompanied it; amongst the Mohammedans as soon as the Christian slave embraces the religion of his master, he is free; but among the followers of the Messiah, the slave may indeed embrace the religion of his master; but he still remains a slave; although a Christian brother.

It is a curious circumstance, that while our missionaries are generously traversing the most inhospitable regions, and endeavoring, with incessant toil, to give the science of Europe and America, together with the Christian revelation, to the benighted pagans, most of the legislatures of our slave holding states have made it a highly penal offense to teach a slave a single letter. While at great expense and waste of valuable lives we are endeavoring to teach the natives of Africa the use of letters, no one durst attempt to do the same thing for the wretched descendants of slavery in America. Thus our slavery chains the soul as well as the body. Would a Mussulman hinder his slave from learning to read the Koran? Surely he would not.

We are often told by slaveholders that they would willingly give freedom to their slaves if they could do it with safety; if they could get rid of them when free; but are they more dangerous when free than when in slavery! But admitting the fact, that owing to their ignorance, stupidity and bad habits, they are unfit for freedom we ourselves have made them so. We debase them to the condition of brutes, and then use that debasement as an argument of perpetuating their slavery.

I will conclude this digression with the eloquent language of President Jefferson on the subject: "Human liberty is the gift of God, and cannot be violated but in his wrath. Indeed I tremble for my country when I reflect that God is just and that his justice cannot sleep forever: that considering numbers, nature, and natural means only, a revolution of the wheel of fortune, an exchange of situation is among the possible events:

it may become probable by supernatural interference. The Almighty has no attribute which can take side with us in such a contest."

But to return. Why this great solicitude of the learned to discover the genealogy of the American Indians. This solicitude is like many other fashionable pursuits of the present day. It is like a voyage to the northern polar regions, or a journey into Africa; in the former of which nothing is seen but immense islands of ice, and in the latter little else than regions of arid deserts; but the voyager and traveler return home rich in discoveries—of red snow—the probable cause of the aurora borealis—or of an hidden catacomb, full of mummies, and the huge head of the lesser Memnon. Besides actual discoveries, both are rich—in conjectures of little or no importance to the world.[1]

We might say to the Englishman, the Frenchman, and German, what is your origin? He knows more of his own genealogy than he does of that of the American Indians. The blood of fifty nations, for aught he can tell to the contrary, runs in his veins. He may be related to the Assyrians, Chaldeans, Egyptians, Greeks, Romans, Copts and many other smaller nations, whose very names have long since been buried in oblivion.

Thus while you are anxiously inquiring for the origin of the poor savages of America, you forget your own. Perhaps at this moment you know nothing of your immediate ancestry, beyond your grandfather, or at the farthest your great-grandfather.

If we should infer a community of origin between the Tartars of Asia and the American Indians, from a resemblance of

---

[1] Many suppose that some of the Indians are of Jewish origin. This may indeed be the case, for at an early period of the Jewish history, Shalmaneser, the king of Assyria, took Samaria after a siege of three years' continuance. "And the king of Assyria did carry away Israel into Assyria, and put them in Halak, and in Habor, by the river Gozan, and in the city of the Medes." From these places it is highly probable many of the Jews found their way into Eastern Tartary, and from thence to America, but with the loss of their natural character, language and religion. Ten of the twelve tribes were carried off by Shalmaneser. After this event, history no longer recognizes those tribes as Jews; thenceforward the kingdom of Israel consisted only of the tribes of Juda, Benjamin, and part of the tribe of Levi. So large a number of prolific people, must have soon associated themselves, by traveling, commerce, and intermarriage, with all the surrounding nations, and of course their descendants would be as likely to find their way to America, as any other people.— II Kings, Chap. 18.—*Notes on Virginia,* p. 222. (D)

color, it would be no more than saying that the same causes will, in similar circumstances, produce the same effects; the sun and air will produce the same effects on man in Tartary that they do in America in the same latitudes. It is now too late, or soon will be so, to find anything like a solution of this question from any resemblance between the languages of these people. The religious worship of savages is everywhere pretty much the same, and therefore throws no light on the subject. On their traditions no reliance can be placed, because to a people who have no written science the past is a region of fabulous uncertainty.

It is enough for the solution of this question that the navigation of the northern Atlantic, and northern Pacific, has at all times been practicable, even to the imperfect navigation of the nations inhabiting their shores, and that they at all times carried on a constant intercourse with each other, especially across the northern Pacific.

But to which continent shall we ascribe the honor of having given population to the other? This is the most important point in this discussion, but can it ever be settled? For my part I am perfectly willing to concede to the old world the honor of having given population to the new. It is much the largest continent, and by far the first in arts and sciences. Besides placing some reliance on the oldest, and not the least authentic history in the world, I can see no reason why the garden of Eden, near the head of the Persian gulf, was not a point from which the whole world might as conveniently be peopled, and in as short a time, as from any other spot which a geographer can point out.

On the whole, the race of mankind constitutes an exclusive genus of animated beings; man is therefore an unit, and as such must have had one common origin, "no matter what color an Indian or an African sun may have burnt upon him." He justly claims a kindred relation to the whole of his race. What though the severe cold of the arctic circles has dwindled their inhabitants down to a dwarfish stature. What though in more fortunate climates we meet with Anakim, or Patagonians, in all the essentials of his physical and moral character man is the same in every region of the globe.

May this paternal relation be everywhere recognized. May a just and enlightened policy, and above all may the holy religion of the good Samaritan, induce the strong to respect the claims of the weak upon his justice and humanity, and "To do unto others as he would they should do unto him."

CHAPTER IV.

Changes in the System of Weather.

Great changes have taken place in our system of weather, since the settlement of the western country, yet these changes have been so gradual that it is no very easy task to recollect or describe them. At the first settlement of the country the summers were much cooler than they are at present. For many years we scarcely ever had a single warm night during the whole summer. The evenings were cool, and the mornings frequently uncomfortably cold. The coldness of the nights was owing to the deep shade of the lofty forest trees, which everywhere covered the ground. In addition to this, the surface of the earth was still further shaded by large crops of wild grass and weeds, which prevented it from becoming heated by the rays of the sun during the day. At sun down the air began to become damp and cool, and continued to increase in coldness until warmed by the sunshine of the succeeding day. This wild herbage afforded pasture for our cattle and horses from spring till the onset of winter. To enable the owner to find his beasts, the leader of each flock of cattle, horses and sheep, was furnished with a bell, suspended to the neck by a leathern or iron collar. Bells, therefore, constituted a considerable article of traffic in early times.

One distressing circumstance resulted from the wild herbage of our wilderness. It produced innumerable swarms of gnats, mosquitoes and horse flies. These distressing insects gave such annoyance to man and beast that they may justly be ranked among the early plagues of the country. During that part of the season in which they were prevalent, they made the cattle poor and lessened the amount of their milk. In plowing they were very distressing to the horses. It was customary to build large fires of old logs about the forts, the smoke of which kept the flies from the cattle, which soon learned to change their position, with every change of wind, so as to keep themselves constantly in the smoke.

Our summers in early times were mostly very dry. The beds of our large creeks, excepting in the deep holes, presented nothing but naked rocks. The mills were not expected to do any grinding after the latter end of May, excepting for a short time after a thunder gust; our most prudent housekeepers, therefore, took care to have their summer stock of flour ground in the months of March and April. If this stock was expended too soon there were no resources but those of the hominy block or hand mill. It was a frequent saying among our farmers that three good rains were sufficient to make a crop of corn, if they happened at the proper times. The want of rain was compensated in some degree by heavy dews, which were then more common than of late, owing to the shaded situation of the earth, which prevented it from becoming either warm or dry, by the rays of the sun, during even the warmest weather. Frost and snow set in much earlier in former times than of late. I have known the whole crop of corn in Greenbrier destroyed by frost on the night of the twenty-second of September. The corn in this district of country was mostly frost-bitten at the same time. Such early frosts, of equal severity, have not happened for some time past. Hunting snows usually commenced about the middle of October. November was regarded as a winter month, as the winter frequently set in with severity during that month, and sometimes at an early period of it.

For a long time after the settlement of the country we had an abundance of snow, in comparison to the amount we usually have now. It was no unusual thing to have snows from one to three feet in depth, and of long continuance. Our people often became tired of seeing the monotonous aspect of the country so long covered with a deep snow, and "longed to see the ground bare once more." I well remember the labor of opening roads through those deep snows, which often fell in a single night, to the barn, spring, smoke house and corn crib. The labor of getting wood, after a deep fall of snow, was in the highest degree disagreeable. A tree, when fallen, was literally buried in the snow, so that the driver of the horses had to plunge the whole length of his arms into it to get the long chain around the butt end of the tree to haul it home. The depth of the snows, the extreme cold and length of our winters, were indeed distressing to the first settlers, who were but poorly provided with clothing, and whose cabins were mostly very open and uncomfortable. Getting wood, making fires, feeding the stock, and going to mill, were considered sufficient employment for any family, and truly those labors left them little time for anything else.

As our roads, in early times, did not admit of the use of sleighs, the only sport we had in the time of a deep snow was that of racing about on the crust of its surface. This was formed by a slight thaw succeeded by a severe frost. On this crust we could travel over logs, brush, and owing to great drifts of snow in many places, over the highest fences. These crusts were often fatal to the deer. Wolves, dogs and men could pursue them without breaking through the crust. The deer, on the contrary, when pursued, owing to the smallness of their hoofs, always broke through it unless when it was uncommonly hard. The hunters never killed the deer in the dead of winter, as their skins and flesh were then of but little value. Taking advantage of them in the time of a crust they held a dishonorable practice, and they always relieved them from the pursuit of wolves and dogs whenever it fell in their way to do so. Foreigners, however, who were not in the habit of hunting, often pursued and caught them on the crust for the sake of informing their friends in the old country by letter that they had killed a deer.

An incident happened in my father's neighborhood which for some time was highly satisfactory to the hunters, as it looked like a providential punishment for taking advantage of the deer in time of a crust, as well as a means of putting an end to the unlawful sport.

A Captain Thomas Wells,[1] a noted warrior, hunter and trapper, was informed by one of his neighbors who came to his house to borrow a bag, that a deer had been killed by the wolves, the night before, not far from his house, and that the deer had not been wholly devoured. They concluded that as the wolves would visit the place the succeeding night, for the purpose of finishing their prey, they might catch one of them in a wolf trap. They accordingly set a large trap in the head of a spring, close by the relics of the deer. The spring had melted the snow as it fell, and it was then covered with a thick coat of dry leaves; under these leaves the trap was concealed.

Shortly after they had finished their work a couple of new comers from Ireland, in pursuit of a deer with dogs, came to the place, and seeing the bones of the deer called a halt to look at them. One of them, whose feet happened to be very cold, stepped on the dry leaves over the spring, and placed one of his feet in the wolf trap, which instantly fastened on his foot with its merciless jaws. With great labor, difficulty and delay, the foot was extricated from the trap. The first house they called at, after the accident, was that of the man who had assisted Capt. Wells to set the trap. They complained bitterly of the occurrence, and said that they had wrought full half an hour before they could get the wicked thing off the foot. They wondered whether there was no law in America to punish people for setting such wicked things about the woods, to catch people by the feet. The gentleman heard their complaint, without letting them know that he had any hand in setting the trap. Fortunately the trap struck the Hibernian across the sole of his shoe, which being thick and frozen prevented the mischief it would otherwise have done him; if the jaws of the trap had reached his ankle, the bones of his leg must have been broken to pieces by them. The

[1] Thomas Wells, here named, lived on the farm where Thos. M. Patterson now resides in Cross Creek township.—(*Simpson.*)

jokes that were carved out of this event throughout the neighborhood, and the high glee with which the hunters related the tale, served to show the foreigners the detestation in which the practice of killing deer in the winter season was held, and in a great measure put a stop to their sport.

But to return. The spring of the year in former times was pretty much like our present springs. We commonly had an open spell of weather during the latter part of February, denominated by some *pawwawing days* and by others *weather breeders.* The month of March was commonly stormy and disagreeable throughout. It was a common saying that we must not expect spring until the *borrowed days,* that is, the three first days of April were over. Sugar was often made in the early part of April. It sometimes happened that a great part of April was but little better than March, with regard to storms of rain, snow and a cold chilling air. I once noticed forty frosts after the first day of April; yet our fruit that year was not wholly destroyed. We never considered ourselves secure from frost until the first ten days of Mav had past. During these days we never failed of having cold, stormy weather, with more or less frost.

On the whole, although the same variable system of weather continues, our springs were formerly somewhat colder, and accompanied with more snow, than they are now, but the change, in these respects, is no way favorable to vegetation, as our latest springs are uniformly followed by the most fruitful seasons. It is a law of the vegetable world that the longer the vegetative principle is delayed, the more rapid when put in motion. Hence those northern countries which have but a short summer, and no spring, are amongst the most fruitful countries in the world. In Russia, Sweden and Denmark, the transition from winter to summer occupies but a very few days; yet a failure of a crop in those countries is but a rare occurrence: while in our latitudes, vegetation prematurely put in motion, and then often checked "by the laggering rear of winter's frost," frequently fails of attaining its ultimate perfection.

From this history of the system of the weather of our early times, it appears that our seasons have already undergone great and important changes. Our summers are much warmer, our falls much milder and longer, and our winters shorter by at least one month, and accompanied with much less snow and cold than formerly. What causes have effected these changes in our system of weather, and what may we reasonably suppose will be the ultimate extent of this revolution, already so apparent, in our system of weather?

In all countries the population of a desert by civilized and agricultural people has had a great effect on its climate.

Italy, which is now a warm country, with very mild winters was, in the time of Horace and Virgil, as cold and as subject to deep snows as the western country was at its first settlement. Philosophy has attributed the change of the seasons in that country to the clearing of its own forests, together with those of France to the north, and those of Germany to the east and north of Italy.[1] The same cause has produced the same effect in our country. Every acre of cultivated land must increase the heat of our summers, by augmenting the extent of the surface of the ground denuded of its timber, so as to be acted upon and heated by the rays of the sun.

The future prospect of the weather throughout the whole extent of the western country is not very flattering. The thermometer in the hottest parts of our summer months already ranges from ninety to one hundred degrees. A frightful degree of heat for a country as yet not half cleared of its native timber! When we consider the great extent of the valley of the Mississippi, so remote from any sea to furnish its cooling breezes, without mountains to collect the vapors, augment and diversify the winds, and watered only by a few rivers, which in the summer time are diminished to a small amount of water, we have every data for the unpleasant conclusion that the climate of the western regions will ultimately become intensely hot and subject to distressing calms and droughts of long continuance.

---

[1] Vides, ut alta stet nive candidum
Soracte; nec jam sustineant onus
Sylvæ laborantes; geluque,
Flumina constiterint acuto?—*Hor., lib.* 1, *Ode* ix.
—(D)

Already we begin to feel the effects of the increase of the heat of summer in the noxious effluvia of the stagnant water of the ponds and low grounds along our rivers. These fruitful sources of pestilential exhalations have converted large tracts of our country into regions of sickness and death, while the excessive heat and dryness of our settlements, remote from the large water courses, have been visited by endemic dysenteries in their most mortal states. Thus the most fortunate regions of the earth have drawbacks from their advantages which serve in some degree to balance the condition of their inhabitants with that of the people of countries less gifted by nature in point of soil, climate and situation.

The conflict for equilibrium between the rarified air of the south and the dense atmosphere of the north will continue forever the changeable state of weather in this country, as there is no mountainous barrier between us and the northern regions of our continent.

CHAPTER V.

Beasts and Birds.

The reader need not expect that this chapter will contain a list of all the beasts and birds which were tenants of the western wilderness at the time of its first settlement. I shall only briefly notice a few of those classes which have already totally or partially disappeared from the country, together with those which have emigrated here with our population. This enumeration, as far as it goes, will serve to show the natural historian a distinction between those beasts and birds which are naturally tenants of the wilderness and refuse the society of man, and those which follow his footsteps from one region to another, and although partially wild yet subsist in part upon his labors.

The buffalo and elk have entirely disappeared from this section of the country. Of the bear and deer but very few remain. The wolves, formerly so numerous, and so destructive to the cattle, are now seldom heard of in our older settlements. It may seem strange that this ferocious and cunning animal, so long the scourge of the mountainous districts of Europe, should have so suddenly disappeared from our infant country. The sagacity of the wolves bids defiance to the most consummate craft of the hunters, many of whom, throughout life, never obtained a single chance to shoot at one of them. Sometimes, indeed, they outwitted them by pit-falls and steel traps; but no great number were killed by either of these means; nor had the price set upon their scalps by the state legislatures any great effect in diminishing their number and depredations. By what means then did their destruction happen? On this subject I will hazard the opinion that a greater number of them were destroyed by hydrophobia than by all other means put together. That this disease took place amongst them at an early period is evident from the fact that nearly forty years ago a Captain Rankin of Raccoon creek, in Washington county, Pa., was bitten by a mad wolf. A few years ago Mr. John M'Camant of this county met with the same misfortune. In both cases the wolf was killed, and I am sorry to add both these men died, after having suffered all the pains and horrors accompanying that most frightful of all diseases, that inflicted by the bite of a rabid animal.

An animal so ferocious as a wolf, and under the influence of madness, bites everything he can reach; of course the companions of his own den and thicket are the first victims of his rage. Hence, a single wolf would be the means of destroying the whole number of his fellows, in his immediate neighborhood at least. In the advanced state of the disease they lose their native wildness, leave their dens and thickets and seek the flocks and herds about farm houses, and in some instances have attempted to enter the houses themselves for the purpose of doing mischief.

The buzzards, or vultures, grey and bald eagles, ravens, or as they were generally called corbies, were very numerous here in former times. It was no uncommon thing to see from fifty to one hundred of them perched on the trees over a single carcase of carrion. All these large carnivorous birds have nearly disappeared from our settlements.

The wild turkeys, which used to be so abundant as to supply no inconsiderable portion of provision for the first settlers, are now rarely seen.

The different kinds of wood-peckers still remain in the country, with the exception of the largest of that genus of birds, the wood-cock, which is now very scarce.

The black and grey squirrels still remain in the country. These beautiful but destructive little animals gave great annoyance to the first settlers of our country, by devouring large quantities of their corn in the fields before it was fit for gathering. There is something singular in the history of the squirrels. Sometimes in the course of a few years they become so numerous as to threaten the destruction of whole crops; when, as if by common consent, they commence an emigration from west to east, crossing the river in countless numbers. At the commencement of their march they are very fat, and furnish an agreeable article of diet; but towards its conclusion they become sickly and poor, with large worms attached to their skins. After this emigration they are scarce for some years, then multiply, emigrate, and perish as before. The cause of this phenomenon is, I believe, unknown. It cannot be the want of food; for the districts of countries which they leave are often as fruitful or more so than those to which they direct their course.

The terrible panther, as well as the wild cat, have also taken their leave of us.

Thus, in far less time than it cost the Jews to rid themselves of the serpents and beasts of prey which infested the "hill country of Judea," we have freed ourselves from those which belonged to our country. Our flocks and herds are safe from their annoyance, and our children are not torn to pieces by "a she bear out of the wood."

In return for the beasts and birds which have left us, we have gained an equal number from the Atlantic side of the mountains, and which were unknown at the first settlement of the country.

Our mornings and evenings are now enlivened with the matins and vespers of a great variety of singing birds, which have slowly followed the emigration from the other side of the mountain.

The honey bees are not natives of this country; but they always keep a little in advance of the white population. We formerly had some professed bee hunters; but the amount of honey obtained from the woods was never considerable, owing to the want of a sufficient quantity of flowers to furnish it.

Crows and black birds have of late become very plenty. They were not natives of the wilderness.

Rats, which were not known here for several years after the settlement of the country, took possession of it, in its whole extent, in one winter season. Children of twelve years old, and under, having never heard their name, were much surprised at finding a new kind of mice, as they called them, with smooth tails.

Opossums were late comers into the country. Fox-squirrels have but a very few years ago made their appearance on this side of the mountains.

Thus our country has exchanged its thinly scattered population of savages for a dense population of civilized inhabitants, and its wild beasts and large, carnivorous fowls, for domesticated animals and fowls, and others which although wild are inoffensive in their habits, and live at least partially on the labors of man. This has been effected here perhaps in less time than such important changes were ever effected in any other region of the earth.

The cases of the two unfortunate victims of the hydrophobia, here alluded to, deserve some notice.

Capt. Rankin was bitten by the wolf in his own door. Hearing in the dead of night a noise among his beasts in the yard, he got up and opened the upper part of his door, which was a double one. The wolf instantly made a spring to get into the house. Rankin, with great presence of mind, caught the wolf in his arms as he was passing over the lower half of the door and held him fast on its upper edge, and against the door post, until a man belonging to the household jumped out of bed, got a knife and cut the wolf's throat; but the wolf in the mean time bit him severely in the wrist. If I recollect rightly he lived but a short time afterwards.[1]

Mr. John M'Cammant, who lived but a few miles from this place on the road to Washington, met a similar death, much in the same way. Hearing an uproar among his beasts, not far from the house, he went to see what was the matter. He had not gone far before the wolf sprang at him and bit him severely in the left breast. Being a very strong, resolute man, he caught the wolf by the jaws, and held them apart, calling on an apprentice lad to bring an axe to knock the wolf on the head. He came with all speed, but finding he had no chance of striking the wolf, without risking an injury to his master, he dropped the axe, ran back to the house and got a butcher knife, with which he cut the wolf's throat. It was between seven and eight weeks before the virus took effect, so as to produce the symptoms of the terrible disease which followed.

From the time I first heard of his being bitten by the wolf I anticipated the consequence with horror, and the more so because he applied to a physician who had the reputation of curing the bite of a mad animal with a single pill. Placing confidence in this nostrum, he neglected all other medical aid. In this pill I had no confidence, having previously seen and examined one of them, and found it made of ingredients possessed of scarcely any medicinal efficacy whatever. On the Thursday preceding his death he became slightly indisposed. On Friday and Saturday he had the appearance of a person taking an intermittent fever. On Sunday the hydrophobia came on. It was then I first saw him. Having never seen the disease before, I was struck with consternation at his appearance. Every sense appeared to have acquired an hundred fold excitability. The slightest im-

[1] Capt. Zachariah Rankin died on the farm now occupied by Alex McCalmont, near Hickory, Washington county, Pa., about the 20th of October, 1785. His will as seen in the register's office at Washington, Pa., is dated Oct. 17, 1785, and is witnessed by Robert Lysle, Thomas Cherry and Isaac Wells. He died three days after he wrote his will. He was attended by Robert Lysle, Aaron Lysle, John Lysle, James Edgar, and some others whose names I have forgotten. He was buried in the old Cherry grave yard, in Mt. Pleasant township, Washington county.—(*Simpson.*)

pression upon any of them gave him a thrill of the deepest horror. Noise, the sight of colored clothing, the sudden passage of any person between him and the light of the window or candle, affected him beyond description.

On Sunday night his convulsive fits came on. He was then fastened by his hands and feet to the bed posts, to prevent him from doing mischief. At three o'clock on Monday evening he became delirious, his fits ceased, and at two o'clock in the morning death put a period to his sufferings.[1]

It is impossible for language to describe this terrible disease. The horror of mind which he continually suffered was equal to that which would be felt by the most timid lady on being compelled to go alone at midnight into a grave yard, with an entire certainty of seeing a ghost in the most frightful form which a disordered imagination ever ascribed to a departed spirit. He several times requested the physicians to bleed him to death. Several veins were opened but the blood had so far lodged itself in engorgements in the viscera that none could be discharged from the veins. He then requested that some of his limbs might be cut off, that the same object might be effected that way. Finding this request would not be complied with, he looked up to his rifle and begged of me with tears in his eyes to take it down and shoot him through the head, saying " I will look at you with delight and thankfulness, while you are pulling the trigger. In doing this you will do right. I know from your countenance that you pity me; but you know not the thousandth part of what I suffer. You ought to put an end to my misery, and God himself will not blame you for doing so." What made these requests the more distressing, was the circumstance that they did not proceed from any derangement of mind; on the contrary, excepting during the time of his fits, which lasted only a few seconds at a time, he was in the full exercise of his understanding. His

[1] John McCamant died in February, 1807. He was bitten December 25, 1806. He was buried at Lower Buffalo church, Brooke county, W. Va. About 1854 his remains were disintered and removed to Washington, Pa., by his daughter, Mrs. Joseph Henderson. Mr. McCamant's residence was on the Wellsburg pike, the first farm on the Virginia side, west of Dr. Parkinson's as one goes from Independence to Wellsburg. Jacob Dimit, the last man who helped attend McCamant, died December 2, 1883.—(*Simpson.*)

discourse until about three o'clock on Monday evening was quite rational. He requested prayers to be made for him, and deliberately gave directions about the place of his interment, and funeral sermon, all which requests were complied with.

The reader, no doubt, wishes to know as much as possible concerning the famous pill, an improper reliance on which terminated in the death of Mr. M'Cammant. I have had an opportunity of examining two of them at a considerable distance of time apart. The first I saw was about five times as large as one of Anderson's pills, and composed of Burgundy pitch and green rue. The second was made of the same material, with a narrow strip of paper rolled up in the middle of it. The paper contained about a dozen ill-shapen letters, but not so arranged as to spell any word in any language with which I am acquainted. The physician who gave those pills reported that he got the recipe for making them from a priest of Abyssinia. Such is the superstition which still remains attached to the practice of the healing art, and from which, in all likelihood, it will never be separated. But why then the celebrity of this pill, as a preventive of canine madness? Has it never had the effect ascribed to it? Certainly never.

Far the greater number of those who are said to be bitten by rabid animals have been bitten by animals either not really mad, or not in such a state of madness as to communicate the disease.

An event which fell under my own observation several years ago will serve to explain this matter. Several children, one of whom was my own, were said to have been bitten by a mad cat, which was instantly killed. On inquiry I found that there was no report of mad animals in the neighborhood. I then gave it as my opinion that the apparent madness of the cat proceeded only from caterwauling. This did not satisfy any one but myself, so I had to treat the children as I should have if the cat had been really mad, and thus got the credit of curing four cases of canine madness: a credit which I never deserved.

A few years ago a gentleman of my neighborhood brought me his daughter who he said had been bitten by a mad cat. I asked if the cat was a male one; he answered in the affirmative.

He said he had imprisoned him in a closet. I am glad of that, said I, keep him there a few days, and you will find him as well as ever he was; and so it turned out.

Dogs are subject to a similar madness from the same cause. In this state, like cats, they are apt to bite even their best friends. In this case the animal is reported to be mad and instantly killed. In such cases these pills, as well as other nostrums for this disease, do wonders; that is where there is nothing to be done.[1]

---

[1] Mr. Doddridge does not do justice to this cure that Mr. McCamant used. It was a pill gotten from Dr. Marchand, of Fayette county, Pa., and there was no doubt it cured many, or prevented them from going mad. Dr. Marchand bound all who got the pill from him that they would never use liquor of any kind. McCamant disregarded this injunction and the consequence was he went mad and died. The Hon. Joseph R. Reed, of Iowa, his mother and brother, were bitten in 1839 by a mad dog. The brother went mad and died. Joseph and his mother got this pill and were cured. Mrs. Reed died in 1874. Mr. Reed himself was alive in 1888. But this cure is now lost to the world, as the last of the Marchands who knew its secret died in the army during the civil war.—(*Simpson.*)

Dr. Doddridge does not specifically state that the pills which were believed to cure hydrophobia came from Dr. Marchand of Fayette county; this statement is by Simpson. The Marchands were prominent citizens, and widely known professionally. Dr. David Marchand, a native of Berne, Switzerland, settled in 1770 on Little Sewickley Creek, about six miles southwest of Greensburg, Westmoreland county, Pa. He is said to have been a physician of rare ability; certainly his practise was very extensive in Westmoreland and adjoining counties. He died July 22, 1809. His three sons, Daniel, David and Louis, all became physicians. Dr. Daniel settled in Uniontown, Pa., and Dr. Louis in Jefferson township, Fayette county, Pa., five miles below Brownsville, on the Monongahela river. After some years of rural practise, following his graduation in 1809, in Philadelphia, from the University of Pennsylvania, Dr. Louis Marchand went to Uniontown to take up the practise of his brother Daniel, who had died there March 13, 1822. Dr. Louis died in 1857. (See Ellis' History of Fayette County.) It was some one, or likely all, of this Marchand family of doctors who, according to Simpson, prescribed the pill reputed to be a specific for rabies. One of Dr. Louis' children was Samuel Sackett Marchand, also a doctor, who practised in Westmoreland county. He enlisted in Co. H., 136th regiment, Pennsylvania Volunteers (Col. Bayne's) and was wounded at Fredericksburg, Dec. 13, 1862, dying in Libby prison Feb. 28, 1863. This is the Marchand referred to by Simpson as the last who knew the secret of the pill that would cure the rabies. David Marchand, Jr., served two terms in congress. —(J. S. R.)

CHAPTER VI.

Number and Variety of Serpents.

Among the plagues of the Jews, at the time of their settlement in the land of Canaan, that of the serpents, which abounded in that country, was not the least. In like manner the early settlers of this country were much annoyed by serpents. Of the poisonous kinds of them we had but two, the rattlesnake and the copper-head, both of which were very numerous in every section of the country, but especially the rattlesnake. We had also different kinds of black snakes, with a number of lesser sorts, but these last are not poisonous. The bite of the rattlesnake was frequently mortal, always extremely painful; that of the copper-head not much less so.

Let the reader imagine the situation of our first settlers, with regard to those poisonous reptiles, when informed that an harvest day seldom passed in which the laborers did not meet with more or less of them. The reaper busily employed with his sickle was suddenly alarmed by the whiz of a rattlesnake at his feet; he instantly retreated, got a club, and giving the snake a blow or two finished his execution by striking the point of the sickle through its head and holding it up to the view of the company. It was then thrown aside by the root of a tree, or in a bunch of bushes, and then labor recommenced. This often happened a half dozen times in the course of a single day. This was not the worst. Owing to the heavy dews and growth of rank weeds among the small grain, it was requisite to let the grain lie in grips a day or more to dry before it was bound up. The rattlesnakes often hid themselves under these handfulls of grain, and hence it often happened that they were taken up in the arms of those who were employed in gathering and binding them. If the laborer happened to be even an old man, stiffened with toil and the rheumatism, he dropped all and sprang away with all the agility of a boy of sixteen, and however brave in other respects it was some time before the tremor of his limbs and the palpitation of his heart wore off.

Terrible as the serpents were to men, they were still more so to our women, to whose lot it generally fell to pull the flax. The flax patch was commonly near the grain field. While the men were reaping the grain the women were pulling the flax. The rattlesnakes were often met with among the flax. When this happened the women always screamed with all their might. A race then took place among the younger reapers, to decide who should have the honor of killing the snake. In the race each one picked up a club, and the first of them who reached the serpent instantly despatched him. This was a little piece of chivalry with which the girls were well pleased. Very few women had the hardihood to attack and kill a rattlesnake. At the sight of one of them they always gave a loud shriek, as if conscious of being the weaker vessel; in similar circumstances a man never does this, as he has no one to depend upon for protection but himself. I have often seen women so overcome with terror at the sight of a rattlesnake as to become almost incapable of moving.

Every season, for a long time, a number of our people were bitten by those poisonous reptiles. Some of them died; those of them who escaped death generally suffered a long and painful confinement, which left some of them in an infirm state of health for the rest of their lives.

In the fall these reptiles congregate together in cavities among the rocks, where it is said that they remain in a dormant state during the winter. Whether this is the fact or not I cannot tell, never having seen one of their dens opened.

These dens were common all over the country, and many of them well known to our people, who much dreaded the egress of their poisonous inhabitants, in the spring of the year, not only on account of themselves, but also on account of their beasts, many of which were killed by the bites of the snakes.

There was a den in the neighborhood of my father's place, and I well remember a rare piece of sport of the children belonging to the farms about it. It was on a warm day in the spring of the year, when we knew that the snakes were out among the leaves sunning themselves. We encircled the den, including several acres of ground, by parting the leaves so as to prevent the fire from spreading through the woods. On the inside of this ring we set fire to the dry leaves. In a short time we had the fun of seeing the snakes jumping and writhing in the blaze of the leaves. After the burning was over we collected a considerable pile of our burnt snakes.

I have heard of but two attempts to demolish the dens of the snakes. The first was somewhere in the Alleghany mountain. My informant told me that by the time they had killed about ninety of them they became so sickened by the stench of the serpents that they were obliged to quit the work, although there was still a great number of them in view. The next attempt to destroy a snake den took place between New Lancaster and Columbus in the state of Ohio. The snakes had chosen one of the old Indian graves, composed mainly of stone, for their residence. They gave such annoyance to the settlers in its neighborhood that they assembled for the purpose of demolishing it. In doing so they found several hundred snakes together with a vast quantity of the bones of those of them which through a long series of years had perished in the den. These were intermingled with the bones of those human beings for whose sepulture the mound had been erected.

Do these reptiles possess that power of fascination which has so frequently been ascribed to them? Many of them as I have seen I never witnessed an instance of the exercise of this power. I have several times seen birds flying about them, approaching close to their heads, and uttering noises which seemed to indicate the greatest distress; but on examination always found that the strange conduct of the bird was owing to an approach of the snake to the nest containing its young.

That such cases as those above mentioned are often mistaken for instances of the exercise of the power of fascination is quite certain; nevertheless that this power exists there can be no doubt. The greater number of the early settlers say that they have been witnesses of the exercise of this power, and their testimony is worthy of credit. It seems from some reports worthy of belief that even mankind as well as birds and beasts are subject to this fascinating power of serpents.

A Mr. Walter Hill, a laborer in Maryland in early times, informed me that once in the spring of the year, himself and a fellow laborer were directed by their employer to clean out the barn. In doing this they found a rattlesnake among the rubbish. Instead of killing, they threw it into a hogshead, with a view to have some sport with him after they had finished their work. Accordingly in the evening, when the work was done, my informant stooped over the top of the hogshead to take a look at the snake, when instantly he said, he became sick at the stomach, giddy headed, and partially blind. His head sunk downwards towards that of the serpent, which was elevated some distance above its coil. The eyes of the snake were steadily fixed on his and looked, as he expressed himself, like balls of fire. His companion observing his approach to the snake pulled him away. It was sometime before he came to himself. I have heard of an instance of the fascination of a young lady of New Jersey.

This power of fascination is indeed a strange phenomenon. Yet, according to the usual munificence of nature, the poor miserable snake, which inherits the hatred of all animated nature, ought to have some means of procuring subsistence, as well as of defense: but he has no teeth or claws to aid him in catching his prey, nor feet to assist him in flight or pursuit. His poison, however, enables him to take revenge for the hatred entertained against him, and his power of charming procures him a scanty supply of provision. But what is this power of fascination? Is there any physical agency in it? I think it must be admitted that there is some physical agency employed in this matter, although we may not be able to ascertain what it is. If there be no such agency employed in fascination by serpents, it must be effected by a power similar to that which superstition ascribes to charms, amulets, spells and incantations. A power wholly imaginary, unknown to the laws of nature, and which philosophy totally rejects as utterly impossible. On this subject I will hazard the opinion that the charm under consideration is effected by means of an intoxicating odor which the serpent has the power of emitting.

That the rattlesnakes have the power of giving out a very offensive vapor I know by experience, having often smelt them in warm sunny days, especially after a shower of rain, when plowing in the field. This often happened when I did not see any of them; but it always excited a painful apprehension that I should speedily meet with some of them. The odor of a serpent is an odor *sui generis*. A person once accustomed to it can never mistake it for anything else.

I have heard it said, although I cannot vouch for the truth of it, that a snake, when in the act of charming, appears, by the alternate expansion and depression of its sides, to be engaged in the act of blowing with all its might.

I think it every way probable, that in every instance of fascination, the position of the snake is to the windward of the victim of its charm. But why should this intoxicating odor draw its victim to the source from whence it issues. Here I must plead ignorance, to be sure; but does anything more happen to the bird or beast in this case than happens to mankind in consequence of the use of those intoxicating gases, or fluids, furnished by the art of chemistry.

A person affected by the exhilarating gas clings to the jar and sucks the pipe after he has inhaled its whole contents; and is not the madness occasioned by inhaling this gas equal to that which takes place in the bird or squirrel when under the influence of the charm of the serpent? The victims of this serpentine fascination scream and run, or flutter about awhile, and then resign themselves to their fate. In like manner the person who inhales the gas is instantly deprived of reason, becomes frantic, and acts the madman; but should he continue to inhale this gas only for a short time death would be the consequence. The same observation may be made with regard to alcohol, the basis of ardent spirits, a habit of using which occasions a repetition of the intoxicating draught, until, in spite of every consideration of honor, duty and interest, the indulgence ends in a slow but inevitable suicide.

My reader, I hope, will not complain of the length of this article. He perhaps has never seen one of the poisonous reptiles which so much annoyed his forefathers; but in gratitude he ought to reflect on the appalling dangers attendant on the settlement of his native country. The first settler at night knew not where to set his foot without danger of being assailed by the fangs of a serpent. Even his cabin was not secure from the invasion of the snakes. In the day time, if in the woods, he knew not in what bunch of weeds or grass he might provoke a rattlesnake by the tread of his foot, or from behind what tree or log he might be met by the bullet or tomahawk of an Indian.

CHAPTER VII.

Indigenous Fruits of the Country.

After having described the western wilderness, an account of its native fruits cannot be improper. To the botanist and agriculturalist this history cannot fail of being acceptable. To the former it will serve to show the great improvement which cultivation has made upon the indigenous fruits of the forest. To the latter it will point out what plants may yet be cultivated with success, although hitherto neglected. For instance, should he inquire whether this country is calculated by nature for the cultivation of the vine, he has only to ask whether the country in its original state produced the fruit of the vine. Those early settlers who profited by the indication with regard to the cultivation of the apple tree, furnished by the growth of the crab apple in the country, derived great advantage from their correct philosophy, in the high price of their fruit, while those who neglected this indication, and delayed planting their trees until they witnessed the growth of fruit on the trees of their neighbors, were left several years in the rear in this respect.

In giving the history of our native fruits I shall follow the order in which they ripened from spring until winter, our manner of gathering them, with some remarks on the present state of those of them which still remain in the country.

The first fruit which ripened in the country was the wild strawberry. It grew on poor land, on which there was no timber. There were many such places of small extent, on the points of hills along the creeks. They were denominated *bald knobs*. The fruit was small, and much sourer than the cultivated strawberry. It was not abundant in any place.

The service trees were the first in bloom in the spring. Their beautiful little flowers made a fine appearance through the woods, in the month of April. The berries were ripe in June. They are sweet, with a very slight mixture of acidity, and a very agreeable flavor. The service trees grew abundantly along the small water courses, and more thinly over the hills at a distance from them. A few of these trees still remain, but their fruit is mostly devoured by the great number of small birds which have accompanied the population of the country. Our time for gathering the service berries, as well as other fruits, was Sunday, and in large companies, under the protection of some of our warriors in arms. In doing this a great number of the trees were cut down, so that our crop of them was lessened every year. This fruit may be considered as lost to the country, for although the trees might be cultivated in gardens, the berries would all be devoured by the small birds before they would be fully ripe.

Blackberries grew in abundance in those places where, shortly before the settlement of the country, the timber had been blown down by hurricanes. Those places we called the *fallen timber*. When ripe, which was in the time of harvest, the children and young people resorted to the fallen timber in large companies, under a guard, for the purpose of gathering the berries, of which tarts were often made for the harvest table. The fallen timber, owing to a new growth of trees, no longer produces those berries, but enough of them are to be had along the fences on most of our farms.

Wild raspberries of an agreeable flavor were found in many places, but not plentifully anywhere.

Gooseberries of a small size, and very full of thorns, but of an agreeable taste, grew in some places in the woods. The amount of them was but small. Whatever may be the reason, this fruit does not succeed well when transplanted into gardens, where they flower abundantly, but shed the berries before they become ripe.

Whortleberries were never abundant in this section of the country, but they were so in many places in the mountains.

Wild plums were abundant in rich land. They were of various colors and sizes, and many of them of an excellent flavor. The wild plums of late years have, like our damson plums, fallen off prematurely. The beetle bug, or curculio, an insect unknown to the country at its first settlement, but now numerous everywhere, perforates the green fruit for the deposition of its egg. This occasions a flow of the juice of the fruit, so that it becomes gummy and falls off.

An indifferent kind of fruit, called buckberries, used to grow on small shrubs on poor ridges. This fruit has nearly vanished from the settled parts of the country.

Our fall fruits were winter and fall grapes; the former grew in the bottom lands. They were sour, of little value; and seldom used. The fall grapes grew on the high grounds, particularly in the fallen timber land. Of these grapes we had several varieties, and some of them large and of an excellent flavor. We still have the wild grapes; but not in such abundance as formerly. In process of time they will disappear from the country.

Black haws grew on large bushes along the moist bottoms of small water courses. They grew in large clusters, and ripened with the first frosts in the fall. Children were very fond of them. Red haws grew on the white thorn bushes. They were of various kinds. The sugar haws, which are small, grow in large clusters, and when ripe and free from worm, and semi transparent, were most esteemed. I have a row of about forty trees of the white thorn in my garden, which were raised from the haws. The berries when ripe are large, and make a fine appearance, and being almost free from worms the children are very fond of eating them.

Wild cherries were abundant in many places. To most people they are very agreeable fruit. They are now becoming scarce.

Pawpaws were plenty along the great water courses and on the rich hills. Some people are fond of eating them. Scarcely any beast will touch them; even the omnivorous hog never eats them. It is said that raccoons are fond of them. They are still plenty in many places.

The crab apple was very abundant along the smaller water courses. The foliage of the tree which bears this fruit is like that of the domestic apple tree but not so large. The tree itself is smaller, of a slower growth than the orchard tree, and the wood of a much firmer texture. It blossoms a little later than our orchards, and when in bloom makes a noble appearance, and fills the surrounding air with a delicious fragrance. The crab appears to be a tree of great longevity. Sour as the crab apples were, the children were fond of eating them, especially when in the winter season they could find them under the leaves, where, defended from the frost, they acquired a fine golden color, a fragrant smell, and lost much of their sourness. One or more of these indigenous apple trees ought to be planted in every orchard, in honor of their native tenancy of our forests, as well as for the convenience of our ladies, who are very fond of them for preserves, but are sometimes unable to procure them.

Of hickory nuts we had a great variety; some of the larger shell bark nuts, with the exception of the thickness of their shells, were little inferior to the English walnut. Of white walnuts, we generally had a great abundance. Of black walnuts, many varieties as to size and amount of kernel. Hazel and chestnuts were plenty in many places.

Thus a munificent providence had furnished this region of the earth with the greater number of fruits which are to be found in the old world; but owing to the want of cultivation, they were inferior in size and flavor to the same kinds of fruit in Europe. It has been my fate, as well as that of many others in this country, to use, in infancy and youth, the native fruits of the wilderness, and in more advanced age to enjoy the same kinds of fruits in their most improved state. The salutary effects of the cultivation of these fruits are, therefore, present to our senses, and we cannot fail to appreciate them.

It may not be amiss to notice in this place the changes which have taken place in the growth and bearing of some of our fruit trees since the settlement of the country.

My father planted peach trees at an early period. For some time a crop of peaches once in three or four years was as much as we expected. After some time these trees became so far naturalized to the climate as to bear almost every year. The same observation applies, although in a less degree, to the apple trees which were first planted in the country. Their fruit was frequently wholly killed by the frost. This has not happened for many years past. The pear and heart cherry trees, although they blossomed abundantly, bore but little fruit for many years; but in process of time they afforded abundant crops. Such was the effect of their becoming naturalized to our climate.

The peach and pear trees did very well until the year 1806, when a long succession of rainy seasons commenced, during which the trees overgrew themselves, and the falls being warm and rainy they continued their growth until the onset of winter. Their branches were then full of sap, and as water occupies a greater space when frozen than when fluid, the freezing of the water they contained bursted the texture of their wood, and rendered them unfit for the transmission of sap the next season. This fact leads to the conclusion that those soft-wooded fruit trees ought to be planted in the highest situations, and poorest land, where they will have the slowest possible growth. The few dry seasons we have had latterly, have, in some measure, restored the peach trees. If such seasons should continue for any length of time, the peaches and pears will again become plenty.

If annual plants, as well as trees, possess the faculty of becoming naturalized to soils and climates remote from those in which they are indigenous, what great advantages may we not reasonably anticipate for the future prosperity of our country, from this important law of the vegetable world? If, by a slow progress from south to north, the period of the growth of a plant may be shortened to three-fourths, or even less than that, of the time of its growth in the south, the sugar cane, already transplanted from the islands of the West Indies to the shores of the Mississippi, may slowly travel up that river and its branches to latitudes far north of any region which has heretofore witnessed its growth. The cotton plant and coffee tree, in all probability, will take the same course.

The conclusions of philosophy, with regard to the future, are prophetic, when correctly drawn from the unerring test of experience. In the prospect here presented of the practicability of naturalizing the plants of the south to the temperate latitudes far north of their native region, it is only saying that what has happened to one plant may under similar treatment happen to another. For example. How widely different is the large squaw corn, in its size and the period of its growth, from the Mandan corn. The latter ripens under the fortieth degree of north latitude; and yet the squaw and Mandan corn are not even different species; but only varieties of the same plant. The squaw corn might travel slowly to the north, and ultimately dwindle down into Mandan corn; while the Mandan corn, by being transplanted to the south, increases in size and lengthens the period of its growth.

The cherry tree, a native of Cerasia, was once cultivated as a tender exotic plant in Italy. It now grows in the open air as far north as St. Petersburg in Russia. The palma christi, the plant which furnishes the beans of which the castor oil is made, is a native of the tropical regions, yet it now flourishes and bears fruit abundantly in our latitudes! I once saw a plant of this kind in a garden in this town, the seed of which had come from the West Indies, among coffee. The plant was large and vigorous; but owing to its too great a removal, at once, from its native soil and climate, it bore no beans.

These observations have been made to show that the independence of our country may be vastly augmented by a proper attention to the laws of nature with regard to the vegetable world, so that we may hereafter cultivate within our own country the precious fruits even of the tropical regions.

CHAPTER VIII.

Account of a Hermit.

A man of the name of Thomas Hardie,[1] who from his mode of living was properly entitled to the appellation of hermit, lived in the neighborhood of my father's place. His appearance, dress, and deportment, are among the earliest impressions of my memory.

He was an Englishman, by birth and education, and an ordained clergyman of the Church of England. He must have been a man of profound learning. Some of his books in Greek and German fell into my hands after his death. His marginal remarks in the Greek books showed clearly that he had read them with great attention.

His appearance was in the highest degree venerable.

He was pretty far advanced in age; his head was bald, his hair gray, and his chin decorated with a large well shapen beard. His dress was a long robe which reached to his feet, held together with a girdle about his loins. This he called his phylactery. His clothes were all fastened together with hooks and eyes. Buttons and buckles were abominations in his view.

In the time of the Indian war he went about wherever he chose, without arms, believing, as he said, that no Indian would hurt him; accordingly so it turned out, although he frequently exposed himself to danger.

---

[1] This Thomas Hardie lived on the farm now occupied by Robert Vance, in Independence township.—(*Simpson.*)

His conversation must have been of the most interesting kind. He seemed to be master of every science and possessed an inexhaustible fund of anecdotes. He frequently entertained pretty large companies with relations of events in England and other parts. In all his anecdotes and historical relations he was the only speaker; for he knew everything and his hearers nothing.

But, however entertaining this hermit's conversation and anecdotes, they were conducted in a very singular way. When speaking he seldom kept his seat, but paced the floor from one side of the house to the other, sometimes with a slow, measured step, sometimes in a quick and irregular gait. During all this time he was constantly twitching his beard, and sputtering out tobacco spittle in such a way that its drops were almost as small as those of mist. Sometimes he would walk up to one of his hearers so as to bring his face almost in contact with that of the person to whom he was speaking; he would then speak in a low tone of voice, almost approaching to a whisper; during this time his hearer was apt to be a little annoyed by the particles of tobacco spittle falling on his face and clothing. After talking a while in this way he would whirl about and talk again in a loud tone of voice. Sometimes the hermit would preach to the people in the fort. When he did this he wore a black robe, made like the rest of his robes, in the fashion of a morning gown. Sometimes he put on bands of the common size and shape. At other times he had over his robe a very fine piece of linen, about four feet long and about eighteen inches broad. In the middle of this there was a hole through which he put his head, so that the piece of linen hung down at equal lengths before and behind. This decoration gave him a truly venerable appearance. I think, from the great extent of his learning, he must have been a first rate preacher. In addition to this, to the best of my recollection, his voice and elocution were of the first order. In his public services, particularly in the marriage ceremony, which it fell to his lot to perform very often for our early settlers, he followed the ritual of the Church of England.

This hermit possessed one art the like of which I never witnessed or heard of since. He was in the habit of giving a piece of white paper four or five inches square a single fold, and with a very small pair of scissors which he always carried about him he would soon produce the picture of a buck, an elk, flower-pot, turkey, or anything else he chose. These pictures sometimes had a single, sometimes a double festoon border which had the appearance of fine needlework. While doing this he was commonly engaged in conversation, and appeared to take very little notice of what he was doing. I remember I once asked him to show me how to make such pictures. He answered with apparent chagrin:

"No, I cannot. It is a star in the head, and you don't possess it, therefore say no more about it."

Mr. Hardie, although he professed himself a clergyman of the Church of England, was nevertheless attached to the Dunkard society, I think on the river Lehigh, but whether he came into the country with the Dunkards who made the establishments which gave name to Dunkard creek and Dunkard bottom on Cheat river, I have not been informed. I have, indeed, never been able to obtain the history of the settlement and departure of those people from the country.

Mr. Hardie brought with him into the country an orphan lad, whom he raised in his hermitage, and taught him his religious principles with such effect that when grown up he suffered his beard to grow long. He adopted his master's deportment and mode of conversation. He was not, however, the disciple of his master in every point. After his beard had grown to a tolerable length he engaged in a scout against a couple of Indians who had taken two women and a child prisoners from the neighborhood. The prisoners were recovered in the evening of the second day of their captivity. On this occasion the young Dunkard behaved with the utmost bravery. He fired the first gun, and was first at the Indian camp to save the prisoners from the tomahawk. When the party returned to the fort they unanimously protested that so brave a man should not wear such an ugly beard, and accordingly shaved it off; but he let it grow again. All this, however, did not suit the pacific principles of his master.

This disciple of the hermit departed from his master in another point. He was twice married. This, I believe, displeased the old hermit; for soon after the first marriage of his pupil he went down among his brethren in the lower part of Pennsylvania, where he died.

Although these hermits seemed wholly devoted to the means of securing their future interest, they nevertheless did not entirely neglect the present world; but took care to secure themselves two very valuable tracts of land; the one on Cross Creek, where their first hermitage was erected, the other the place now owned by Dr. John Cuthbertson, on which the second hermitage was established.

When a boy I was often at the latter hermitage for the purpose of receiving instructions in arithmetic from the old hermit; although the old man was a good hand at washing and cooking, yet the apparent poverty and wretchedness of the cabin demonstrated in most impressive manner "that it is not good for man to be alone."

There was something strange in the character and latter end of the younger hermit. During the greater part of his time, especially in his latter years, he was enthusiastically religious. Before eating he commonly read a few verses in his Bible, instead of saying grace. When alone he was often engaged in soliloquies; sometimes he attempted to preach, although he was a great stutterer. Several times he became quite deranged. On one occasion he took it into his head that he ought to be scourged, and actually prepared hickories, stripped himself, and made a mulatto man whip him until he said he had enough. Throughout life, with the exception of his last year, he was remarkably lazy and careless about his worldly affairs, owing to his great devotion to reading and religious exercises. He was the last in the neighborhood at planting, sowing, reaping, and everything else on his farm, so that, although he had an excellent tract of land, he could hardly make out to live. About a year before his death he fell into a consumptive complaint. During this year his former religious impressions seemed entirely to have forsaken his mind. He became completely the man of the world. Whenever any conversation on religious subjects was offered him by his neighbors, who saw that his end was fast approaching, he always replied with some observation about building a barn, a fence, or something else of a worldly nature. During this year he did more worldly business than he ever had done in any ten years of his life before.

I knew an instance of a similar change in the deportment of a gentleman whom I attended in a severe attack of the dropsy. Before his illness he was an easy, good natured, careless man, and a good neighbor; but after his recovery he was excessively avaricious, profane in his language, and a tyrant to his family and neighbors. Both these men appeared to have undergone an entire change in the state of the mind and external deportment.

The question whether the moral system of our nature is not as apt to suffer a deterioration, as to receive an improvement, in consequence of severe and long continued fits of sickness, would be an interesting subject in moral philosophy, and deserves the attention of men of science.

CHAPTER IX.

SETTLEMENT OF THE COUNTRY.

The settlements on this side of the mountains commenced along the Monongahela, and between that river and the Laurel Ridge, in the year 1772. In the succeeding year they reached the Ohio river. The greater number of the first settlers came from the upper parts of the then colonies of Maryland and Virginia. Braddock's trail, as it was called, was the route by which the greater number of them crossed the mountains. A less number of them came by the way of Bedford and Fort Ligonier, the military road from Pennsylvania to Pittsburg. They effected their removals on horses furnished with packsaddles. This was the more easily done, as but few of these early adventurers into the wilderness were encumbered with much baggage.

Land was the object which invited the greater number of these people to cross the mountain, for as the saying then was, "it was to be had here for taking up"; that is, building a cabin and raising a crop of grain, however small, of any kind, entitled the occupant to four hundred acres of land, and a preemption right to one thousand acres more adjoining, to be secured by a land office warrant. This right was to take effect if there happened to be so much vacant land, or any part thereof, adjoining the tract secured by the settlement right.

At an early period the government of Virginia appointed three commissioners to give certificates of settlement rights. These certificates, together with the surveyor's plan, were sent to the land office of the state, where they laid six months, to await any caveat which might be offered. If none was offered the patent then issued.

There was, at an early period of our settlements, an inferior kind of land title denominated a *tomahawk right,* which was made by deadening a few trees near the head of a spring, and marking the bark of some one or more of them with the initials of the name of the person who made the improvement. I remember having seen a number of these tomahawk rights when a boy. For a long time many of them bore the names of those who made them. I have no knowledge of the efficacy of the tomahawk improvement, or whether it conferred any right whatever, unless followed by an actual settlement. These rights, however, were often bought and sold. Those who wished to make settlement on their favorite tracts of land bought up the tomahawk improvements rather than enter into quarrels with those who had made them. Other improvers of the land, with a view to actual settlement, and who happened to be stout veteran fellows, took a very different course from that of purchasing the tomahawk rights. When annoyed by the claimants under those rights they deliberately cut a few good hickories and gave them what was called in those days *a laced jacket,* that is a sound whipping.

Some of the early settlers took the precaution to come over the mountains in the spring, leaving their families behind to raise a crop of corn, and then return and bring them out in the fall. This I should think was the better way. Others, especially those whose families were small, brought them with them in the spring. My father took the latter course. His family was but small and he brought them all with him. The Indian meal which he brought over the mountain was expended six weeks too soon, so that for that length of time we had to live without bread. The lean venison and the breast of the wild turkey we were taught to call bread. The flesh of the bear was denominated meat. This artifice did not succeed very well; after living in this way for some time we became sickly, the stomach seemed to be always empty, and tormented with a sense of hunger. I remember how narrowly the children watched the growth of the potato tops, pumpkin and squash vines, hoping from day to day to get something to answer in the place of bread. How delicious was the taste of the young potatoes when we got them! What a jubilee when we were permitted to pull the young corn for roasting ears! Still more so when it had acquired sufficient hardness to be made into johnny cakes by the aid of a tin grater. We then became healthy, vigorous and contented with our situation, poor as it was.

My father with a small number of his neighbors made their settlements in the spring of 1773.[1] Though they were in a poor and destitute situation, they nevertheless lived in peace; but their tranquility was not of long continuance. Those most atrocious murders of the peaceable inoffensive Indians at Captina and Yellow Creek brought on the war of Lord Dunmore in the spring of the year 1774. Our little settlement then broke up. The women and children were removed to Morris' fort in Sandy

---

[1] Among those who settled in 1773 with Mr. Doddridge was Alexander Wells, who built the mill where Oliver Clemons now lives. John Tennell settled where W. V. Walker now lives. Mr. Wells died in 1813, aged 86 years, and was buried in the old Wells grave yard.—(*Simpson.*)

creek glade, some distance to the east of Uniontown.[2] The fort consisted of an assemblage of small hovels, situated on the margin of a large and noxious marsh, the effluvia of which gave the most of the women and children the fever and ague. The men were compelled by necessity to return home, and risk the tomahawk and scalping knife of the Indians, in raising corn to keep their families from starvation the succeeding winter. Those sufferings, dangers and losses, were the tribute we had to pay to that thirst for blood which actuated those veteran murderers who brought the war upon us! The memory of the sufferers in this war, as well as that of their descendants, still looks back upon them with regret and abhorrence, and the page of history will consign their names to posterity with the full weight of infamy they deserve.

A correct and detailed view of the origin of societies, and their progress from one condition or point of wealth, science and civilization, to another, in these important respects a much higher grade, is always highly interesting even when received through the dusky medium of history, oftentimes but poorly and partially written; but when this retrospect of things past and gone is drawn from the recollections of experience, the impressions which it makes on the heart are of the most vivid, deep and lasting kind. The following history of the state of society, manners and customs of our forefathers is to be drawn from the latter source, and it is given to the world with the recollection that many of my cotemporaries, still living, have, as well as myself, witnessed all the scenes and events herein described, and whose memories would speedily detect and expose any errors the work may contain.

---

[2] Veech's "Monongahela of Old" makes mention of this reference to the father and family of Dr. Doddridge passing over the "Sandy Creek road" in 1774, and Mr. Veech points out that "this was the second road viewed and laid out by order of the court of Fayette county after its erection in 1783. It came from the Ten Mile settlement through Greene county, crossing the river (Monongahela) at Hyde's Ferry, or mouth of Big Whitely, passing by the south side of Masontown, through Haydentown, or by David John's mill, up Laurel Hill, through the Sandy Creek settlement to Daniel McPeak's and into Virginia. Morris Fort was on Sandy Creek, in Virginia, just outside the Fayette county border. It was much resorted to by the early settlers on the upper Monongahela and Cheat rivers, and from Ten Mile."

The municipal, as well as ecclesiastical, institutions of society, whether good or bad, in consequence of their long continued use, give a corresponding cast to the public character of the society whose conduct they direct, and the more so because in the lapse of time the observance of them becomes a matter of conscience. This observation applies, in full force, to that influence of our early land laws, which allowed four hundred acres, and no more, to a settlement right. Many of our first settlers seemed to regard this amount of the surface of the earth as the allotment of divine providence for one family, and believed that any attempt to get more would be sinful. Most of them, therefore, contented themselves with that amount; although they might have evaded the law, which allowed but one settlement right to any one individual, by taking out the title papers in the names of others, to be afterwards transferred to them, as if by purchase. Some few, indeed, pursued this practice; but it was held in detestation.

My father, like many others, believed, that having secured his legal allotment, the rest of the country belonged of right to those who chose to settle in it. There was a piece of vacant land adjoining his tract amounting to about two hundred acres. To this tract of land he had the preemption right, and accordingly secured it by warrant; but his conscience would not permit him to retain it in his family; he therefore gave it to an apprentice lad whom he had raised in his house. This lad sold it to an uncle of mine for a cow and a calf and a wool hat.

Owing to the equal distribution of real property directed by our land laws, and the sterling integrity of our forefathers in their observance of them, we have no districts of *sold land,* as it is called, that is large tracts of land in the hands of individuals, or companies, who neither sell nor improve them, as is the case in Lower Canada and the north-western part of Pennsylvania. These unsettled tracts make huge blanks in the population of the country where they exist.

The division lines between those whose lands adjoined were generally made in an amicable manner, before any survey of them was made, by the parties concerned. In doing this they were guided mainly by the tops of ridges and water courses, but particularly the former. Hence the greater number of farms in the western parts of Pennsylvania and Virginia bear a striking resemblance to an amphitheatre. The buildings occupy a low situation and the tops of the surrounding hills are the boundaries of the tract to which the family mansion belongs.

Our forefathers were fond of farms of this description, because, as they said, they are attended with this convenience "that everything comes to the house down hill." In the hilly parts of the state of Ohio, the land having been laid off in an arbitrary manner, by straight parallel lines, without regard to hill or dale, the farms present a different aspect from those on the east side of the river opposite. There the buildings as frequently occupy the tops of the hills as any other situation.

Our people had become so accustomed to the mode of "getting land for taking it up," that for a long time it was generally believed that the land on the west side of the Ohio would ultimately be disposed of in that way. Hence almost the whole tract of country between the Ohio and Muskingum was parcelled out in tomahawk improvements; but these latter improvers did not content themselves with a single four hundred acre tract apiece. Many of them owned a great number of tracts of the best land, and thus, in imagination, were as "wealthy as a South Sea dream." Many of the land jobbers of this class did not content themselves with marking the trees, at the usual height, with the initials of their names, but climbed up the large beech trees and cut the letters in their bark from twenty to forty feet from the ground. To enable them to identify those trees, at a future period, they made marks on other trees around them as references.

Most of the early settlers considered their land as of little value, from an apprehension that after a few years' cultivation it would lose its fertility, at least for a long time. I have often heard them say that such a field would bear so many crops and another so many, more or less, than that. The ground of this belief concerning the short lived fertility of the land in this country was the poverty of a great proportion of the land in the lower parts of Maryland and Virginia, which, after producing a few crops, became unfit for use and was thrown out into commons.

In their unfavorable opinion of the nature of the soil of our country our forefathers were utterly mistaken. The native weeds were scarcely destroyed before the white clover and different kinds of grass made their appearance. These soon covered the ground, so as to afford pasture for the cattle, by the time the wood range was eaten out, as well as protect the soil from being washed away by drenching rains, so often injurious in hilly countries.

Judging from Virgil's[1] test of fruitful and barren soils, the greater part of this country must possess every requisite for fertility. The test is this: dig a hole of any reasonable dimensions and depth. If the earth which was taken out, when thrown lightly back into it, does not fill up the hole the soil is fruitful; but if it more than fill it up the soil is barren.

Whoever chooses to make this experiment will find the result indicative of the richness of our soil. Even our graves, notwithstanding the size of the vault, are seldom finished with the earth thrown out of them, and they soon sink below the surface of the earth.

CHAPTER X.

House Furniture and Diet.

The settlement of a new country, in the immediate neighborhood of an old one, is not attended with much difficulty, because supplies can be readily obtained from the latter; but the

---

[1] Ante locum capies oculis, alteque jubebis
In solido puteum demitti, omnemque repones
Rursus humum, et pedibus summas œquabis arenas,
Si deerunt: rarum, pecorique et vitibus almis
Aptius uber erit. Sin in sua posse negabunt
Ire loca, et scrobibus superabit terra repletis,
Spissus ager: glebas cunctanes crassaque terga
Expecta, validis terram proscinde juvencis.
Vir. Geo., lib., ii, l. 230.
—(D)

settlement of a country very remote from any cultivated region is a very different thing, because at the outset, food, raiment, and the implements of husbandry are obtained only in small supplies and with great difficulty. The task of making new establishments in a remote wilderness in a time of profound peace is sufficiently difficult; but when, in addition to all the unavoidable hardships attendant on this business, those resulting from an extensive and furious warfare with savages are superadded, toil, privations and sufferings are then carried to the full extent of the capacity of men to endure them.

Such was the wretched condition of our forefathers in making their settlements here. To all their difficulties and privations the Indian war was a weighty addition. This destructive warfare they were compelled to sustain almost single handed, because the revolutionary contest with England gave full employment for the military strength and resources on the east side of the mountains.

The following history of the poverty, labors, sufferings, manners and customs, of our forefathers, will appear like a collection of "tales of olden times" without any garnish of language to spoil the original portraits by giving them shades of coloring which they did not possess. I shall follow the order of things as they occurred during the period of time embraced in these narratives, beginning with those rude accommodations with which our first adventurers into this country furnished themselves at the commencement of their establishments. It will be a homely narrative; yet valuable on the ground of its being real history.

If my reader, when viewing through the medium which I here present the sufferings of human nature in one of its most depressed and dangerous conditions, should drop an involuntary tear, let him not blame me for the sentiment of sympathy which he feels. On the contrary, if he should sometimes meet with a recital calculated to excite a smile or a laugh I claim no credit for his enjoyment. It is the subject matter of the history and not the historian which makes those widely different impressions on the mind of the reader.

In this chapter it is my design to give a brief account of the household furniture and articles of diet which were used by the first inhabitants of our country. A description of their cabins and half-faced camps, and their manner of building them, will be found elsewhere.

The furniture for the table, for several years after the settlement of this country, consisted of a few pewter dishes, plates and spoons; but mostly of wooden bowls, trenchers and noggins. If these last were scarce, gourds and hard shelled squashes made up the deficiency. The iron pots, knives and forks, were brought from the east side of the mountains along with the salt and iron on pack horses. These articles of furniture corresponded very well with the articles of diet on which they were employed. "Hog and hominy" were proverbial for the dish of which they were the component parts. Johnny cake and pone were at the outset of the settlements of the country the only forms of bread in use for breakfast and dinner. At supper, milk and mush was the standard dish. When milk was not plenty, which was often the case, owing to the scarcity of cattle, or the want of proper pasture for them, the substantial dish of hominy had to supply the place of them; mush was frequently eaten with sweetened water, molasses, bear's oil, or the gravy of fried meat.

Every family, besides a little garden for the few vegetables which they cultivated, had another small enclosure containing from half an acre to an acre, which they called a *truck patch,* in which they raised corn for roasting ears, pumpkins, squashes, beans and potatoes. These, in the latter part of the summer and fall, were cooked with their pork, venison and bear meat for dinner, and made very wholesome and well tasted dishes. The standard dinner dish for every log rolling, house raising and harvest day was a pot pie, or what in other countries is called *sea pie.* This, besides answering for dinner, served for a part of the supper also. The remainder of it from dinner, being eaten with milk in the evening, after the conclusion of the labor of the day.

In our whole display of furniture, the delft, china and silver were unknown. It did not then as now require contributions from the four quarters of the globe to furnish the breakfast table, viz: the silver from Mexico; the coffee from the West Indies; the tea from China, and the delft and porcelain from Europe or Asia. Yet our homely fare, and unsightly cabins, and furniture, produced a hardy veteran race, who planted the first footsteps of society and civilization in the immense regions of the west. Inured to hardihood, bravery and labor from their early youth, they sustained with manly fortitude the fatigue of the chase, the campaign and scout, and with strong arms "turned the wilderness into fruitful fields" and have left to their descendants the rich inheritance of an immense empire blessed with peace and wealth.

I well recollect the first time I ever saw a tea cup and saucer and tasted coffee. My mother died when I was about six or seven years of age. My father then sent me to Maryland with a brother of my grandfather, Mr. Alexander Wells, to school. At Colonel Brown's in the mountains, at Stony creek glades, I for the first time saw tame geese, and by bantering a pet gander I got a severe biting by his bill, and beating by his wings. I wondered very much that birds so large and strong should be so much tamer than the wild turkeys. At this place, however, all was right, excepting the large birds which they called geese. The cabin and its furniture were such as I had been accustomed to see in the backwoods, as my country was then called. At Bedford everything was changed. The tavern at which my uncle put up was a stone house, and to make the change still more complete it was plastered in the inside, both as to the walls and ceiling. On going into the dining room I was struck with astonishment at the appearance of the house. I had no idea that there was any house in the world which was not built of logs; but here I looked round the house and could see no logs, and above I could see no joists; whether such a thing had been made by the hands of man, or had grown so of itself, I could not conjecture. I had not the courage to inquire anything about it. When supper came on, "my confusion was worse confounded." A little cup stood in a bigger one with some brownish looking stuff in it, which was neither milk, hominy nor broth; what to do with these little cups and the little spoon belonging to them I could not tell; and I was afraid to ask anything concerning the use of them.

It was in the time of the war, and the company were giving accounts of catching, whipping and hanging the tories. The word *jail* frequently occurred: this word I had never heard before; but I soon discovered, and was much terrified at its meaning, and supposed that we were in much danger of the fate of the tories; for I thought, as we had come from the backwoods, it was altogether likely that we must be tories too. For fear of being discovered I durst not utter a single word. I therefore watched attentively to see what the big folks would do with their little cups and spoons. I imitated them, and found the taste of the coffee nauseous beyond anything I ever had tasted in my life. I continued to drink, as the rest of the company did, with the tears streaming from my eyes, but when it was to end I was at a loss to know, as the little cups were filled immediately after being emptied. This circumstance distressed me very much, as I durst not say I had enough. Looking attentively at the grown persons, I saw one man turn his little cup bottom upwards and put his little spoon across it. I observed that after this his cup was not filled again; I followed his example, and to my great satisfaction the result as to my cup was the same.

The introduction of delft ware was considered by many of the backwoods people as a culpable innovation. It was too easily broken, and the plates of that ware dulled their scalping and clasp knives; tea ware was too small for *men;* they might do for women and children. Tea and coffee were only slops, which in the adage of the day "did not stick by the ribs." The idea was they were designed only for people of quality, who do not labor, or the sick. A genuine backwoodsman would have thought himself disgraced by showing a fondness for those slops. Indeed, many of them have, to this day, very little respect for them.

CHAPTER XI.

Dress of the Indians and First Settlers.

On the frontiers, and particularly amongst those who were much in the habit of hunting, and going on scouts and campaigns, the dress of the men was partly Indian and partly that of civilized nations.

The hunting shirt was universally worn. This was a kind of loose frock, reaching half way down the thighs, with large sleeves, open before, and so wide as to lap over a foot or more when belted. The cap was large, and sometimes handsomely fringed with a ravelled piece of cloth of a different color from that of the hunting shirt itself. The bosom of this dress served as a wallet to hold a chunk of bread, cakes, jerk, tow for wiping the barrel of the rifle, or any other necessary for the hunter or warrior. The belt, which was always tied behind, answered several purposes, besides that of holding the dress together. In cold weather the mittens, and sometimes the bullet-bag, occupied the front part of it. To the right side was suspended the tomahawk and to the left the scalping knife in its leathern sheath. The hunting shirt was generally made of linsey, sometimes of coarse linen, and a few of dressed deer skins. These last were very cold and uncomfortable in wet weather. The shirt and jacket were of the common fashion. A pair of drawers or breeches and leggins were the dress of the thigh and legs; a pair of moccasins answered for the feet much better than shoes. These were made of dressed deer skin. They were mostly made of a single piece with a gathering seam along the top of the foot, and another from the bottom of the heel, without gathers as high as the ankle joint or a little higher. Flaps were left on each side to reach some distance up the legs. These were nicely adapted to the ankles and lower part of the leg by thongs of deer skin, so that no dust, gravel or snow could get within the moccasin.

The moccasins in ordinary use cost but a few hours labor to make them. This was done by an instrument denominated a moccasin awl, which was made of the backspring of an old claspknife. This awl with its buckshorn handle was an appendage of every shot pouch strap, together with a roll of buckskin for mending the moccasins. This was the labor of almost every evening. They were sewed together and patched with deer skin thongs, or whangs, as they were commonly called.

In cold weather the moccasins were well stuffed with deer's hair, or dry leaves, so as to keep the feet comfortably warm; but in wet weather it was usually said that wearing them was "a decent way of going barefooted;" and such was the fact, owing to the spongy texture of the leather of which they were made.

Owing to this defective covering of the feet, more than to any other circumstance, the greater number of our hunters and warriors were afflicted with the rheumatism in their limbs. Of this disease they were all apprehensive in cold or wet weather, and therefore always slept with their feet to the fire to prevent or cure it as well as they could. This practice unquestionably had a very salutary effect, and prevented many of them from becoming confirmed cripples in early life.

In the latter years of the Indian war our young men became more enamored of the Indian dress throughout, with the exception of the matchcoat. The drawers were laid aside and the leggins made longer, so as to reach the upper part of the thigh. The Indian breech clout was adopted. This was a piece of linen or cloth nearly a yard long, and eight or nine inches broad. This passed under the belt before and behind leaving the ends for flaps hanging before and behind over the belt. These flaps were sometimes ornamented with some coarse kind of embroidery work. To the same belts which secured the breech clout, strings which supported the long leggins were attached.

When this belt, as was often the case, passed over the hunting shirt the upper part of the thighs and part of the hips were naked.

The young warrior instead of being abashed by this nudity was proud of his Indian like dress. In some few instances I have seen them go into places of public worship in this dress. Their appearance, however, did not add much to the devotion of the young ladies.

The linsey petticoat and bed gown, which were the universal dress of our women in early times, would make a strange figure in our days. A small home-made handkerchief, in point of elegance, would illy supply the place of that profusion of ruffles with which the necks of our ladies are now ornamented.

They went barefooted in warm weather, and in cold their feet were covered with moccasins, coarse shoes, or shoepacks, which would make but a sorry figure beside the elegant morocco slippers often embossed with bullion which at present ornament the feet of their daughters and grand-daughters.

The coats and bedgowns of the women, as well as the hunting shirts of the men, were hung in full display on wooden pegs round the walls of their cabins, so that while they answered in some degree the place of paper hangings or tapestry they announced to the stranger as well as neighbor the wealth or poverty of the family in the articles of clothing. This practice has not yet been wholly laid aside amongst the backwoods families.

The historian would say to the ladies of the present time, our ancestors of your sex knew nothing of the ruffles, leghorns, curls, combs, rings and other jewels with which their fair daughters now decorate themselves. Such things were not then to be had. Many of the younger part of them were pretty well grown up before they ever saw the inside of a store room, or even knew there was such a thing in the world, unless by hearsay, and indeed scarcely that. Instead of the toilet, they had to handle the distaff or shuttle, the sickle or weeding hoe, contented if they could obtain their linsey clothing and cover their heads with a sun bonnet made of six or seven hundred linen.

CHAPTER XII.

The Fort and other Defenses.

My reader will understand by this term, not only a place of defense, but the residence of a small number of families belonging to the same neighborhood. As the Indian mode of warfare was an indiscrimate slaughter of all ages and both sexes, it was as requisite to provide for the safety of the women and children as for that of the men.

The fort consisted of cabins, blockhouses and stockades. A range of cabins commonly formed one side, at least, of the fort. Divisions or partitions of logs separated the cabins from each other. The walls on the outside were ten or twelve feet high, the slope of the roof being turned wholly inward. A very few of these cabins had puncheon floors, the greater part were earthen. The blockhouses were built at the angles of the fort. They projected about two feet beyond the outer walls of the cabins and stockades. Their upper stories were about eighteen inches every way larger in dimension than the under one, leaving an opening at the commencement of the second story to prevent the enemy from making a lodgment under their walls. In some forts, instead of blockhouses, the angles of the fort were furnished with bastions. A large folding gate made of thick slabs, nearest the spring, closed the fort. The stockades, bastions, cabins and blockhouse walls, were furnished with port holes at proper heights and distances. The whole of the outside was made completely bullet proof.

It may be truly said that necessity is the mother of invention; for the whole of this work was made without the aid of a single nail or spike of iron, and for this reason, such things were not to be had.

In some places less exposed a single blockhouse, with a cabin or two, constituted the whole fort. Such places of refuge may appear very trifling to those who have been in the habit of seeing the formidable military garrisons of Europe and America; but they answered the purpose, as the Indians had no artillery. They seldom attacked, and scarcely ever took one of them.

The families belonging to these forts were so attached to their own cabins on their farms that they seldom moved into their fort in the spring until compelled by some alarm, as they called it; that is, when it was announced by some murder that the Indians were in the settlement.

The fort to which my father belonged was, during the first years of the war, three-quarters of a mile from his farm; but when this fort went to decay, and became unfit for defense, a new one was built at his own house. I well remember that, when a little boy, the family were sometimes waked up in the dead of night by an express with a report that the Indians were at hand. The express came softly to the door, or back window, and by a gentle tapping waked the family. This was easily done, as an habitual fear made us ever watchful and sensible to the slightest alarm. The whole family were instantly in motion. My father seized his gun and other implements of war. My stepmother waked up and dressed the children as well as she could, and being myself the oldest of the children I had to take my share of the burdens to be carried to the fort. There was no possibility of getting a horse in the night to aid us in removing to the fort. Besides the little children, we caught up what articles of clothing and provision we could get hold of in the dark, for we durst not light a candle or even stir the fire. All this was done with the utmost dispatch and the silence of death. The greatest care was taken not to awaken the youngest child. To the rest it was enough to say *Indian* and not a whimper was heard afterwards. Thus it often happened that the whole number of families belonging to a fort who were in the evening at their homes were all in their little fortress before the dawn of the next morning. In the course of the succeeding day their household furniture was brought in by parties of the men under arms.

Some families belonging to each fort were much less under the influence of fear than others, and who, after an alarm had subsided, in spite of every remonstrance, would remove home, while their more prudent neighbors remained in the fort. Such families were denominated *fool hardy* and gave no small amount of trouble by creating such frequent necessities of sending runners to warn them of their danger, and sometimes parties of our men to protect them during their removal.

CHAPTER XIII.

Caravans and Mode of Trade.

The acquisition of the indispensable articles of salt, iron, steel and castings, presented great difficulties to the first settlers of the western country. They had no stores of any kind, no salt, iron, nor iron works; nor had they money to make purchases where those articles could be obtained. Peltry and furs were their only resources before they had time to raise cattle and horses for sale in the Atlantic states.

Every family collected what peltry and fur they could obtain throughout the year for the purpose of sending them over the mountains for barter.

In the fall of the year, after seeding time, every family formed an association with some of their neighbors for starting the little caravan. A master driver was selected from among them who was to be assisted by one or more young men and sometimes a boy or two. The horses were fitted out with pack-saddles, to the hinder part of which was fastened a pair of hobbles made of hickory withes; a bell and collar ornamented his neck. The bags provided for the conveyance of the salt were filled with feed for the horses; on the journey a part of this feed was left at convenient stages on the way down, to support the return of the caravan; large wallets well filled with bread, jerk, boiled ham and cheese furnished provisions for the drivers. At night after feeding, the horses, whether put in pasture or turned out into the woods, were hobbled and the bells were opened.

The barter for salt and iron was made first at Baltimore; Frederick, Hagerstown, Oldtown and Fort Cumberland, in succession, became the place of exchange. Each horse carried two bushels of alum salt weighing eighty four pounds to the bushel. This, to be sure, was not a heavy load for the horses but it was enough, considering the scanty subsistence allowed them on the journey.

The common price of a bushel of alum salt, at an early period, was a good cow and calf; and until weights were introduced, the salt was measured into the half bushel, by hand, as lightly as possible. No one was permitted to walk heavily over the floor while the operation of measuring was going on.

The following anecdote will serve to show how little the native sons of the forest knew of the etiquette of the Atlantic cities.

A neighbor of my father, some years after the settlement of the country, had collected a small drove of cattle for the Baltimore market. Amongst the hands employed to drive them was one who never had seen any condition of society but that of woodsmen. At one of their lodging places in the mountain, the landlord and his hired man, in the course of the night, stole two of the bells belonging to the drove and hid them in a piece of woods. The drove had not gone far in the morning before the bells were missed; and a detachment went back to recover the stolen bells. The men were found reaping in the field of the landlord. They were accused of the theft, but they denied the charge. The torture of sweating according to the custom of that time, that is of suspension by the arms pinioned behind their backs, brought a confession. The bells were procured and hung around the necks of the thieves. In this condition they were driven on foot before the detachment until they overtook the drove, which by this time had gone nine miles. A halt was called and a jury selected to try the culprits. They were condemned to receive a certain number of lashes on the bare back from the hand of each drover.

The man above alluded to was the owner of one of the bells; when it came to his turn to use the hickory, " now," says he to the thief, "you infernal scoundrel, I'll work your jacket nineteen to the dozen; only think what a rascally figure I should make in the streets of Baltimore without a bell on my horse."

The man was in earnest; having seen no horses used without bells he thought they were requisite in every situation.

CHAPTER XIV.

Subsistence by Hunting.

This was an important part of the employment of the early settlers of this country. For some years the woods supplied them with the greater amount of their subsistence, and with regard to some families at certain times, the whole of it; for it was no uncommon thing for families to live several months without a mouthful of bread. It frequently happened that there was no breakfast until it was obtained from the woods. Fur and peltry were the people's money. They had nothing else to give in exchange for rifles, salt and iron, on the other side of the mountains.

The fall and early part of the winter was the season for hunting the deer, and the whole of the winter, including part of the spring, for bears and fur skinned animals. It was a customary saying that fur is good during every month in the name of which the letter R occurs.

The class of hunters with whom I was best acquainted were those whose hunting ranges were on the western side of the river, and at the distance of eight or nine miles from it. As soon as the leaves were pretty well down and the weather became rainy, accompanied by light snows, these men, after acting the part of husbandmen, so far as the state of warfare permitted them to do so, soon began to feel that they were hunters. They became uneasy at home. Everything about them became disagreeable. The house was too warm. The feather bed too soft, and even the good wife was not thought for the time being a proper companion. The mind of the hunter was wholly occupied with the camp and chase. I have often seen them get up early in the morning at this season, walk hastily out and look anxiously to the woods and snuff the autumnal winds with the highest rapture, then return into the house and cast a quick and attentive look at the rifle, which was always suspended to a joist by a couple of buck's horns, or little forks. His hunting dog, understanding the intentions of his master, would wag his tail and by every blandishment in his power express his readiness to accompany him to the woods.

A day was soon appointed for the march of the little cavalcade to the camp. Two or three horses furnished with pack saddles were loaded with flour, Indian meal, blankets and everything else requisite for the use of the hunter.

A hunting camp, or what was called a half-faced cabin, was of the following form: the back part of it was sometimes a large log; at the distance of eight or ten feet from this two stakes were set in the ground a few inches apart, and at the distance of eight or ten feet from these two more, to receive the ends of the poles for the sides of the camp. The whole slope of the roof was from the front to the back. The covering was made of slabs, skins or blankets, or, if in the spring of the year, the bark of hickory or ash trees. The front was left entirely open. The fire was built directly before this opening. The cracks between the logs were filled with moss. Dry leaves served for a bed. It is thus that a couple of men, in a few hours, will construct for themselves a temporary, but tolerably comfortable, defense from the inclemencies of the weather. The beaver, otter, muskrat and squirrel are scarcely their equals in dispatch in fabricating for themselves a covert from the tempest! A little more pains would have made a hunting camp a defense against the Indians. A cabin ten feet square, bullet proof and furnished with port holes, would have enabled two or three hunters to hold twenty Indians at bay for any length of time. But this precaution I believe was never attended to; hence the hunters were often surprised and killed in their camps.

The site for the camp was selected with all the sagacity of the woodsmen, so as to have it sheltered by the surrounding hills from every wind, but more especially from those of the north and west.

An uncle of mine of the name of Samuel Teter occupied the same camp for several years in succession. It was situated on one of the southern branches of Cross creek. Although I lived many years not more than fifteen miles from the place, it was not till within a very few years ago that I discovered its situation. It was shown me by a gentleman living in the neighborhood. Viewing the hills round about it, I soon perceived the sagacity of the hunter in the site for his camp. Not a wind could touch him; and unless by the report of his gun or the sound of his axe, it would have been by mere accident if an Indian had discovered his concealment.

Hunting was not a mere ramble in pursuit of game, in which there was nothing of skill and calculation; on the contrary the hunter, before he set out in the morning, was informed by the state of the weather in what situation he might reasonably expect to meet with his game; whether on the bottoms, sides or tops of the hills. In stormy weather the deer always seek the most sheltered places, and the leeward sides of the hills. In rainy weather, in which there is not much wind, they keep in the open woods on the highest ground.

In every situation it was requisite for the hunter to ascertain the course of the wind, so as to get the leeward of the game. This he effected by putting his finger in his mouth and holding it there until it became warm, then holding it above his head; the side which first becomes cold shows which way the wind blows.

As it was requisite, too, for the hunter to know the cardinal points, he had only to observe the trees to ascertain them. The bark of an aged tree is thicker and much rougher on the north than on the south side. The same thing may be said of the moss, it is much thicker and stronger on the north than on the south sides of the trees.

The whole business of the hunter consists of a succession of intrigues. From morning till night he was on the alert to gain the wind of his game, and approach them without being discovered. If he succeeded in killing a deer, he skinned it and hung it up out of the reach of the wolves, and immediately resumed the chase till the close of the evening, when he bent his course towards his camp; when arrived there he kindled up his fire, and together with his fellow hunter cooked his supper. The supper finished, the adventures of the day furnished the tales for the evening. The spike buck, the two and three pronged buck, the doe and barren doe, figured through their anecdotes with great advantage. It would seem that after hunting awhile on the same ground, the hunters became acquainted with nearly all the gangs of deer within their range, so as to know each flock of them when they saw them. Often some old buck, by the means of his superior sagacity and watchfulness, saved his little gang from the hunter's skill by giving timely notice of his approach. The cunning of the hunter and that of the old buck were staked against each other, and it frequently happened that at the conclusion of the hunting season the old fellow was left free, uninjured tenant of his forest; but if his rival succeeded in bringing him down, the victory was followed by no small amount of boasting on the part of the conqueror.

When the weather was not suitable for hunting, the skins and carcases of the game were brought in and disposed of.

Many of the hunters rested from their labors on the Sabbath day, some from a motive of piety; others said that whenever they hunted on Sunday they were sure to have bad luck all the rest of the week.

CHAPTER XV.

The Wedding and Mode of Living.

For a long time after the first settlement of this country the inhabitants in general married young. There was no distinction of rank and very little of fortune. On these accounts the first impression of love resulted in marriage; and a family establishment cost but a little labor and nothing else. A description of a wedding from the beginning to the end will serve to show the manners of our forefathers and mark the grade of civilization which has succeeded to their rude state of society in the course of a few years.

At an early period the practice of celebrating the marriage at the house of the bride began, and it should seem with great propriety. She also has the choice of the priest to perform the ceremony.

In the first years of the settlement of this country a wedding engaged the attention of a whole neighborhood; and the frolic was anticipated by old and young with eager expectation. This is not to be wondered at, when it is told that a wedding was almost the only gathering which was not accompanied with the labor of reaping, log rolling, building a cabin, or planning some scout or campaign.

In the morning of the wedding day the groom and his attendants assembled at the house of his father for the purpose of reaching the mansion of his bride by noon, which was the usual time for celebrating the nuptials, which for certain must take place before dinner.

Let the reader imagine an assemblage of people without a store, tailor or mantuamaker within a hundred miles; and an assemblage of horses without a blacksmith or saddler within an equal distance. The gentlemen dressed in shoepacks, moccasins, leather breeches, leggins, linsey hunting shirts, and all home made. The ladies dressed in linsey petticoats and linsey or linen bed gowns, coarse shoes, stockings, handkerchiefs and buckskin gloves, if any. If there were any buckles, rings, buttons, or ruffles, they were the relics of old times; family pieces from parents or grand parents. The horses were caparisoned with old saddles, old bridles or halters, and packsaddles, with a bag or blanket thrown over them: a rope or string as often constituted the girth as a piece of leather.

The march, in double file, was often interrupted by the narrowness and obstructions of our horse paths, as they were called, for we had no roads; and these difficulties were often increased, sometimes by the good, and sometimes by the ill will of neighbors, by felling trees and tying grape vines across the way. Sometimes an ambuscade was formed by the way side, and an unexpected discharge of several guns took place, so as to cover the wedding company with smoke. Let the reader imagine the scene which followed this discharge; the sudden spring of the horses, the shrieks of the girls, and the chivalric bustle of their partners to save them from falling. Sometimes, in spite of all that could be done to prevent it, some were thrown to the ground. If a wrist, elbow, or ankle happened to be sprained it was tied with a handkerchief, and little more was thought or said about it.

Another ceremony commonly took place before the party reached the house of the bride, after the practice of making whiskey began, which was at an early period. When the party were about a mile from the place of their destination, two young men would single out to run for the bottle; the worse the path, the more logs, brush and deep hollows the better, as these obstacles afforded an opportunity for the greater display of intrepidity and horsemanship. The English fox chase, in point of danger to the riders and their horses, is nothing to this race for the bottle. The start was announced by an Indian yell; logs, brush, muddy hollows, hill and glen, were speedily passed by the rival ponies. The bottle was always filled for the occasion, so that there was no use for judges; for the first who reached the door was presented with the prize, with which he returned in triumph to the company. On approaching them he announced his victory over his rival by a shrill whoop. At the head of the troop, he gave the bottle first to the groom and his attendants, and then to each pair in succession to the rear of the line, giving each a dram; and then, putting the bottle in the bosom of his hunting shirt, took his station in the company.

The ceremony of the marriage preceded the dinner, which was a substantial backwoods feast of beef, pork, fowls, and sometimes venison and bear meat roasted and boiled, with plenty of potatoes, cabbage, and other vegetables. During the dinner the greatest hilarity always prevailed; although the table might be a large slab of timber, hewed out with a broad axe, supported by four sticks set in auger holes; and the furniture, some old pewter dishes and plates; the rest, wooden bowls and trenchers; a few pewter spoons, much battered about the edges, were to be seen at some tables. The rest were made of horns. If knives were scarce, the deficiency was made up by the scalping knives which were carried in sheaths suspended to the belt of the hunting shirt.

After dinner the dancing commenced, and generally lasted till the next morning. The figures of the dances were three and four handed reels, or square sets and jigs. The commencement was always a square four, which was followed by what was called jigging it off; that is, two of the four would single out for a jig, and were followed by the remaining couple. The jigs were often accompanied with what was called cutting out; that is, when either of the parties became tired of the dance, on intimation, the place was supplied by some one of the company without any interruption of the dance. In this way a dance was often continued till the musician was heartily tired of his situation. Toward the latter part of the night, if any of the company, through weariness, attempted to conceal themselves for the purpose of sleeping, they were hunted up, paraded on the floor, and the fiddler ordered to play "Hang on till to-morrow morning."

About nine or ten o'clock a deputation of the young ladies stole off the bride and put her to bed. In doing this it frequently happened that they had to ascend a ladder instead of a pair of stairs, leading from the dining and ball room to the loft, the floor of which was made of clapboards lying loose and without nails. This ascent, one might think, would put the bride and her attendants to the blush; but as the foot of the ladder was commonly behind the door, which was purposely opened for the occasion, and its rounds at the inner end were well hung with hunting shirts, petticoats, and other articles of clothing, the candles being on the opposite side of the house, the exit of the bride was noticed but by few. This done, a deputation of young men in like manner stole off the groom, and placed him snugly by the side of his bride. The dance still continued; and if seats happened to be scarce, which was often the case, every young man, when not engaged in the dance, was obliged to offer his lap as a seat for one of the girls; and the offer was sure to be accepted. In the midst of this hilarity the bride and groom were not forgotten. Pretty late in the night some one would remind the company that the new couple must stand in need of some refreshment; black Betty, which was the name of the bottle, was called for and sent up the ladder, but sometimes black Betty did not go alone; I have many times seen as much bread, beef, pork and cabbage sent along with her as would afford a good meal for a half dozen hungry men. The young couple were compelled to eat and drink, more or less, of whatever was offered them.

In the course of the festivity if any wanted to help himself to a dram, and the young couple to a toast, he would call out:

"Where is black Betty? I want to kiss her sweet lips." Black Betty was soon handed to him. Then holding her up in his right hand he would say:

"Health to the groom, not forgetting myself; and here's to the bride, thumping luck and big children."

This, so far from being taken amiss, was considered as an expression of a very proper and friendly wish, for big children, especially sons, were of great importance; as we were few in number, and engaged in perpetual hostility with the Indians, the end of which no one could foresee. Indeed many of them seemed to suppose that war was the natural state of man, and therefore did not anticipate any conclusion of it; every big son was therefore considered as a young soldier.

But to return. It often happened that some neighbors or relations, not being asked to the wedding, took offense; and the mode of revenge adopted by them on such occasions was that of cutting off the manes, foretops and tails of the horses of the wedding company. Another method of revenge which was adopted when the chastity of the bride was a little suspected was that of setting up a pair of horns on poles, or trees, on the route of the wedding company. This was a hint to the groom that he might expect to be complimented with a pair of horns himself.

On returning to the infare, the order of procession and the race for black Betty was the same as before. The feasting and dancing often lasted for several days, at the end of which the whole company were so exhausted with loss of sleep that several days' rest were requisite to fit them to return to their ordinary labors.

Should I be asked why I have presented this unpleasant portrait of the rude manners of our forefathers, I in my turn would ask my reader, why are you pleased with the histories of the blood and carnage of battles? Why are you delighted with the fictions of poetry, the novel and romance? I have related truth, and only truth, strange as it may seem. I have depicted a state of society and manners which are fast vanishing from the memory of man, with a view to give the youth of our country a knowledge of the advantages of civilization, and to give contentment to the aged by preventing them from saying "that former times were better than the present."

CHAPTER XVI.

The House Warming.

I will proceed to state the usual manner of settling a young couple in the world.

A spot was selected on a piece of land of one of the parents, for their habitation. A day was appointed shortly after their marriage for commencing the work of building their cabin. The fatigue party consisted of choppers, whose business it was to fell the trees and cut them off at proper lengths. A man with a team for hauling them to the place, and arranging them, properly assorted, at the sides and ends of the building, a carpenter, if such he might be called, whose business it was to search the woods for a proper tree for making clapboards for the roof. The tree for this purpose must be straight grained and from three to four feet in diameter. The boards were split four feet long, with a large frow, and as wide as the timber would allow. They were used without planing or shaving. Another division was employed in getting puncheons for the floor of the cabin; this was done by splitting trees, about eighteen inches in diameter, and hewing the faces of them with a broad axe. They were half the length of the floor they were intended to make. The materials for the cabin were mostly prepared on the first day and sometimes the foundation laid in the evening. The second day was allotted for the raising.

In the morning of the next day the neighbors collected for the raising. The first thing to be done was the election of four corner men, whose business it was to notch and place the logs. The rest of the company furnished them with the timbers. In the meantime the boards and puncheons were collecting for the floor and roof, so that by the time the cabin was a few rounds high the sleepers and floor began to be laid. The door was made by sawing or cutting the logs in one side so as to make an opening about three feet wide. This opening was secured by upright pieces of timber about three inches thick through which holes were bored into the ends of the logs for the purpose of pinning them fast. A similar opening, but wider, was made at the end for the chimney. This was built of logs and made large to admit of a back and jambs of stone. At the square, two end logs projected a foot or eighteen inches beyond the wall to receive the butting poles, as they were called, against which the ends of the first row of clapboards was supported. The roof was formed by making the end logs shorter until a single log formed the comb of the roof. On these logs the clapboards were placed, the ranges of them lapping some distance over those next below them and kept in their places by logs placed at proper distances upon them

The roof and sometimes the floor were finished on the same day of the raising. A third day was commonly spent by a few carpenters in leveling off the floor, making a clapboard door and a table. This last was made of a split slab and supported by four round legs set in auger holes. Some three-legged stools were made in the same manner. Some pins stuck in the logs at the back of the house supported some clapboards which served for shelves for the table furniture. A single fork, placed with its lower end in a hole in the floor and the upper end fastened to a joist, served for a bedstead by placing a pole in the fork with one end through a crack between the logs of the wall. This front pole was crossed by a shorter one within the fork, with its outer end through another crack. From the front pole, through a crack between the logs of the end of the house, the boards were put on which formed the bottom of the bed. Sometimes other poles were pinned to the fork a little distance above these, for the purpose of supporting the front and foot of the bed, while the walls were the supports of its back and head. A few pegs around the walls for a display of the coats of the women, and hunting shirts of the men, and two small forks or buck's horns to a joist for the rifle and shot pouch, completed the carpenter work.

In the mean time masons were at work. With the heart pieces of the timber of which the clapboards were made they made billets for chunking up the cracks between the logs of the cabin and chimney; a large bed of mortar was made for daubing up those cracks; a few stones formed the back and jambs of the chimney.

The cabin being finished, the ceremony of house warming took place before the young couple were permitted to move into it. The house warming was a dance of a whole night's continuance, made up of the relations of the bride and groom and their neighbors. On the day following the young couple took possession of their new mansion.

CHAPTER XVII.

Labor and its Discouragements.

The necessary labors of the farms along the frontiers were performed with every danger and difficulty imaginable. The whole population of the frontiers huddled together in their little forts left the country with every appearance of a deserted region; and such would have been the opinion of a traveler concerning it, if he had not seen, here and there, some small fields of corn or other grain in a growing state.

It is easy to imagine what losses must have been sustained by our first settlers owing to this deserted state of their farms. It was not the full measure of their trouble that they risked their lives, and often lost them, in subduing the forest, and turning it into fruitful fields; but compelled to leave them in a deserted state during the summer season, a great part of the fruits of their labors was lost by this untoward circumstance. Their sheep and hogs were devoured by the wolves panthers and bears. Horses and cattle were often let into their fields, through breaches made in their fences by the falling of trees, and frequently almost the whole of a little crop of corn was destroyed by squirrels and raccoons, so that many families, and after an hazardous and laborious spring and summer, had but little left for the comfort of the dreary winter.

The early settlers on the frontiers of this country were like Arabs of the desert of Africa, in at last two respects; every man was a soldier, and from early in the spring till late in the fall, was almost continually in arms. Their work was often carried on by parties, each one of whom had his rifle and everything else belonging to his war dress. These were deposited in some central place in the field. A sentinel was stationed on the outside of the fence, so that on the least alarm the whole company repaired to their arms, and were ready for the combat in a moment. Here, again, the rashness of some families proved a source of difficulty. Instead of joining the working parties, they went out and attended their farms by themselves, and in case of alarm an express was sent for them, and sometimes a party of men to guard them to the fort. These families, in some instances, could boast that they had better crops, and were every way better provided for the winter than their neighbors. In other instances their temerity cost them their lives.

In military affairs, when every one concerned is left to his own will, matters are sure to be but badly managed. The whole frontiers of Pennsylvania and Virginia presented a succession of military camps or forts. We had military officers, that is to say, captains and colonels, but they, in many respects, were only nominally such. They could advise but not command. Those who chose to follow their advice did so to such an extent as suited their fancy or interest. Others were refractory and thereby gave much trouble. These officers would lead a scout or campaign. Those who thought proper to accompany them did so, those who did not remained at home. Public odium was the only punishment for their laziness or cowardice. There was no compulsion to the performance of military duties, and no pecuniary reward when they were performed.

It is but doing justice to the first settlers of this country to say that instances of disobedience of families and individuals to the advice of our officers were by no means numerous. The greater number cheerfully submitted to their directions with a prompt and faithful obedience.

CHAPTER XVIII.

The Mechanic Arts.

In giving the history of the state of the mechanic arts, as they were exercised at an early period of the settlement of this country, I shall present a people driven by necessity to perform works of mechanical skill far beyond what a person enjoying all the advantages of civilization would expect from a population placed in such destitute circumstances.

My reader will naturally ask where were their mills for grinding grain? Where their tanners for making leather? Where their smith shops for making and repairing their farming utensils? Who were their carpenters, tailors, cabinet workmen, shoemakers, and weavers? The answer is, those manufacturers did not exist, nor had they any tradesmen, who were professedly such. Every family were under the necessity of doing every thing for themselves as well as they could.

The hominy block and hand mills were in use in most of our houses. The first was made of a large block of wood about three feet long, with an excavation burned in one end, wide at the top and narrow at the bottom, so that the action of the pestle on the bottom threw the corn up to the sides toward the top of it, from whence it continually fell down into the centre. In consequence of this movement the whole mass of the grain was pretty equally subjected to the strokes of the pestle. In the fall of the year, while the Indian corn was soft, the block and pestle did very well for making meal for johnny cake and mush, but were rather slow when the corn became hard.

The sweep was sometimes used to lessen the toil of pounding grain into meal. This was a pole of some springy elastic wood, thirty feet long or more; the butt end was placed under the side of a house, or a large stump; this pole was supported by two forks, placed about one-third of its length from the butt end so as to elevate the small end about fifteen feet from the ground; to this was attached, by a large mortise, a piece of a sapling about five or six inches in diameter and eight or ten feet long. The lower end of this was shaped so as to answer for a pestle. A pin of wood was put through it at a proper height, so that two persons could work at the sweep at once. This simple machine very much lessened the labor, and expedited the work. I remember that when a boy I put up an excellent sweep at my father's. It was made of a sugar tree sapling. It was kept going almost constantly from morning till night by our neighbors for several weeks.

In the Greenbriar country, where they had a number of saltpetre caves, the first settlers made plenty of excellent gun powder by the means of these sweeps and mortars.

A machine, still more simple than the mortar and pestle, was used for making meal while the corn was too soft to be beaten. It was called a grater. This was a half circular piece of tin, perforated with a punch from the concave side, and nailed by its edges to a block of wood. The ears of corn were rubbed on the rough edges of the holes, while the meal fell through them on the board or block to which the grater was nailed, which, being in a slanting direction, discharged the meal into a cloth or bowl place for its reception. This to be sure was a slow way of making meal; but necessity has no law.

The hand mill was better than the mortar and grater. It was made of two circular stones, the lowest of which was called the bed stone, the upper one the runner. These were placed in a hoop, with a spout for discharging the meal. A staff was let into a hole in the upper surface of the runner, near the outer edge, and its upper end through a hole in a board fastened to a joist above, so that two persons could be employed in turning the mill at the same time. The grain was put into the opening in the runner by hand. These mills are still in use in Palestine, the ancient country of the Jews. To a mill of this sort our Saviour alluded, when, with reference to the destruction of Jerusalem, He said, "Two women shall be grinding at a mill, the one shall be taken and the other left." This mill is much preferable to that used at present in upper Egypt for making the dhourra bread. It is a smooth stone, placed on an inclined plane upon which the grain is spread, which is made into meal by rubbing another stone up and down upon it.

Our first water mills were of that description denominated tub mills. It consists of a perpendicular shaft, to the lower end of which an horizontal wheel of about four or five feet diameter is attached; the upper end passes through the bedstone and carries the runner, after the manner of a trundlehead. These mills were built with very little expense, and many of them answered the purpose very well.

Instead of bolting cloths, sifters were in general use. These were made of deer skins in the state of parchment, stretched over a hoop and perforated with a hot wire.

Our clothing was all of domestic manufacture. We had no other resource for clothing, and this, indeed, was a poor one. The crops of flax often failed, and the sheep were destroyed by the wolves. Linsey, which is made of flax and wool, the former the chain and the latter the filling, was the warmest and most substantial cloth we could make. Almost every house contained a loom, and almost every woman was a weaver.

Every family tanned their own leather. The tan vat was a large trough sunk to the upper edge in the ground. A quantity of bark was easily obtained every spring, in clearing and fencing the land. This, after drying, was brought in and in wet days was shaved and pounded on a block of wood, with an axe or mallet. Ashes was used in place of lime for taking off the hair. Bear's oil, hog's lard and tallow, answered the place of fish oil. The leather, to be sure, was coarse; but it was substantially good. The operation of currying was performed by a drawing knife with its edge turned, after the manner of a currying knife. The blacking for the leather was made of soot and hog's lard.

Almost every family contained its own tailors and shoemakers. Those who could not make shoes could make shoepacks. These, like moccasins, were made of a single piece of leather with the exception of a tongue piece on the top of the foot. This was about two inches broad and circular at the lower end. To this the main piece of leather was sewed, with a gathering stitch. The seam behind was like that of a moccasin. To the shoepack a sole was sometimes added. The women did the tailor work. They could all cut out and make hunting shirts, leggins and drawers.

The state of society which existed in our country at an early period of its settlement is well calculated to call into action every native mechanical genius. This happened in this country. There was, in almost every neighborhood, some one whose natural ingenuity enabled him to do many things for himself and his neighbors, far above what could have been reasonably expected. With the few tools which they brought with them into the country they certainly performed wonders. Their plows, harrows with their wooden teeth, and sleds, were in many instances well made. Their cooper ware, which comprehended everything for holding milk and water, was generally pretty well executed. The cedar ware, by having alternately a white and red stave, was then thought beautiful. Many of their puncheon floors were very neat, their joints close and the top even and smooth. Their looms, although heavy, did very well. Those who could not exercise these mechanic arts were under the necessity of giving labor, or barter, to their neighbors in exchange for the use of them, so far as their necessities required.

An old man in my father's neighborhood had the art of turning bowls from the knots of trees, particularly those of the ash. In what way he did it, I do not know: or whether there was much mystery in his art. Be that as it may, the old man's skill was in great request as well turned wooden bowls were amongst our first rate articles of household furniture.

My brothers and myself once undertook to procure a fine suit of these bowls made of the best wood, the ash. We gathered all we could find on our father's land and took them to the artist, who was to give, as the saying was, one-half for the other. He put the knots in a branch before his door. A freshet came and swept them all away. Not one of them was ever found. This was a dreadful misfortune. Our anticipation of an elegant display of new bowls was utterly blasted in a moment, as the poor old man was not able to repair our loss, or any part of it.

My father possessed a mechanical genius of the highest order, and necessity, which is the mother of invention, occasioned the full exercise of his talents. His farming utensils were the best in the neighborhood. After making his loom, he often used it as a weaver. All the shoes belonging to the family were made by himself. He always spun his own shoe thread. Saying that no woman could spin *shoe thread* as well as he could. His cooper ware was made by himself. I have seen him make a small, neat kind of wooden ware called set work, in which the staves were all attached to the bottom of the vessel by the means of a groove cut in them by a strong clasp knife, and small chisel, before a single hoop was put on. He was sufficiently the carpenter to build the best kind of houses then in use, that is to say first a cabin, and afterwards the hewed log house, with a shingled roof. In his latter years he became sickly, and not being able to labor he amused himself with tolerably good imitations of cabinet work.

Not possessing sufficient health for service on the scouts, and campaigns, his duty was that of repairing the rifles of his neighbors when they needed it. In this business he manifested a high degree of ingenuity. A small depression on the surface of a stump or log and a wooden mallet were his instruments for straightening the gun barrel when crooked. Without the aid of a bow string he could discover the smallest bend in a barrel. With a bit of steel, he could make a saw for deepening the furrows, when requisite. A few shots determined whether the gun might be trusted.

Although he never had been more than six weeks at school he was nevertheless a first rate penman, and a good arithmetician. His penmanship was of great service to his neighbors in writing letters, bonds, deeds of conveyance, etc.

Young as I was, I was possessed of an art which was of great use. It was that of weaving shot-pouch straps, belts and garters. I could make my loom and weave a belt in less than one day. Having a piece of board about four feet long, an inch auger, spike gimlet, and a drawing knife, I needed no other tools or materials for making my loom. It frequently happened that my weaving proved serviceable to the family, as I often sold a belt for a day's work, or making an hundred rails. So that, although a boy, I could exchange my labor for that of a full grown person for an equal length of time.

CHAPTER XIX.

Diseases and their Remedies.

This, amongst a rude and illiterate people, consisted mostly of specifics. As far as I can recollect them, they shall be enumerated, together with the diseases for which they were used.

The diseases of children were mostly ascribed to worms, for the expulsion of which a solution of common salt was given. The dose was always large. I well remember, having been compelled to take half a table spoon full, when quite small. To the best of my recollection it generally answered the purpose. Scrapings of pewter spoons was another remedy for the worms. This dose was also large, amounting, I should think, from twenty to forty grains. It was commonly given in sugar. Sulphate of iron, or green copperas, was a third remedy for the worms. The dose of this was also larger than we should venture to give at this time.

For burns a poultice of Indian meal was a common remedy. A poultice of scraped potatoes was also a favorite remedy with some people. Roasted turnips, made into a poultice, was used by others. Slippery elm bark was often used in the same way. I do not recollect that any internal remedy or bleeding was ever used for burns.

The croup, or what was then called the *bold hives,* was a common disease among the children, many of whom died of it. For the cure of this, the juice of roasted onions or garlic was given in large doses. Wall-ink was also a favorite remedy with many of the old ladies. For fevers, sweating was the general remedy. This was generally performed by means of a strong decoction of Virginia snake root. The dose was always very large. If a purge was used, it was about half a pint of a strong decoction of white walnut bark. This, when intended for a purge, was peeled downwards; if for a vomit, it was peeled upwards. Indian physic, or bowman root, a species of epicacuanha was frequently used for a vomit, and sometimes the pocoon or blood root.

For the bite of a rattle, or copper snake, a great variety of specifics was used. I remember when a small boy to have seen a man bitten by a rattlesnake brought into the fort on a man's back. One of the company dragged the snake after him by a forked stick fastened in its head. The body of the snake was cut into pieces of about two inches in length, split open in succession, and laid on the wound to draw out the poison, as they expressed it. When this was over, a fire was kindled up in the fort yard and the whole of the serpent burned to ashes, by way of revenge for the injury he had done. After this process was over, a large quantity of chestnut leaves was collected and boiled in a pot. The whole of the wounded man's leg and part of his thigh were placed in a piece of chestnut bark, fresh from the tree, and the decoction poured on the leg so as to run down into the pot again; after continuing this process for some time, a quantity of the boiled leaves were bound to the leg. This was repeated several times a day. The man got well; but whether owing to the treatment bestowed on his wound is not so certain.

A number of native plants were used for the cure of snake bites. Among them the white plantain held a high rank. This was boiled in milk and the decoction given the patient in large quantities. A kind of fern, which, from its resemblance to the leaves of walnut, was called walnut fern, was another remedy. A plant with fibrous roots, resembling the seneka-snake root, of a black color and a strong, but not disagreeable smell, was considered and relied on as the Indian specific for the cure of the sting of a snake. A decoction of this root was also used for the cure of colds. Another plant which very much resembles the one above mentioned, but violently poisonous, was sometimes mistaken for it and used in its place. I knew two young women who, in consequence of being bitten by rattlesnakes, used the poisonous plant instead of the other, and nearly lost their lives by the mistake. The roots were applied to their legs in the form of a poultice; the violent burning and swelling, occasioned by the inflammation, discovered the mistake in time to prevent them from taking any of the decoction, which, had they done, it would have been instantly fatal. It was with difficulty that the part to which the poultice was applied was saved from mortification, so that the remedy was far worse than the disease.

Cupping, sucking the wound, and making deep incisions which were filled with salt and gun powder, were amongst the remedies for snake bits. It does not appear to me that any of the internal remedies used by the Indians and the first settlers of this country, were well adapted for the cure of the disease occasioned by the bite of a snake. The poison of a snake, like that of a bee or wasp, must consist of an highly concentrated and very poisonous acid, which instantly inflames the part to which it is applied. That any substance whatever can act as a specific for the decomposition of this poison seems altogether doubtful. The cure of the fever occasioned by this animal poison must be effected with reference to those general indications which are regarded in the cure of other fevers of equal force. The internal remedies alluded to, so far as I am acquainted with them, are possessed of little or no medical efficacy. They are not emetics, cathartics, or sudorifics. What then? They are harmless substances which do wonders in all those cases in which there is nothing to be done.

The truth is, the bite of a rattle or copper snake in a fleshy or tenderous part, where the blood vessels are neither numerous nor large, soon healed under any kind of treatment. But when the fangs of the serpent, which are hollow and eject the poison through an orifice near the points, penetrate a blood vessel of any considerable size, a malignant and incurable fever was generally the immediate consequence, and the patient often expired in the first paroxysm. The same observations apply to the effects of the bite of serpents when inflicted on beasts. Horses were frequently killed by them, as they were commonly bitten somewhere about the nose, in which the blood vessels are numerous and large. I once saw a horse die of the bite of a rattlesnake. The blood, for some time before he expired, exuded in great quantity through the pores of the skin.

Cattle were less frequently killed, because their noses are of a grisly texture, and less furnished with blood vessels than those of a horse. Dogs were sometimes bitten, and being naturally physicians they commonly scratched a hole in some damp place and held the wounded part in the ground till the inflammation abated. Hogs, when in tolerable order, were never hurt by them, owing to their thick subtratum of fat between the skin, muscular flesh and blood vessels. The hog generally took immediate revenge for the injury done him by instantly tearing to pieces and devouring the serpent which inflicted it.

The itch, which was a very common disease in early times, was commonly cured by an ointment made of brimstone and hog's lard.

Gun shot, and other wounds, were treated with slippery elm bark, flax seed and other such like poultices. Many lost their lives from wounds which would now be considered trifling and easily cured. The use of the lancet and other means of depletion, in the treatment of wounds, constituted no part of their cure in this country in early times.

My mother died in early life of a wound from the tread of a horse, which any person in the habit of letting blood might have cured by two or three bleedings, without any other remedy. The wound was poulticed with spikenard roots and soon terminated in an extensive mortification.[1]

Most of the men of the early settlers of this country were affected with the rheumatism. For relief from this disease the hunters generally slept with their feet to the fire. From this practice they certainly derived much advantage. The oil of rattlesnakes, geese, wolves, bears, raccoons, ground-hogs and polecats, was applied to swelled joints and bathed in before the fire.

The pleurisy was the only disease which was supposed to require blood letting; but in many cases a bleeder was not to be had.

---

[1] Mrs. Doddridge was killed about 1777 by horses running away with a sled. Her body was buried on the Doddridge farm, but in 1824 was removed, with the remains of her husband, to Wellsburg. Mr. Doddridge was absent from home when his wife was killed. He had gone east for their salt.—(*Simpson.*)

Coughs, and pulmonary consumptions, were treated with a great variety of syrups, the principal ingredients of which were commonly spikenard and elecampane. These syrups certainly gave but little relief.

Charms and incantations were in use for the cure of many diseases. I learned, when young, the incantation in German for the cure of burns, stopping blood, for the toothache, and the charm against bullets in battle; but for the want of faith in their efficacy I never used any of them.

The erysipelas, or St. Anthony's fire, was circumscribed by the blood of a black cat. Hence there was scarcely a black cat to be seen whose ears and tail had not been frequently cropped, for a contribution of blood.

Whether the medical profession is productive of most good or harm may still be a matter of dispute with some philosophers who never saw any condition of society in which there were no physicians, and therefore could not be furnished a proper test for deciding the question. Had an unbeliever in the healing art been amongst the early inhabitants of this country, he would have been in a proper situation to witness the consequences of the want of the exercise of this art. For many years in succession there was no person who bore even the name of a doctor within a considerable distance of the residence of my father. For the honor of the medical profession, I must give it as my opinion, that many of our people perished for want of medical skill and attention.

The pleurisy was the only disease which was, in any considerable degree, understood by our people. A pain in the side called for the use of the lancet, if there was any to be had; but owing to its sparing use, the patient was apt to be left with a spitting of blood, which sometimes ended in consumption. A great number of children died of the croup. Remittent and intermittent fevers were treated with warm drinks, for the purpose of sweating. The patients were denied the use of cold water and fresh air. Many of them died. Of those who escaped, not a few died afterwards of the dropsy, or consumption; or were left with paralytic limbs. Deaths in child bed were not unfrequent. Many, no doubt, died of the bite of serpents, in consequence of an improper reliance on specifics possessed of no medical virtue.

My father died of an hepatitis, at the age of about forty-six. He had labored under this disease for thirteen years. The fever which accompanied it was called " the dumb ague," and the swelling in the region of the liver, " the ague cake." The abscess bursted and discharged a large quantity of matter which put a period to his life in about thirty hours after the commencement. of the discharge.

Thus I, for one, may say, that in all human probability, I lost both my parents for want of medical aid.

CHAPTER XX.

Games and Diversions.

These were such as might be expected among a people who, owing to their circumstances as well as education, set a higher value on physical than on mental endowments, and on skill in hunting and bravery in war than on any polite accomplishments, or fine arts.

Amusements are, in many instances, either imitations of the business of life, or, at least, of some of its particular objects of pursuit; on the part of young men belonging to nations in a state of warfare, many amusements are regarded as preparations for the military character which they are expected to sustain in future life. Thus, the war dance of savages is a pantomime of their stratagems and horrid deeds of cruelty in war, and the exhibition prepares the minds of their young men for a participation in the bloody tragedies which they represent. Dancing, among civilized people, is regarded not only as an amusement suited to the youthful period of human life, but as a means of inducing urbanity of manners and a good personal deportment in public. Horse racing is regarded by the statesman as a preparation, in various ways, for the equestrian department of warfare; it is said that the English government never possessed a good cavalry until, by the encouragement given to public races, their breed of horses was improved. Games, in which there is a mixture of chance and skill, are said to improve the understanding in mathematical and other calculations.

Many of the sports of the early settlers of this country were imitative of the exercises and stratagems of hunting and war. Boys were taught the use of the bow and arrow at an early age; but although they acquired considerable adroitness in the use of them, so as to kill a bird or squirrel sometimes, yet it appears to me that in the hands of the white people the bow and arrow could never be depended upon for warfare or hunting, unless made and managed in a different manner from any specimens of them which I ever saw. In ancient times the bow and arrow must have been deadly instruments in the hands of the barbarians of our country; but I much doubt whether any of the present tribes of Indians could make much use of the flint arrow heads which must have been so generally used by their forefathers.

Fire arms, wherever they can be obtained, soon put an end to the use of the bow and arrow; but independently of this circumstance, military, as well as other arts, sometimes grow out of date and vanish from the world. Many centuries have elapsed since the world has witnessed the destructive accuracy of the Benjamites in their use of the sling and stone; nor does it appear to me that a diminution in the size and strength of the aborigines of this country has occasioned a decrease of accuracy and effect in their use of the bow and arrow. From all the ancient skeletons which have come under my notice, it does not appear that this section of the globe was ever inhabited by a larger race of human beings than that which possessed it at the time of its discovery by the Europeans.

One important pastime of our boys was that of imitating the noise of every bird and beast in the woods. This faculty was not merely a pastime, but a very necessary part of education, on account of its utility in certain circumstances. The imitations of the gobbling and other sounds of wild turkeys often brought those keen eyed and ever watchful tenants of the forest within the reach of the rifle. The bleating of the fawn brought her dam to her death in the same way. The hunter often collected a company of mopish owls to the trees about his camp, and amused himself with their hoarse screaming; his howl would raise and obtain responses from a pack of wolves, so as to inform him of their neighborhood, as well as guard him against their depredations.

This imitative faculty was sometimes requisite as a measure of precaution in war. The Indians, when scattered about in a neighborhood, often collected together by imitating turkeys by day and wolves or owls by night. In similar situations our people did the same. I have often witnessed the consternation of a whole neighborhood in consequence of a few screeches of owls. An early and correct use of this imitative faculty was considered as an indication that its possessor would become in due time a good hunter and a valiant warrior.

Throwing the tomahawk was another boyish sport, in which many acquired considerable skill. The tomahawk with its handle of a certain length will make a given number of turns in a given distance. Say in five steps it will strike with the edge, the handle downwards; at the distance of seven and a half, it will strike with the edge, the handle upwards, and so on. A little experience enabled the boy to measure the distance with his eye, when walking through the woods, and strike a tree with his tomahawk in any way he chose.

The athletic sports of running, jumping and wrestling, were the pastimes of boys, in common with the men. A well grown boy, at the age of twelve or thirteen years, was furnished with a small rifle and shot pouch. He then became a fort soldier, and had his port hole assigned him. Hunting squirrels, turkeys and raccoons soon made him expert in the use of his gun.

Dancing was the principal amusement of our young people of both sexes. Their dances, to be sure, were of the simplest forms. Three and four handed reels and jigs. Contra dances, cotillions and minuets, were unknown. I remember to have seen, once or twice, a dance which was called the Irish trot, but I have long since forgotten its figure.

Shooting at marks was a common diversion among the men, when their stock of ammunition would allow it; this, however, was far from being always the case. The present mode of shooting off hand was not then in practice. This mode was not considered as any trial of the value of a gun; nor, indeed, as much of a test of the skill of a marksman. Their shooting was from a rest, and at as great distance as the length and weight of the barrel of the gun would throw a ball on a horizontal level. Such was their regard to accuracy, in these sportive trials of their rifles, and of their own skill in the use of them, that they often put moss, or some other soft substance, on the log or stump from which they shot, for fear of having the bullet thrown from the mark, by the spring of the barrel. When the rifle was held to the side of a tree for a rest, it was pressed against it as lightly as possible, for the same reason.

Rifles of former times were different from those of modern date; few of them carried more than forty-five bullets to the pound. Bullets of less size were not thought sufficiently heavy for hunting or war.

Dramatic narrations, chiefly concerning Jack and the giant, furnished our young people with another source of amusement during their leisure hours. Many of these tales were lengthy, and embraced a considerable range of incident. Jack, always the hero of the story, after encountering many difficulties, and performing many great achievements, came off conqueror of the giant. Many of these stories were tales of knight errantry, in which some captive virgin was released from captivity and restored to her lover. These dramatic narrations concerning Jack and the giant bore a strong resemblance to the poems of Ossian, the story of the Cyclops and Ulysses, in the Odyssey of Homer, and the tale of the giant and Great-heart, in the *Pilgrim's Progress*. They were so arranged, as to the different incidents of the narration, that they were easily committed to memory. They certainly have been handed down from generation to generation, from time immemorial. Civilization has, indeed, banished the use of those ancient tales of romantic heroism; but what then? it has substituted in their place the novel and romance.

It is thus that in every state of society the imagination of man is eternally at war with reason and truth. That fiction should be acceptable to an unenlightened people is not to be wondered at, as the treasures of truth have never been unfolded to their mind; but that a civilized people themselves should in so many instances, like barbarians, prefer the fairy regions of fiction to the august treasures of truth developed in the sciences of theology, history, natural and moral philosophy, is truly a sarcasm on human nature. It is as much as to say that it is essential to our amusement; that, for the time being, we must suspend the exercise of reason, and submit to a voluntary deception.

Singing was another, but no very common, amusement among our first settlers. Their tunes were rude enough, to be sure. Robin Hood furnished a number of our songs, the balance were mostly tragical. These last were denominated "love songs about murder;" as to cards, dice, back-gammon and other games of chance, we knew nothing about them. These are amongst the blessed gifts of civilization.

CHAPTER XXI.

The Witchcraft Delusion.

I shall not be lengthy on this subject. The belief in witchcraft was prevalent among the early settlers of the western country. To the witch was ascribed the tremendous power of inflicting strange and incurable diseases, particularly on children, of destroying cattle by shooting them with hair balls, and a great variety of other means of destruction, of inflicting spells and curses on guns and other things, and lastly of changing men into horses, and after bridling and saddling them, riding them in full speed over hill and dale to their frolics and other places of rendezvous. More ample powers of mischief than these cannot well be imagined.

Wizards were men supposed to possess the same mischievous powers as the witches; but these were seldom exercised for bad purposes. The powers of the wizards were exercised almost exclusively for the purpose of counteracting the malevolent influences of the witches of the other sex. I have known several of those witch masters, as they were called, who made a public profession of curing the diseases inflicted by the influence of witches, and I have known respectable physicians who had no greater portion of business in the line of their profession than many of those witch masters had in theirs.

The means by which the witch was supposed to inflict diseases, curses and spells, I never could learn. They were occult sciences, which no one was supposed to understand, excepting the witch herself, and no wonder, as no such arts ever existed in any country.

The diseases of children supposed to be inflicted by witchcraft were those of the internal organs, dropsy of the brain, and the rickets. The symptoms and cure of these destructive diseases were utterly unknown in former times in this country. Diseases which could neither be accounted for nor cured were usually ascribed to some supernatural agency of a malignant kind.

For the cure of the diseases inflicted by witchcraft, the picture of the supposed witch was drawn on a stump or piece of board and shot at with a bullet containing a little bit of silver. This silver bullet transferred a painful and sometimes a mortal spell on that part of the witch corresponding with the part of the portrait struck by the bullet. Another method of cure was that of getting some of the child's water, which was closely corked up in a vial and hung up in a chimney. This complemented the witch with a strangury which lasted as long as the vial remained in the chimney. The witch had but one way of relieving herself from any spell inflicted on her in any way, which was that of borrowing something, no matter what, of the family to which the subject of the exercise of her witchcraft belonged. I have known several poor old women much surprised at being refused requests which had usually been granted without hesitation, and almost heart broken when informed of the cause of the refusal.

When cattle or dogs were supposed to be under the influence of witchcraft they were burnt in the forehead by a branding iron, or when dead burned wholly to ashes. This inflicted a spell upon the witch which could only be removed by borrowing, as above stated.

Witches were often said to milk the cows of their neighbors. This they did by fixing a new pin in a new towel for each cow intended to be milked. This towel was hung over her own door, and by the means of certain incantations the milk was extracted from the fringes of the towel after the manner of milking a cow. This happened when the cows were too poor to give much milk.

The first German glass blowers in this country drove the witches out of their furnaces by throwing living puppies into them.

The greater or less amount of belief in witchcraft, necromancy and astrology, serves to show the relative amount of philosophical science in any country. Ignorance is always associated with superstition, which, presenting an endless variety of sources of hope and fear, with regard to the good or bad fortunes of life, keep the benighted mind continually harassed with groundless, and delusive, but strong and often deeply distressing impressions of a false faith. For this disease of the mind there is no cure but that of philosophy. This science shows to the enlightened reason of man that no effect whatever can be produced in the physical world without a corresponding cause. This science announces that the death bell is but a momentary morbid motion of the ear, and the death watch the noise of a bug in the wall, and that the howling of the dog, and the croaking of the raven are but the natural languages of the beast and fowl, and no way prophetic of the death of the sick. The comet, which used to shake pestilence and war from its fiery train, is now viewed with as little emotion as the movements of Jupiter and Saturn in their respective orbits.

An eclipse of the sun, and an unusual freshet of the Tiber, shortly after the assassination of Julius Cæsar by Cassius and Brutus, threw the whole of the Roman empire into consternation. It was supposed that all the gods of heaven and earth were enraged and about to take revenge for the murder of the emperor; but since the science of astronomy foretells in the calendar the time and extent of the eclipse, the phenomenon is not viewed as a miraculous and portentous, but as a common and natural event.

That the pythoness and wizard of the Hebrews, the monthly soothsayers, astrologers and prognosticators of the Chaldeans, and the sybils of the Greeks and Romans, were merely mercenary impostors, there can be no doubt. To say that the pythoness and all others of her class were aided in their operations by the intervention of familiar spirits does not mend the matter, for spirits, whether good or bad, possess not the power of life and death, health and disease, with regard to man or beast. Prescience is an incommunicable attribute of God, and therefore spirits cannot foretell future events.

The afflictions of Job, through the intervention of Satan, were miraculous. The possessions mentioned in the New Testament, in all human probability, were maniacal diseases, and if, at their cures the supposed evil spirits spoke with an audible voice, these events were also miraculous, and effected for a special purpose. But from miracles no general conclusions can be drawn with regard to the divine government of the world. The conclusion is that the powers professed to be exercised by the occult science of necromancy and other arts of divination were neither more or less than impostures.

Among the Hebrews the profession of arts of divination was thought deserving capital punishment, because the profession was of pagan origin, and of course incompatible with the profession of theism, and a theocratic form of government. These jugglers perpetrated a debasing superstition among the people. They were also swindlers, who divested their neighbors of large sums of money, and valuable presents, without an equivalent. On the ground then, of fraud alone, according to the genius of the criminal codes of ancient governments, this offense deserved capital punishment.

But is the present time better than the past with regard to a superstitious belief in occult influences? Do no traces of the polytheism of our fore-fathers remain among their Christian descendants? This inquiry must be answered in the affirmative. Should an almanac maker venture to give out the Christian calendar without a column containing the signs of the zodiac, the calendar would be condemned as being totally deficient and the whole impression would remain on his hands.

But what are these signs? They are constellations of the zodiac, that is clusters of stars, twelve in number, within and including the tropics of Cancer and Capricorn. These constellations resemble the animals after which they are named. But what influence do these clusters of stars exert on the animal and the plant. Certainly none at all; and yet we are taught that the northern constellations govern the divisions of living bodies alternately from the head to the reins, and in like manner the southern from the reins to the feet. The sign then makes a skip from the feet to Aries, who again assumes the government of the head, and so on. About half of these constellations are friendly divinities and exert a salutary influence on the animal and the plant. The others are malignant in their temper, and govern only for evil purposes. They blast, during their reign, the seed sown in the earth and render medicine and operations of surgery unsuccessful.

We have read of the Hebrews worshipping the host of heaven, whenever they relapsed into idolatry, and these same constellations were the hosts of heaven which they worshipped. We, it is true, make no offering to these hosts of heaven, but we give them our faith and confidence. We hope for physical benefits from those of them whose dominion is friendly to our interests, while the reign of the malignant ones is an object of dread and painful apprehension. Let us not boast very much of our science, civilization, or even Christianity while this column of the relics of paganism still disgraces the Christian calendar.

I have made these observations with a view to discredit the remnants of superstition still existing among us. While dreams, the howling of the dog, croaking of a raven are prophetic of future events we are not good Christians. While we are dismayed at the signs of heaven we are for the time being pagans. Life has real evils enough to contend with, without imaginary ones.

CHAPTER XXII.

Law, Morality and Religion.

In the section of the country where my father lived there was, for many years after the settlement of the country, "neither law nor gospel." Our want of legal government was owing to the uncertainty whether we belonged to the state of Virginia or Pennsylvania. The line, which at present divides the two states, was not run until some time after the conclusion of the revolutionary war. Thus it happened that during a long period of time we knew nothing of courts, lawyers, magistrates, sheriffs, or constables. Every one was therefore at liberty "to do whatever was right in his own eyes."

As this is a state of society which few of my readers have ever witnessed, I shall describe it minutely as I can, and give in detail those moral maxims which, in a great degree, answered the important purposes of municipal jurisprudence.

In the first place, let it be observed that in a sparse population, where all the members of the community are well known to each other, and especially in a time of war, where every man capable of bearing arms is considered highly valuable as a defender of his country, public opinion has its full effect and answers the purposes of legal government better than it would in a dense population, and in time of peace.

Such was the situation of our people along the frontiers of our settlements. They had no civil, military or ecclesiastical laws, at least none that were enforced, and yet "they were a law unto themselves" as to the leading obligations of our nature in all the relations in which they stood to each other. The turpitude of vice and the majesty of moral virtue were then as apparent as they are now, and they were then regarded with the same sentiments of aversion or respect which they inspire at the present time. Industry in working and hunting, bravery in war, candor, honesty, hospitality, and steadiness of deportment, received their full reward of public confidence among our rude forefathers, as well as among their better instructed and more polished descendants. The punishments which they inflicted upon offenders, by the imperial court of public opinion, were well adapted for the reformation of the culprit, or his expulsion from the community.

The punishment for idleness, lying, dishonesty, and ill fame generally, was that of "hating the offender out," as they expressed it. This mode of chastisement was like the *atimea* of the Greeks. It was a public expression, in various ways, of a general sentiment of indignation against such as transgressed the moral maxims of the community to which they belonged. This commonly resulted either in the reformation or banishment of the person against whom it was directed.

At house raisings, log rollings and harvest parties, every one was expected to do his duty faithfully. A person who did not perform his share of labor on these occasions was designated by the epithet of *Lawrence,* or some other title still more opprobrious; and when it came to his turn to require the like aid from his neighbors, the idler soon felt his punishment in their refusal to attend to his calls.

Although there was no legal compulsion to the performance of military duty, yet every man of full age and size was expected to do his full share of public service. If he did not do so he was "hated out as a coward." Even the want of any article of war equipments, such as ammunition, a sharp flint, a priming wire, a scalping knife or tomahawk, was thought highly disgraceful. A man who, without a reasonable cause, failed to go on a scout or campaign, when it came to his turn, met with an expression of indignation in the countenances of all his neighbors, and epithets of dishonor were fastened upon him without mercy.

Debts, which make such an uproar in civilized life, were but little known among our forefathers at the early settlement of this country. After the depreciation of the continental paper they had no money of any kind; everything purchased was paid for in produce or labor. A good cow and calf was often the price of a bushel of alum salt. If a contract was not punctually fulfilled, the credit of the delinquent was at an end.

Any petty theft was punished with all the infamy that could be heaped on the offender. A man on a campaign stole from his comrade a cake out of the ashes in which it was baking. He was immediately named *the bread rounds.* This epithet of reproach was bandied about in this way; when he came in sight of a group of men, one of them would call "Who comes there?" Another would answer, "The bread rounds." If any one meant to be more serious about the matter, he could call out, "Who stole a cake out of the ashes?" Another replied by giving the name of the man in full; to this a third would give confirmation exclaiming, "That is true and no lie." This kind of *tongue-lashing* he was doomed to bear for the rest of the campaign, as well as for years after his return home.

If a theft was detected in any of the frontier settlements, a summary mode of punishment was always resorted to. The first settlers, as far as I knew of them, had a kind of innate or hereditary detestation of the crime of theft, in any shape or degree, and their maxim was that "a thief must be whipped." If the theft was of something of some value, a kind of jury of the neighborhood, after hearing the testimony, would condemn the culprit to Moses's law, that is, to forty stripes save one. If the theft was of some small article, the offender was doomed to carry on his back the flag of the United States, which then consisted of thirteen stripes. In either case, some able hands were selected to execute the sentence, so that the stripes were sure to be well laid on. This punishment was followed by a sentence of exile. He then was informed that he must decamp in so many days and be seen there no more on penalty of having the number of stripes doubled.

For many years after the law was put in operation in the western part of Virginia the magistrates themselves were in the habit of giving those who were brought before them on charges of small thefts the liberty of being sent to jail or taking a whipping. The latter was commonly chosen and was immediately inflicted, after which the thief was ordered to clear out.

In some instances stripes were inflicted, not for the punishment of an offense, but for the purpose of extorting a confession from suspected persons. This was the torture of our early times, and no doubt sometimes very unjustly inflicted.

If a woman was given to tattling and slandering her neighbors, she was furnished, by common consent, with a kind of patent right to say whatever she pleased without being believed. Her tongue was then said to be harmless, or to be no scandal.

With all their rudeness, these people were given to hospitality, and freely divided their rough fare with a neighbor or stranger, and would have been offended at the offer of pay. In their settlements and forts they lived, they worked, they fought and feasted, or suffered together, in cordial harmony. They were warm and constant in their friendships. On the other hand they were revengeful in their resentments. And the point of honor sometimes led to personal combats. If one man called another a liar, he was considered as having given a challenge which the person who received it must accept, or be deemed a coward, and the charge was generally answered on the spot with a blow. If the injured person was decidedly unable to fight the aggressor he might get a friend to do it for him. The same thing took place on a charge of cowardice, or any other dishonorable action; a battle must follow and the person who made the charge must fight either the person against whom he made the charge or any champion who chose to espouse his cause. Thus circumstanced, our people in early times were much more cautious of speaking evil of their neighbors than they are at present.

Sometimes pitched battles occurred in which time, place and seconds were appointed beforehand. I remember having seen one of those pitched battles in my father's fort, when a boy. One of the young men knew very well beforehand that he should get the worst of the battle, and no doubt repented the engagement to fight; but there was no getting over it. The point of honor demanded the risk of battle. He got his whipping; they then shook hands and were good friends afterwards.

The mode of single combats in those days was dangerous in the extreme; although no weapons were used, fists, teeth and feet were employed at will, but above all the detestable practice of gouging, by which eyes were sometimes put out, rendered this mode of fighting frightful indeed; it was not, however, so destructive as the stiletto of an Italian, the knife of a Spaniard, the small sword of the Frenchman, or the pistol of the American or English duelist.

Instances of seduction and bastardy did not frequently happen in our early times. I remember one instance of the former, in which the life of the man was put in jeopardy by the resentment of the family to which the girl belonged. Indeed, considering the chivalrous temper of our people, this crime could not then take place without great personal danger from the brothers or other relations of the victims of seductions, family honor being then estimated at a high rate.

I do not recollect that profane language was much more prevalent in our early times than at present.

Among the people with whom I was most conversant, there was no other vestige of the Christian religion than a faint observation of Sunday, and that merely as a day of rest for the aged, and a play day for the young. The first Christian service I ever heard was in the garrison church in Baltimore county in Maryland, where my father had sent me to school. I was then about ten years old. The appearance of the church, the windows of which were Gothic, the white surplice of the minister, and the responses in the service, overwhelmed me with surprise. Among my schoolfellows in that place, it was a matter of reproach to me that I was not baptized, and why? Because, as they said, I had no name. Such was their notion of the efficacy of baptism.

CHAPTER XXIII.

Cruelty to Slaves and Servants.

If some of my readers should complain of the introduction of too great a portion of my own history, and that of my family, into this work, I trust I shall not be considered blamable for having given the narrative of the horrid cruelties exercised upon slaves and servants, which I was doomed to witness in my early years, together with the lasting impressions which the view of these tortures made upon my infant mind.

On the death of my mother, which happened when I was about eight years old, my father sent me, under the care of a relation, to Maryland for the purpose of being sent to school.

When I arrived there I was in a new world. I had left the backwoods behind me. I had exchanged its rough manners and poor living for the buildings, plenty and polish of civilized life. Everything I saw and heard confounded me. I learnt, after some time, that there were rich and poor masters, slaves and convicts, and I discovered that the poor servants and convicts were under entire subordination to their masters. I saw that the slaves and convicts lived in filthy hovels called kitchens, and that they were poor, ragged and dirty, and kept at hard labor; while their masters and families lived in large houses, were well clothed and fed and did as they pleased. The reason of this difference in the condition of men and women of the same race of beings I could not comprehend. Having no idea of crime, I thought it could not be otherwise than unjust, that some should have so little and others so much, and that one should work so hard and others perform no labor.

My residence was in a neighborhood where slaves and convicts were numerous, and where tortures inflicted upon them had become the occurrences of almost every day, so that they were viewed with indifference by the whole population of the neighborhood, as matters of course. Thus it is that custom reconciles human nature, with all its native sympathies, to the grossest barbarities, and hardens the heart against the intrusion of feeling at the sight of the most exquisite suffering of a fellow creature.

Not so with me, who never had witnessed such tortures; I had not been long in my new habitation, before I witnessed a scene which I shall never forget. A convict servant, accused of some trivial offense, was doomed to the whip. Tied with his arms extended upwards to the limb of a tree, and a bundle of hickories thrown down before him, he was ordered to look at them and told that they should all be worn out on him, and a great many more, if he did not make a confession of the crime alleged against him. The operation began by tucking up the shirt over his head, so as to leave his back and shoulders naked. The master then took two of the hickories in his hand, and by forward and backhanded strokes, each of which sounded like a wagon whip, and applied with the utmost rapidity and with his whole muscular strength, in a few seconds lacerated the shoulders of the poor miserable sufferer, with not less than fifty scourges, so that in a little time the whole of his shoulders had the appearance of a mass of blood, streams of which soon began to flow down his back and sides; he then made a confession of his fault. A fault not worth naming; but this did not save him from further torture. He had put his master "to the trouble of whipping him and he must have a little more." His trousers were then unbuttoned and suffered to fall down about his feet, two new hickories were selected from the bundle, and so applied that in a short time his posteriors, like his shoulders, exhibited nothing but laceration and blood. A consultation was then held between the master and the bystanders, who had been coolly looking on, in which it was humanely concluded "that he got enough." A basin of brine and a cloth were ordered to be brought; with this his stripes were washed or salted as they called it. During this operation the suffering wretch writhed and groaned as if in the agonies of death. He was then untied and told to go home and mistress would tell him what to do.

From this scene of torture I went home with a heavy heart, and wished myself in the backwoods again; nor did the frequency of witnessing such scenes lessen, in any degree, the horror which they first occasioned in my mind.

It frequently happened that torture was inflicted upon slaves and convicts in a more protracted manner than in that above described. When the victim of cruelty was doomed by his master to receive the lash, several of his neighbors were called on, for their assistance. They attended at the time and place appointed. A jug of rum and water were provided for the occasion. After the trembling wretch was brought forth and tied up, the number of lashes which he was to receive was determined on, and by lot, or otherwise, it was decided who should begin the operation; this done, the torture commenced; at the conclusion of the first course, the operator, pretending great weariness, called for a drink of rum and water, in which he was joined by the company. A certain time was allowed for the subject of their cruelty *to cool*, as they called it. When the allotted time had expired, the next hand took his turn, and in like manner ended with a drink, and so on until the appointed number of lashes were all imposed. This operation lasted several hours, sometimes half a day, at the conclusion of which the sufferer, with his hands swollen with the cords, was unbound and suffered to put on his shirt. His executioners, to whom the operation was rather a frolic than otherwise, returned home from the scene of their labor half drunk. Another method of punishment, still more protracted than this, was that of dooming a slave to receive so many lashes, during several days in succession; each of those whippings, excepting the first, was called "tickling up the old scabs."

A couple of wagoners in the neighborhood, having caught a man, as they said, in the act of stealing something from the wagon, stripped him and fastened him to the hinder part of the wagon, got out their jug of rum and amused themselves by making scores on his back for wagers. He that could make the deepest score was to have the first dram. Sometimes the cuts appearing to be equal, no decision could be had until the second or third trial was made. This sport was continued for several hours, until the poor fellow was almost killed, and the wagoners both drunk.

Female servants, both white and black, were subjected to the whip in common with the males. Having to pass through the yard of a neighbor, on my way to school, it happened that on going my usual route in a cold snowy morning, when I came within view of the house I was much surprised at seeing a naked woman standing at the whipping post and her master with a hickory in his hand. When I got to the place I stopped to see what was going on; after the woman had received a certain number of lashes, a female black slave was ordered from the kitchen, stripped and fastened by the irons of the whipping post; her scars exhibited the stripes and corrugations of former years. Both these women had handkerchiefs tied around their eyes, to prevent them from seeing when the blow was coming. The hickory used by this man was a forked one, twisted together and tied. A hickory of this kind, owing to the inequality of its surface, gives the greater pain. With this he scored the backs of these two women alternately; but for what length of time I do not know; being shocked at the sight, I hurried on to school and left the master at his work.

I might here relate many other methods of torture, of which I have been eye witness among these people, such as the thumb screw, sweating, the birch, etc., but it is enough, the heart sickens at the recollection of such cruelties.

Some time ago I made inquiry of a gentleman who had recently removed from the neighborhood in which I had lived in Maryland, to this country, concerning the present state of the families of my former acquaintance in Maryland; he informed me that of the whole number of those families, only three or four of their descendants remain possessors of the estates of their forefathers; of the others, their sons had become dissipated, sold their lands, and had either perished in consequence of intemperance, or left the country, so that the places which once knew those families as princes of the land now know them no more. Thus it is that in moral and physical respects at least "the sins of the fathers are visited upon the children to the third and fourth generation."

If the very sanctuaries built by the former hierarchy of the slave states, in which the oppressors used the ritual of the Christian service, with hands reeking with the blood of slaves, have long since ceased to be vocal with the songs of Zion, and have passed to other hands, or even fallen to decay, it is only saying that God is just.

The recollection of the tortures which I witnessed so early in life is still a source of affliction to my mind. Twenty-four hours never pass during which my imagination does not present me with the afflicting view of the slave or servant writhing beneath the lashes of his master, and cringing from the brine with which he salted his stripes.

During my stay of three years, in the region of slavery, my only consolation was, that the time would come in which the master and slave would exchange situations; that the former would receive the punishment due to his cruelty, while the latter should find rest from his toils and sufferings in the kingdom of Heaven. The master I regarded as Dives who, after "being clothed in purple and fine linen and faring sumptuously every day," must soon "lift up his eyes in hell, being in torment." The slave was Lazarus, who, after closing his sufferings in death, was to be "carried by the angels into Abraham's bosom."

From this afflicting state of society I returned to the back-woods a republican, without knowing the meaning of the term, that is, with an utter detestation of an arbitrary power of one man over another.

On reading this recital the historian will naturally reflect that personal, real, or political slavery, has, at all times, been the condition of almost the whole human race; that the history of man is the history of *oppressors* and the *victims* of oppression. Wars, bastiles, prisons, crosses, gibbets, tortures, scourges and fire, in the hands of despots, have been the instruments of spreading desolation and misery over the earth. The philosopher regards those means of destruction, and their extensive use, in all ages, as indices of the depravity and ferocity of man. From the blood-stained pages of history he turns with disgust and horror, and pronounces an involuntary anathema on the whole of his race. But is the condition of the world still to remain the same? Are the moral impressions of our nature to be forever sacrificed at the shrine of lawless ambition? Is man, as heretofore, to be born only to destroy, or be destroyed? Does the good Samaritan see no rational ground of hope of better things for future ages? We trust he does, and that ages yet to come will witness the fulfillment of his benevolent wishes and predictions.

The American revolution was the commencement of a new era in the history of the world. The issue of that eventful contest snatched the sceptre from the hands of the monarch, and placed it where it ought to be, in the hands of the people.

On the sacred altar of liberty it consecrated the rights of man, surrendered him the right and the power of governing himself, and placed in his hands the resources of his country as munitions of war for his defense. The experiment was indeed bold and hazardous; but the success has hitherto more than justified the most sanguine anticipations of those who made it. The world has witnessed, with astonishment, the rapid growth and confirmation of our noble fabric of freedom. From our distant horizon we have reflected a strong and steady blaze of light on ill-fated Europe, from time immemorial involved in the fetters and gloom of slavery. Our history has excited a general and ardent spirit of inquiry into the nature of our civil institutions, and a strong wish, on the part of the people in distant countries, to participate in our blessings.

But will an example, so portentous of evil to the chiefs of despotic institutions, be viewed with indifference by those who now sway the sceptre with unlimited power over the many millions of their vassals? Will they adopt new measures of defense against the influence of that thirst for freedom, so widely diffused and so rapidly gaining strength throughout their empires? Will they make no effort to remove from the world those free governments whose example gives them so much annoyance? The measures of defense will be adopted, the effort will be made; for power is never surrendered without a struggle.

Already nations which from the earliest period of their history have constantly crimsoned the earth with each other's blood have become a band of brothers for the destruction of every germ of human liberty. Every year witnesses an association of the monarchs of those nations, in unhallowed conclave, for the purpose of concerting measures for effecting their dark designs. Hitherto the execution of those measures has been, alas! too fatally successful.

It would be impolitic and unwise in us to calculate on escaping the hostile notice of the despots of continental Europe; already we hear, like distant thunder, their expressions of indignation and threats of vengeance. We ought to anticipate the gathering storm without dismay; but not with indifference. In viewing the dark side of the prospect before us, one source of consolation of much magnitude, presents itself. It is confidently expected that the brave and potent nation with whom we have a common origin will not risk the loss of that portion of liberty, which at the expense of so much blood and treasure, they have secured for themselves, by an unnatural association with despots for the unholy purpose of making war on the freedom of the few nations of the earth which possess any considerable portion of that invaluable blessing; on the contrary it is hoped by us that they will, if necessity should require, employ the bravery of their people, their immense resources and the trident of the ocean, in defense of their own liberties and by consequence those of others.

Legislators, fathers of our country! lose no time, spare no expense in hastening on the requisite means of defense, for meeting with safety, and with victory, the impending storm which, sooner or later, must fall upon us.

CHAPTER XXIV.

Western Civilization.

The causes which led to the present state of civilization of the western country are subjects which deserve some consideration.

The state of society and manners of the early settlers, as presented in these Notes, shows very clearly that their grade of civilization was, indeed, low enough. The descendants of the English cavaliers from Maryland and Virginia, who settled mostly along the rivers, and the descendants of the Irish, who settled the interior parts of the country, were neither of them remarkable for science or urbanity of manners. The former were mostly illiterate, rough in their manners, and addicted to the rude diversions of horse racing, wrestling, jumping, shooting, dancing, etc. These diversions were often accompanied with personal combats, which consisted of blows, kicks, biting and gouging. This mode of fighting was what they called *rough and tumble*. Sometimes a previous stipulation was made to use the fists only. Yet these people were industrious, enterprising, generous in their hospitality, and brave in the defense of their country.

These people, for the most part, formed the cordon along the Ohio river on the frontiers of Pennsylvania, Virginia and Kentucky, which defended the country against the attacks of the Indians during the revolutionary war. They were the janizaries of the country, that is, they were soldiers, when they chose to be so, and when they chose laid down their arms. Their military service was voluntary and of course received no pay.

With the descendants of the Irish I had but little acquaintance, although I lived near them. At an early period they were comprehended in the Presbyterian church, and were, therefore, more reserved in their deportment than their frontier neighbors, and from their situation, being less exposed to the Indian warfare, took less part in that war.

The patriot of the western region finds his love of the country and national pride augmented to the highest grade when he compares the political, moral and religious character of his people with that of the inhabitants of many large divisions of the old world. In Asia and Africa generation after generation passes without any change in the moral and religious character, or physical condition of the people.

On the Barbary coast the traveler, if a river lies in his way, and happens to be high, must either swim it or wait until it subsides. If the traveler is a Christian he must have a firman and a guard. Yet this was once the country of the famous Carthagenians.

In upper Egypt the people grind meal for their dhoura bread by rubbing it between two flat stones. This is done by women.

In Palestine the grinding of grain is still performed by an ill constructed hand mill, as in the days of our Saviour. The roads to the famous city of Jerusalem are still almost in the rude state of nature.

In Asiatic Turkey merchandise is still carried on by caravans, which are attended with a military guard, and the naked walls of the caravansera is their fortress and place of repose at night instead of a place of entertainment. The streets of Constantinople, instead of being paved, are, in many places, almost impassable from mud, filth, and the carcasses of dead beasts. Yet this is the metropolis of a great empire.

Throughout the whole of the extensive regions of Asia and Africa man, from his cradle to his grave, sees no change in the aspect of anything around him; unless from the desolations of war. His dress, his ordinary salutations of his neighbors, his diet and his mode of eating it, are prescribed by his religious institutions, and his rank in society, as well as his occupation, are determined by his birth. Steady and unvarying as the lapse of time in every department of life, generation after generation beats the dull monotonous round. The Hindoo would sooner die a martyr at the stake than sit on a chair or eat with a knife and fork.

The descendant of Ishmael is still "a wild man," hungry, thirsty and half naked; beneath a burning sun he traverses the immense and inhospitable desert of Sahara, apparently without any object, because his fore-fathers did so before him. Throughout life he subsists on camel's milk and flesh, while his only covering from the inclemency of weather is a flimsy tent of camel's hair; his single, solitary virtue is that of hospitality to strangers; in every other respect he is a thief and a robber.

The Chinese still retain their alphabet of thirty-six thousand *hieroglyphics*. They must never exchange it for one of twenty letters, which would answer an infinitely better purpose.

Had we pursued the course of the greater number of the nations of the earth we should have been at this day treading in the footsteps of our forefathers, from whose example in any respect we should have thought it criminal to depart, in the slightest degree.

Instead of a blind or superstitious imitation of the manners and customs of our forefathers, we have thought and acted for ourselves, and we have changed ourselves and everything around us. The linsey and coarse linen of the first settlers of the country have been exchanged for the substantial and fine fabrics of Europe and Asia; the hunting shirt for the fashionable coat of broadcloth, and the moccasin for boots and shoes of tanned leather. The dresses of our ladies are equal in beauty, fineness and fashion, to those of the cities and countries of Europe and Atlantic America.

It is not enough that persevering industry has enabled us to purchase the "purple and fine linen" from foreigners and to use their porcelain and glassware whether plain, engraved or gilt. We have nobly dared to fabricate those elegant, comfortable and valuable productions of art for ourselves. A well founded prospect of large gains from useful arts and honest labor has drawn to our country a large number of the best artizans of other countries. Their mechanic arts, immensely improved by American genius, have hitherto realized the hopeful prospect which induced their emigration to our infant country.

The horse paths, along which our forefathers made their laborious journeys over the mountains, for salt and iron, were soon succeeded by wagon roads, and those again by substantial turnpikes, which, as if by magic enchantment, have brought the distant region not many years ago denominated the backwoods, into a close and lucrative connection with our great Atlantic cities. The journey over the mountains, formerly considered so long, so expensive and even perilous, is now made in a very few days, and with accommodations not displeasing to the epicure himself. Those giants of North America, the different mountains composing the great chain of the Alleghany, formerly so frightful in their aspect, and presenting so many difficulties in their passage, are now scarcely noticed by the traveler in his journey along the graduated highways by which they are crossed.

The rude sports of former times have been discontinued. Athletic trials of muscular strength and activity, in which there certainly is not much of merit, have given way to the more noble ambition for mental endowments and skill in useful arts. To the rude and often indecent songs, but roughly and unskillfully sung, have succeeded the psalm, the hymn, and swelling anthem. To the clamorous boast, the provoking banter, the biting sarcasm, the horrid oath and imprecation, have succeeded urbanity of manners and a course of conversation enlightened by science, and chastened by mental attention and respect.

Above all the direful spirit of revenge, the exercise of which so much approximated the character of many of the first settlers of our country to that of the worst of savages, is now unknown. The Indian might pass in safety among those whose remembrance still bleeds at the recollection of the loss of their relatives, who have perished under the tomahawk and scalping-knife of the savages.

The Moravian brethren may dwell in safety on the sites of the villages desolated, and over the bones of their brethren and forefathers murdered by the more than savage ferocity of the whites. Nor let it be supposed that the return of peace produced this salutary change of feeling towards the tawny sons of the forest. The thirst of revenge was not wholly allayed by the balm of peace. Several Indians fell victims to the private vengeance of those who had recently lost their relations in the war, for some years after it had ceased.

If the state of society and manners, from the commencement of the settlements in this country during the lapse of many years, owing to the sanguinary character of the Indian mode of warfare, and other circumstances, was in a state of retrogression, as was evidently the case; if ignorance is more easily induced than science; if society more speedily deteriorates than improves; if it be much easier for the civilized man to become wild than for the wild man to become civilized; what means have arrested the progress of the early inhabitants of the western region towards barbarism? What agents have directed their influence in favor of science, morals and piety?

The early introduction of commerce was among the first means of changing, in some degree, the exterior aspect of the population of the country, and giving a new current to public feeling and individual pursuit. The huntsman and warrior, when he had exchanged his hunter's dress for that of the civilized man, soon lost sight of his former occupations and assumed a new character and a new line of life; like the soldier, who, when he receives his discharge, and lays aside his regimentals, soon loses the feeling of a soldier, and even forgets, in some degree, his manual exercise. Had not commerce furnished the means of changing the dresses of our people and the furniture of their houses, had the hunting shirt, moccasin and leggins continued to be the dress of our men, had the three legged stool, the noggin, the trencher and wooden bowl, continued to be the furniture of our houses, our progress towards science and civilization would have been much slower.

It may seem strange that so much importance is attached to the influence of dress in giving the moral and intellectual character of society.

In all the institutions of despotic governments we discover evident traces of the highest grade of human sagacity and foresight. It must have been the object of the founders of those governments to repress the genius of man, divest the mind of every sentiment of ambition, and prevent the cognizance of any rule of life excepting that of a blind obedience to the despot and his established institutions of religion and government; hence the canon laws of religion, in all governments despotic in principle, have prescribed the costume of each class of society, their diet, and their manner of eating it; even their household furniture is in like manner prescribed by law. In all these departments no deviation from the law or custom is permitted, or even thought of. The whole science of human nature, under such governments, is that of a knowledge of the duties of the station of life prescribed by parentage and the whole duty of man that of a rigid performance of them; while reason, having nothing to do with either the one or the other, is never cultivated.

Even among Christians those founders of religious societies have succeeded best who have prescribed a professional costume for their followers, because every time the disciple looks at his dress he is put in mind of his obligations to the society to which he belongs, and he is, therefore, the less liable to wander into strange pastures.

The English government could never subdue the *esprit de corps* of the north of Scotland until after the rebellion of '45. The prohibition of wearing the tartan plaid, the kilt and the bonnet, amongst Highlanders, broke down the spirit of the clans.

I have seen several of the Moravian Indians, and wondered that they were permitted to wear the Indian dress; their conduct, when among the white people, soon convinced me that the conversion of those whom I saw was far from being complete.

There can be little doubt but that if permission should be given by the supreme power of the Mussulman faith for a change, at the will of each individual, in dress, household furniture, and in eating and drinking, the whole Mohammedan system would be overthrown in a few years. With a similar permission the Hindoo superstition would share the same fate. We have yet some small districts of country where the costume, cabins, and in some measure the household furniture of their ancestors, are still in use. The people of these districts are far behind their neighbors in every valuable endowment of human nature. Among them the virtues of chastity, temperance and industry bear no great value, and schools and places of worship are but little regarded. In general every one "does what is right in his own eyes."

In short, why have we so soon forgotten our forefathers, and everything belonging to our former state? The reason is, everything belonging to our former state has vanished from our view; we meet with nothing to put us in remembrance of them. The recent date of the settlement of our country is no longer a subject of reflection. Its immense improvements present to the imagination the results of the labors of several centuries, instead of the work of a few years; and we do not often take the trouble to correct the false impression.

The introduction of the mechanic arts has certainly contributed, not a little, to the morals and scientific improvement of the country. The carpenter, the joiner and mason have displaced the rude, unsightly and uncomfortable cabin of our forefathers by comfortable and in many instances elegant mansions of stone, brick, hewn or sawed timbers.

The ultimate objects of civilization are the moral and physical happiness of man. To the latter, the commodious mansion house, with its furniture, contributes essentially. The family mansions of the nations of the earth furnish the criteria of the different grades of their moral and mental condition. The savages universally live in tents, wigwams or lodges covered with earth. Barbarians, next to these, may indeed have habitations something better, but of no value and indifferently furnished. Such are the habitations of the Russian, Tartar and Turkish peasantry.

Such is the effect of a large, elegant and well furnished house on the feelings and deportment of a family, that if you were to build one for a family of savages, by the occupancy of it they would lose their savage character; or if they did not choose to make the exchange of that character for that of civilization, they would forsake it for the wigwam and the woods.

This was done by many of the early stock of backwoodsmen, even after they built comfortable houses for themselves. They no longer had the chance of "*a fall hunt*," the woods pasture was eaten up. They wanted "*elbow room.*" They therefore sold out and fled to the forest of the frontier settlements, choosing rather to encounter the toil of turning the wilderness into fruitful fields a second time, and even risk an Indian war, rather than endure the inconveniences of a crowded settlement. Kentucky first offered a resting place for those pioneers, then Indiana and now the Missouri, and it cannot be long before the Pacific ocean will put a final stop to the westward march of those lovers of the wilderness.

Substantial buildings have the effect of giving value to the soil and creating an attachment to the family residence. Those who have accustomed themselves to poetry, ancient or modern, need not be told how finely and how impressively the household gods, the blazing hearth, the plentiful board and the social fireside, figure in poetical imagery. And this is not "Tying up nonsense for a song;" they are realities of life in its most polished states; they are among its best and most rational enjoyment; they associate the little family community in parental and filial affection and duty, in which even the well clothed child feels its importance, claims and duties.. The amount of attachment to the family mansion furnishes the criterion of the relative amount of virtue in the members of a family. If the head of a family should wander from the path of parental duty and become addicted to vicious habits, in proportion as his virtue suffers a declension, his love of his home and family abates until at last, any place, however base and corrupting it may be, is more agreeable to him than the once *dulce domum.* If a similar declension in virtue happens on the part of the maternal chief of the family mansion, the first effect of her deviation from the path of maternal virtue is that "Her feet abideth not in her own house." The same observations apply to children. When the young man or woman, instead of manifesting a strong attachment for the family mansion, is "given to outgoing" to places of licentious resort, their moral ruin may be said to be at no great distance.

Architecture is of use even in the important province of religion. Those who build no houses for themselves build no temples for the service of God, and of course derive the less benefit from the institutions of religion. While our people lived in cabins their places ot worship were tents, as they were called, their seats logs, their communion tables rough slabs of hewn timber, and the covering of the worshipers the leaves of the forest trees. Churches have succeeded to tents, with their rude accommodations for public worship. The very aspect of those sacred edifices fills the mind of the beholder with a religious awe, and as to the most believing and sincere, it serves to increase the fervor of devotion. Patriotism is augmented by the sight of the majestic forum of justice, the substantial public highway and bridge, with its long succession of ponderous arches.

Rome and Greece would, no doubt, have fallen much sooner had it not been for the patriotism inspired by their magnificent public edifices; had it not been for these, their histories would have been less complete and lasting than they have been.

Emigration has brought to the western regions the wealth, science and arts of our eastern brethren and even of Europe. These we hope have suffered no deterioration in the western country. They have contributed much to the change which has been effected in the moral and scientific character of our country.

The ministry of the gospel has contributed, no doubt immensely, to the happy change which has been effected in the state of our western society. At an early period of our settlements three Presbyterian clergymen commenced their clerical labors in our infant settlements. The Rev. Joseph Smith, the Rev. John M'Millan, and the Rev. Mr. Bowers, the two latter of whom are still living. They were pious, patient, laborious men, who collected their people into regular congregations, and did all for them that their circumstances would allow. It was no disparagement to them that their first churches were the shady groves, and their first pulpits a kind of tent, constructed of a few rough slabs and covered with clapboards. "He who dwelleth not exclusively in temples made with hands," was propitious to their devotions. From the outset they prudently resolved to create a ministry in the country, and accordingly established little grammar schools at their own houses or in their immediate neighborhoods. The course of education which they gave their pupils was, indeed, not extensive; but the piety of those who entered into the ministry more than made up the deficiency. They formed societies most of which are now large and respectable, and in point of education their ministry has much improved.

About the year 1792 an academy was established at Cannonsburg, in Washington county, in the western part of Pennsylvania, which was afterwards incorporated under the name Jefferson college. The means possessed by the society for the undertaking were indeed but small; but they not only erected a tolerable edifice for the academy, but created a fund for the education of such pious young men as were desirous of entering into the ministry, but unable to defray the expenses of their education. This institution has been remarkably successful in its operations. It has produced a large number of good scholars in all the literary professions and added immensely to the science of the country.

Next to this, Washington college, situated in the county town of the county of that name, has been the means of diffusing much of the light of science through the western country.

Too much praise cannot be bestowed on those good men who opened these fruitful sources of instruction for our infant country at so early a period of its settlement. They have immensely improved the departments of theology, law, medicine and legislation in the western regions.

At a later period the Methodist society began their labors in the western parts of Virginia and Pennsylvania; their progress at first was slow, but their zeal and perseverance at length overcame every obstacle, so that they are now one of the most numerous and respectable societies in this country. The itinerant plan of their ministry is well calculated to convey the gospel throughout a thinly scattered population. Accordingly, their ministry has kept pace with the extension of our settlements. The little cabin was scarcely built, and the little field fenced in, before these evangelical teachers made their appearance amongst them, collected them into societies and taught them the worship of God. Had it not been for the labors of these indefatigable men, our country, as to a great extent of its settlements, would have been at this day a semi-barbaric region. How many thousands and tens of thousands of the most ignorant and licentious of our population have they instructed, and reclaimed from the error of their ways? They have restored to society even the most worthless, and made them valuable and respectable as citizens, and useful in all the relations of life. Their numerous and zealous ministry bids fair to carry on the good work to any extent which our settlements and population may require.

With the Catholics I have but little acquaintance, but have every reason to believe that in proportion to the extent of their flocks they have done well. In this country they have received the Episcopal visitations of their bishops. In Kentucky they have a cathedral, a college and a bishop. In Indiana they have a monastery of the order of St. Trap, which is also a college, and a bishop. Their clergy, with apostolic zeal, but in an unostentatious manner, have sought out and ministered to their scattered flocks throughout the country; and as far as I know, with good success.

The societies of Friends, in the western country, are numerous and their establishments in good order. Although they are not much in favor of a classical education they are, nevertheless, in the habit of giving their people a substantial English education. Their habits of industry and attention to useful arts and improvements are highly honorable to themselves, and worthy of imitation.

The Baptists in the state of Kentucky took the lead in the ministry, and with great success. Their establishments are, as I have been informed, at present numerous and respectable in that state. A great and salutary revolution has taken place in this community of people. Their ministry was formerly quite illiterate; but they have turned their attention to science and have already erected some very respectable literary establishments in different parts of America.

The German Lutheran and Reformed churches in our country, as far as I know of them, are doing well. The number of the Lutheran congregations is said to be at least one hundred, that of the Reformed, it is presumed, is about the same amount. It is remarkable that throughout the whole extent of the United States the Germans, in proportion to their wealth, have the best churches, organs and grave yards.

It is a fortunate circumstance that those of our citizens who labor under the disadvantage of speaking a foreign language are blessed with a ministry so evangelical as that of these very numerous and respectable communities.

The Episcopalian church, which ought to have been foremost in gathering their scattered flocks, have been the last, and done the least of any Christian community in the evangelical work. Taking the western country in its whole extent, at least one-half of its population was originally of Episcopalian parentage; but, for want of a ministry of their own, have associated with other communities. They had no alternative but that of changing their profession or living and dying without the ordinances of religion. It can be no subject of regret that those ordinances were placed within their reach by other hands, whilst they were withheld by those by whom, as a matter of right and duty, they ought to have been given. One single chorea episcopus, or suffragan bishop, of a faithful spirit, who twenty years ago should have "ordained them elders in every place" where they were needed, would have been the instrument of forming episcopal congregations over a great extent of country, and which by this time would have become large, numerous and respectable; but the opportunity was neglected, and the consequent loss to this church is irreparable. So total a neglect of the spiritual interests of so many valuable people, for so great a length of time, by a ministry so near at hand, is a singular and unprecedented fact in ecclesiastical history, the like of which never occurred before.

It seems to me that if the twentieth part of the Christian people of any other community had been placed in Siberia, and dependent on any other ecclesiastical authority, in this country, that that authority would have reached them many years ago with the ministration of the gospel. With the earliest and most numerous episcopacy in America, not one of the eastern bishops has ever yet crossed the Alleghany mountains, although the dioceses of two of them comprehended large tracts of country on the western side of the mountains. It is hoped that the future diligence of this community will make up, in some degree, for the negligence of the past. There is still an immense void in this country which it is their duty to fill up. From their respectability on the ground of antiquity among the reformed churches, the science of their patriarchs, who have been the lights of the world, from their number and great resources, even in America, she ought to hasten to fulfill the just expectations of her own people, as well as those of other communities, in contributing her full share to the science, piety, and civilization of our country.

From the whole of our ecclesiastical history, it appears that, with the exception of the Episcopal church, all our religious communities have done well for their country.

The author begs that it may be understood that with the distinguishing tenets of our religious societies he has nothing to do, nor yet with the excellencies or defects of their ecclesiastical institutions. They are noticed on no other ground than that of their respective contributions to the science and civilization of the country.

The last, but not the least, of the means of our present civilization are our excellent forms of government and the administration of the laws. In vain, as means of general reformation, are schools, colleges, and a ministry of the gospel only; without the best of order a land of liberty is a land of crime as well as of virtue.

It is often mentioned as a matter of reproach to England that, in proportion to her population, they have more convictions, executions and transportations than any other country in Europe. Should it be asked what is the reason of the prevalence of crime in England? Is it that human nature is worse there than elsewhere? No. There is more liberty there than elsewhere in Europe, and that is the true and only solution of the matter in question. Where a people are at liberty to learn what they choose, to think and act as they please, and adopt any profession for a living or a fortune, they are much more liable to fall into the commission of crime than a people who, from their infancy, have been accustomed to the dull, monotonous march of despotism, which chains each individual to the rank and profession of his forefathers; and does not permit him to wander into the strange and devious paths of hazardous experiments.

In America, should a stranger read awhile our numerous publications of a religious nature, the reports of missionary and Bible societies, at first blush he would look upon the Americans as a nation of saints; let him lay these aside and read the daily newspapers, he will change his opinion and for the time being consider them as a nation abounding in crimes of the most atrocious dye. Both portraits are true.

The greater the amount of freedom the greater the necessity of a steady and faithful administration of justice; but more especially of criminal justice, because a general diffusion of science, while it produces the most salutary effects on a general scale, produces also the worst of crimes, by creating the greater capacity for their commission. There is scarcely any art or science which is not in some hands, and certain circumstances, made an instrument of the most atrocious vices. The arts of navigation and gunnery, so necessary for the wealth and defense of a nation, have often degenerated into the crime of piracy. The beautiful art of engraving, and the more useful art of writing, have been used by the fraudulent for counterfeiting all kinds of public and private documents of credit. Were it not for science and freedom, the important professions of theology and physic would not be so frequently assumed by the pseudo priest and the quack, without previous acquirements, without right, and for purposes wholly base and unwarrantable.

The truth is, the western country is the region of adventure. If we have derived some advantage from the importation of science, arts and wealth, we have on the other hand been much annoyed and endangered, as to our moral and political state, by an immense importation of vice, associated with a high grade of science and the most consummate art, in the pursuit of wealth by every description of unlawful means. The steady administration of justice has been our only safety from destruction by the pestilential influence of so great an amount of moral depravity in our infant country.

Still it may be asked whether facts warrant the belief that the scale is fairly turned in favor of science, piety and civilization; whether in regard to these important endowments of our nature, the present time is better than the past, and the future likely to be better than the present. Whether we may safely consider our political institutions so matured and settled that our personal liberty, property and sacred honor are not only secured to us for the present, but likely to remain the inheritance of our children for generations yet to come.

Society in its best state resembles a sleeping volcano, as to the amount of latent moral evil which it always contains. It is enough for public safety, and all that can reasonably be expected, that the good preponderate over the evil. The moral and political means which have been so successfully employed for preventing a revolutionary explosion have, as we trust, procrastinated the danger of such an event for a long time to come. If we have criminals they are splendidly pursued and brought to justice.

The places of our country which still remain in their native state of wilderness do not, as in many other countries, afford notorious lodgements for thieves. Our hills are not, as in the wilderness of Judea, hills of robbers. The ministry of the holy gospel is enlightening the minds of our people with the best of all sciences, that of God himself, His divine government and man's future state.

Let it not be thought hard that our forums of justice are so numerous, the style of their architecture so imposing, and the business which occupies them so multifarious; they are the price which freedom must pay for its protection. Commerce, circulating through its million channels, will create an endless variety of litigated claims. Crimes of the deepest dye, springing from science and liberty themselves, require constantly the vigilance and coercions of criminal justice. Even the poorest of our people are solicitous for the education of their children. Thus the great supports of our moral and political state, resting on their firmest basis, public opinion and attachment to our government and laws, promise stability for generations yet to come.

CHAPTER XXV.

Indian Mode of Warfare.

Preliminary observations on the character of the Indian mode of warfare and its adoption by the white people.

This is a subject which presents human nature in its most revolting features as subject to a vindictive spirit of revenge and a thirst for human blood leading to an indiscriminate slaughter of all ranks, ages and sexes, by the weapons of war or by torture.

The history of man is, for the most part, one continued detail of bloodshed, battles and devastations. War has been from the earliest periods of history the almost constant employment of individuals, clans, tribes and nations. Fame, one of the most potent objects of human ambition, has at all times been the delusive but costly reward of military achievements. The triumph of conquest, the epithet of greatness, the throne and the sceptre, have uniformly been purchased by the conflict of battle, and garments rolled in blood.

If the modern European laws of warfare have softened in some degree the horrid features of national conflicts by respecting the rights of private property and extending humanity to the sick, wounded and prisoners, we ought to reflect that this amelioration is the effect of civilization only. The natural state of war knows no such mixture of mercy with cruelty. In his primitive state man knows no object in his wars but that of the extermination of his enemies, either by death or captivity.

The wars of the Jews were exterminatory in their object. The destruction of a whole nation was often the result of a single campaign. Even the beasts themselves were sometimes included in the general massacre. The present war between the Greeks and Turks is a war upon the ancient model; a war of utter extermination.

It is, to be sure, much to be regretted that our people so often followed the cruel examples of the Indians in the slaughter of prisoners, and sometimes women and children; yet let them receive a candid hearing at the bar of reason and justice before they are condemned, as barbarians, equally with the Indians themselves. History scarcely presents an example of a civilized nation carrying on a war with barbarians without adopting the method of warfare of the barbarous nation. The ferocious Suwarrow, when at war with the Turks, was as much of a savage as the Turks themselves. His slaughters were as indiscriminate as theirs; but during his wars against the French, in Italy, he faithfully observed the laws of civilized warfare.

Were the Greeks now at war with a civilized nation we should hear nothing of the barbarities which they have committed on the Turks; but, being at war with barbarians, the principle of self-defense compels them to retaliate on the Turks the barbarities which they commit on them.

In the last rebellion in Ireland, that of united Irishmen, the government party were not much behind the rebels in acts of lawless cruelty. It was not by the hands of the executioner, alone, they perished. Summary justice, as it was called, was sometimes inflicted. How many perished under the torturing scourge of the drummer for the purpose of extorting confessions! These extra judicial executions were attempted to be justified on the ground of the necessity of the case.

Our revolutionary war has a double aspect; on the one hand we carried on a war with the English, in which we observed the maxims of civilized warfare with the utmost strictness; but the brave, the potent, the magnanimous nation of our forefathers had associated with themselves, as auxiliaries, the murderous tomahawk and scalping knife of the Indian nations around our defenseless frontiers, leaving those barbarous sons of the forest to their own savage mode of warfare, to the full indulgence of all their native thirst for human blood. On them, then, be the blame of all the horrid features of this war between civilized and savage men, in which the former were compelled, by every principle of self defense, to adopt the Indian mode of warfare in all its revolting and destructive features.

Were those who were engaged in the war against the Indians less humane than those who carried on the war against their English allies? No. They were not. Both parties carried on the war on the same principle of reciprocity of advantages and disadvantages. For example, the English and Americans take each one thousand prisoners. They are exchanged. Neither army is weakened by the arrangement. A sacrifice is indeed made to humanity, in the expense of taking care of the sick, wounded and prisoners; but this expense is mutual. No disadvantages result from all the clemency of modern warfare excepting an augmentation of the expenses of war. In this mode of warfare those of the nation, not in arms, are safe from death by the hands of soldiers. No civilized warrior dishonors his sword with the blood of helpless infancy, old age, or that of the fair sex. He aims his blows only at those whom he finds in arms against him. The Indian kills indiscriminately. His object is the total extermination of his enemies. Children are victims of his vengeance because, if males, they may hereafter become warriors, or if females, they may become mothers. Even the fœtal state is criminal in his view. It is not enough that the fœtus should perish with the murdered mother, it is torn from her pregnant womb and elevated on a stick or pole, as a trophy of victory and an object of horror, to the survivors of the slain.

If the Indian takes prisoners, mercy has but little concern in the transaction; he spares the lives of those who fall into his hands for the purpose of feasting the feelings of ferocious vengeance of himself and his comrades by the torture of his captive, or to increase the strength of his nation by his adoption into an Indian family, or for the purpose of gain, by selling him for a higher price than his scalp would fetch, to his Christian allies of Canada; for be it known that those allies were in the constant practice of making presents for scalps, and prisoners, as well as furnishing the means for carrying on the Indian war, which for so many years desolated our defenseless frontiers. No lustration can ever wash out this national stain. The foul blot must remain as long as the page of history shall convey the record of the foul transaction to future generations.

The author would not open wounds which have, alas! already bled so long, but for the purpose of doing justice to the memory of his forefathers and relatives, many of whom perished in the defense of their country by the hands of the merciless Indians.

How is a war of extermination, and accompanied with such acts of atrocious cruelty, to be met by those on whom it is inflicted? Must it be met by the lenient maxims of civilized warfare? Must the Indian captive be spared his life? What advantage would be gained by this course? The young white prisoners, adopted into Indian families, often became complete Indians, but in how few instances did ever an Indian become civilized. Send a cartel for an exchange of prisoners, the Indians knew nothing of this measure of clemency in war; the bearer of the white flag for the purpose of effecting the exchange would have exerted his humanity at the forfeit of his life. Should my countrymen be still charged with barbarism in the prosecution of the Indian war, let him who harbors this unfavorable impression concerning them portray in imagination the horrid scenes of slaughter which frequently met their view in the course of the Indian war. Let him, if he can bear the reflection, look at helpless infancy, virgin beauty and hoary age, dishonored by the ghastly wounds of the tomahawk and scalping knife of the savage. Let him hear the shrieks of the victims of the Indian torture by fire, and smell the surrounding air, rendered sickening by the effluvia of their burning flesh and blood. Let him hear the yells, and view the hellish features of the surrounding circle of savage warriors, rioting in all the luxuriance of vengeance, while applying the flaming torches to the parched limbs of the sufferers, and then suppose those murdered infants, matrons, virgins and victims of torture, were his friends and relations, the wife, sister, or brother; what would be his feelings? After a short season of grief he would say, "I will now think only of revenge."

Philosophy shudders at the destructive aspect of war in any shape; Christianity, by teaching the religion of the good Samaritan, altogether forbids it; but the original settlers of the western regions, like the greater part of the world, were neither philosophers nor saints. They were "men of like passions with others," and therefore adopted the Indian mode of warfare from necessity, and a motive of revenge, with the exception of burning their captives alive, which they never did; if the bodies of savage enemies were sometimes burned, it was not until after they were dead.

Let the voice of nature, and the law of nations plead in favor of the veteran pioneers of the desert regions of the west. War has hitherto been a prominent trait in the moral system of human nature, and will continue such until a radical change shall be effected in favor of science, morals and piety, on a general scale.

In the conflicts of nations, as well as those of individuals, no advantages are to be conceded. If mercy may be associated with the carnage and devastations of war, that mercy must be reciprocal; but a war of utter extermination must be met by a war of the same character; or by an overwhelming force which may put an end to it, without a sacrifice of the helpless and unoffending part of hostile nations; such a force was not at the command of the first inhabitants of this country. The sequel of the Indian war goes to show that in a war with savages, the choice lies between extermination and subjugation. Our government has wisely and humanely pursued the latter course.

The author begs to be understood that the foregoing observations are not intended as a justification of the whole of the transactions of our people with regard to the Indians during the course of the war. Some instances of acts of wanton barbarity occurred on our side, which have received, and must continue to receive, the unequivocal reprobation of all the civilized world. In the course of this history it will appear that more deeds of wanton barbarity took place on our side than the world is now acquainted with.

CHAPTER XXVI.

THE WAR OF 1763.

The treaty of peace between his British majesty and the kings of France, Spain and Portugal, concluded at Paris on the 10th of February, 1763, did not put an end to the Indian war against the frontier parts and back settlements of the colonies of Great Britain. The spring and summer of 1763, as well as those of 1764, deserve to be memorable in history for the great extent and destructive results of a war of extermination carried on by the united force of all the Indian nations of the western country, along the shore of the northern lakes and throughout the whole extent of the frontier settlements of Pennsylvania, Virginia and North Carolina.

The events of this war as they relate to the frontier of Pennsylvania and the shores of the lakes are matters of history already, and therefore shall be no farther related here than is necessary to give a connected view of the military events of those disastrous seasons. The massacre by the Indians in the south-western part of Virginia, so far as they have come to the knowledge of the author, shall be related more in detail.

The English historians attribute this terrible war to the influence of the French Jesuits over the Indians,[1] but whether with much truth and candor, is, to say the least of it, extremely doubtful.

The peace of 1763, by which the provinces of Canada were ceded to Britain, was offensive to the Indians; especially, as they very well knew that the English government, on the

---

[1] *History of England,* vol. x, p. 399.

ground of this treaty, claimed the jurisdiction of the western country generally; and as an Indian sees no difference between the right of jurisdiction and that of possession, they considered themselves as about to be dispossessed of the whole of their country as rapidly as the English might find it convenient to take possession of it. In this opinion they were confirmed by the building of forts on the Susquehanna, on lands to which the Indians laid claim. The forts and posts of Pittsburg, Bedford, Ligonier, Niagara, Detroit, Presque Isle, St. Joseph, and Michilimackinac, were either built, or improved and strengthened, with additions to their garrisons. Thus the Indians saw themselves surrounded on the north and east by a strong line of forts, while those of Bedford, Ligonier and Pittsburg, threatened an extension of them into the heart of their country. Thus circumstanced the aborigines of the country had to choose between the prospects of being driven to the inhospitable regions of the north and west; of negotiating with the British government for continuance of the possession of their own land, or of taking up arms for its defense. They chose the latter course, in which a view of the smallness of their numbers and scantiness of their resources ought to have taught them that, although they might do much mischief, they could not ultimately succeed; but the Indians, as well as their brethren of the white skin, are often driven by their impetuous passions to rash and destructive enterprises, which reason, were it permitted to give its counsel, would disapprove. The plan resolved on by the Indians for the prosecution of the war was that of a general massacre of all the inhabitants of the English settlements in the western country, as well as of those on the lands on the Susquehanna, to which they laid claim.

Never did military commanders of any nation display more skill, or their troops more steady and determined bravery, than did those red men of the wilderness in the prosecution of their gigantic plan for the recovery of their country from the possession of the English. It was, indeed, a war of utter extermination on an extensive scale, a conflict which exhibited human nature in its native state, in which the cunning of the fox is associated with the cruelty of the tiger. We read the history of this war with feelings of the deepest horror; but why? On the part of the savages, theirs was the ancient mode of warfare, in which there was nothing of mercy. If science, associated with the benign influence of the Christian system, has limited the carnage of war to those in arms, so as to give the right of life and hospitality to women, infancy, old age, the sick, wounded and prisoners, may not a farther extension of the influence of those powerful but salutary agents put an end to war altogether? May not future generations read the history of our civilized warfare with equal horror and wonder, that, with our science and piety, we had wars at all!

The English traders among the Indians were the first victims in this contest. Out of one hundred and twenty of them, among the different nations, only two or three escaped being murdered. The forts of Presque Isle, St. Joseph and Michilimackinac were taken, with a general slaughter of their garrisons. The fortresses of Bedford, Ligonier, Niagara, Detroit and Pitt were with difficulty preserved from being taken. It was a principal object with the Indians to get possession of Detroit and Fort Pitt either by assault or famine. The former was attempted with regard to Detroit. Fort Pitt, being at a considerable distance from the settlements, where alone supplies could be obtained, determined the savages to attempt its reduction by famine.

In their first attempt on Fort Detroit the Indians calculated on taking possession of it by stratagem. A large number of Indians appeared before the place under pretense of holding a congress with Major Gladwin, the commandant. He was on his guard and refused them admittance. On the next day, about five hundred of the Indians arrived in arms and demanded leave to go into the fort to hold a treaty. The commandant refused to admit a greater number than forty. The Indians understood his design of detaining them as hostages for the good conduct of their comrades on the outside of the fort, and therefore did not send them into the place. The whole number of men in the fort and on board two vessels of war in the river did not exceed one hundred and ten or twelve; but by the means of cannons they possessed they made shift to keep the Indians at a distance and convince them that they could not take the place. When the Indians were about to retire Captain Dalyell arrived at the fort with a considerable reinforcement for the relief of the place. He made a sortie against the breast works which the Indians had thrown up with two hundred and forty-five men. This detachment was driven back with the loss of seventy men killed and forty-two wounded. Captain Dalyell was among the slain. Of one hundred men who were escorting a large quantity of provisions to Detroit, sixty-seven were massacred.

Fort Pitt had been invested for some time before Captain Ecayer had the least prospect of relief. In this situation he and his garrison had resolved to stand it out to the last extremity and even perish of famine rather than fall into the hands of the savages; notwithstanding the fort was a bad one, the garrison weak, and the country between the fort and Ligonier was in possession of the savages, and his messengers killed or compelled to return back. In this situation Col. Bouquet was sent by General Amherst to the relief of the place, with a large quantity of provisions under a strong escort. This escort was attacked by a large body of Indians in a narrow defile on Turtle creek, and would have been entirely defeated had it not been for a successful stratagem employed by the commander for extricating themselves from the savage army. After sustaining a furious contest, from one o'clock till night, and for several hours the next morning, a retreat was pretended, with a view to draw the Indians into a close engagement. Previously to this movement four companies of infantry and grenadiers were placed in ambuscade. The plan succeeded. When the retreat commenced the Indians thought themselves secure of victory, and pressing forward with great vigor fell into the ambuscade and were dispersed with great slaughter. The loss on the side of the English was above one hundred killed and wounded; that of the Indians could not have been less. This loss was severely felt by the Indians, as in addition to the number of warriors who fell in the engagement, several of the most distinguished chiefs were amongst the slain. Fort Pitt, the reduction of which they had much at heart, was now placed out of their reach by being effectually relieved and supplied with the munitions of war.

The historian of the western region of our country cannot help regarding Pittsburg, the present flourishing emporium of the northern part of that region, and its immediate neighborhood, as classic ground, on account of the memorable battles which have taken place for its possession in the infancy of our settlements. Braddock's defeat, Major Grant's defeat, its conquest by Gen. Forbes, the victory over the Indians above related by Major Bouquet, serve to show the importance in which this post was held in early times, and that it was obtained and supported by the English government at the price of no small amount of blood and treasure. In the neighborhood of this place, as well as in the war-worn regions of the old world, the plough share of the farmer turns up, from beneath the surface of the earth, the broken and rusty implements of war, and the bones of the slain in battle.

It was in the course of this war that the dreadful massacre at Wyoming took place, and desolated the fine settlements of the New England people along the Susquehanna. The extensive and indiscriminate slaughter of both sexes and all ages by the Indians, at Wyoming and other places, so exasperated a large number of men, denominated the *Paxton boys*, that they rivalled the most ferocious of the Indians themselves in deeds of cruelty which have dishonored the history of our country by the record of the shedding of innocent blood without the slightest provocation; deeds of the most atrocious barbarity.

The Canestoga Indians had lived in peace for more than a century in the neighborhood of Lancaster. Their number did not exceed forty. Against these unoffending descendants of the first friends of the famous William Penn the Paxton boys first directed their more than savage vengeance. Fifty-seven of them, in military array, poured into their little village and instantly murdered all whom they found at home, to the number of fourteen men, women and children. Those of them who did not happen to be at home at the massacre were lodged in the jail of Lancaster for safety. But alas! This precaution was unavailing. The Paxton boys broke open the jail door and murdered the whole of them, in number from fifteen to twenty. It was in vain that these poor defenseless people protested their innocence and begged for mercy on their knees. Blood was the order of the day with those ferocious Paxton boys. The death of the victims of their cruelties did not satisfy their rage for slaughter; they mangled the dead bodies of the Indians with their scalping knives and tomahawks in the most shocking manner, scalping even the children and chopping off the hands and feet of most of them. The next object of those Paxton boys was the murder of the Christian Indians of the villages of Wequetank and Nain. From the execution of this infernal design they were prevented by the humane interference of the government of Pennsylvania, which removed the inhabitants of both places under a strong guard to Philadelphia for protection. They remained under guard from November, 1763, until the close of the war in December, 1764; the greater part of this time they occupied the barracks of the city. The Paxton boys twice assembled in great force, at no great distance from the city, with a view to assault the barracks and murder the Indians; but owing to the military preparations made for their reception they at last reluctantly desisted from the enterprise.

While we read, with feelings of the deepest horror, the record of the murders which have, at different periods, been inflicted on the unoffending Christian Indians, of the Moravian profession, it is some consolation to reflect that our government has had no participation in those murders; but on the contrary has at all times afforded them all the protection which circumstances allowed.

The principal settlements in Greenbriar were those of Muddy creek and the Big Levels, distant about fifteen or twenty miles from each other. Before these settlers were aware of the existence of the war, and supposing that the peace made with the French comprehended their Indian allies also, about sixty Indians visited the settlement on Muddy creek. They made the visit under the mask of friendship. They were cordially received and treated with all the hospitality which it was in the power of these new settlers to bestow upon them; but on a sudden, and without any previous intimation of anything like an hostile intention, the Indians murdered, in cold blood, all the men belonging to the settlement and made prisoners of the women and children. Leaving a guard with their prisoners, they then marched to the settlement in the Levels, before the fate of the Muddy creek settlement was known. Here, as at Muddy creek, they were treated with the most kind and attentive hospitality, at the house of Mr. Archibald Glendennin, who gave the Indians a sumptuous feast of three fat elks, which he had recently killed. Here a scene of slaughter, similar to that which had recently taken place at Muddy creek, occurred at the conclusion of the feast. It commenced with an old woman, who having a very sore leg showed it to an Indian, desiring his advice how she might cure it. This request he answered with a blow of the tomahawk, which instantly killed her. In a few minutes all the men belonging to the place shared the same fate. The women and children were made prisoners. In the time of the slaughter a negro woman while at the spring near the house where it happened killed her own child for fear it would fall into the hands of the Indians, or hinder her from making her escape.

Mrs. Glendennin, whose husband was among the slain, and herself, with her children, prisoners, boldly charged the Indians with perfidy and cowardice in taking advantage of the mask of friendship to commit murder. One of the Indians, exasperated at her boldness, and stung, no doubt, at the justice of her charge against them, brandished his tomahawk over her head and dashed her husband's scalp in her face. In defiance of all his threats, the heroine still reiterated the charges of perfidy and cowardice against the Indians.

On the next day, after marching about ten miles, while passing through a thicket, the Indians forming a front and rear guard, Mrs. Glendennin gave her infant to a neighbor woman, stepped into the bushes without being perceived by the Indians, and made her escape. The cries of the child made the Indians enquire for the mother. She was not to be found.

"Well," says one of them, "I will soon bring the cow to her calf," and taking the child by the feet beat its brains out against a tree.

Mrs. Glendennin returned home, in the course of the succeeding night, and covered the corpse of her husband with fence rails. Having performed this pious work for her murdered husband she chose, as a place of safety, a cornfield where, as she related, her heroic resolution was succeeded by a paroxysm of grief and despondency, during which she imagined she saw a man with the aspect of a murderer standing within a few steps of her. The reader of this narrative, instead of regarding this fit of despondency as a feminine weakness on the part of this daughter of affliction, will commiserate her situation of unparalleled destitution and distress. Alone, in the dead of night, the survivor of all the infant settlements of that district, while all her relatives and neighbors of both settlements were either prisoners or lying dead, dishonored by ghastly wounds of the tomahawk and scalping knife of the savages, her husband and her children amongst the slain.

It was some days before a force could be collected in the eastern part of Bottetourt and the adjoining country for the purpose of burying the dead.

Of the events of this war, in the south-western frontier of Virginia, and in the country of Holstein, the then western part of North Carolina, the author has not been informed further than that, on the part of the Indians, it was carried on with the greatest activity, and its course marked with many deeds of the most atrocious cruelty, until late in the year 1764, when a period was put to this sanguinary contest by a treaty made with the Indian nations by Sir William Johnson at the German Flats.

The perfidy and cruelties practiced by the Indians, during the war of 1763 and 1764, occasioned the revolting and sanguinary character of the Indian wars which took place afterwards. The Indians had resolved on the total extermination of all the settlers of our north and south-western frontiers, and being no longer under the control of their former allies, the French, they were at full liberty to exercise all their native ferocity and riot in the indulgence of their innate thirst for blood.

CHAPTER XXVII.

Gov. Dunmore's War.

After the conclusion of the Indian war by the treaty made with the chiefs by Sir William Johnson at the German Flats, in the latter part of 1764, the western settlements enjoyed peace until the spring of 1774. During this period of time the settlements increased with great rapidity along the whole extent of the western frontier. Even the shores of the Ohio, on the Virginia side, had a considerable population as early as the year 1774.

Devoutly might humanity wish that the record of the causes which led to the destructive war of 1774 might be blotted from the annals of our country; but as it is now too late to efface it the black-lettered list must remain, a dishonorable blot in our national history; good however may spring out of evil. The injuries inflicted upon the Indians in early times by our forefathers may induce their descendants to show *justice* and *mercy* to the diminished posterity of those children of the wilderness whose ancestors perished in cold blood under the tomahawk and scalping knife of the white savages.

In the month of April, 1774, a rumor was circulated that the Indians had stolen several horses from some land jobbers on the Ohio and Kanawha rivers. No evidences of the fact having been adduced leads to the conclusion that the report was false. This report, however, induced a pretty general belief that the Indians were about to make war upon the frontier settlements; but for this apprehension there does not appear to have been the slightest foundation. In consequence of this apprehension of being attacked by the Indians, the land jobbers ascended the river and collected at Wheeling. On the 27th of April it was reported in Wheeling that a canoe containing two Indians and some traders was coming down the river and then not far from the place. On hearing this the commandant of the station, Capt. Cresap, proposed taking a party to go up the river and kill the Indians. This project was vehemently opposed by Col. Zane, the proprietor of the place. He stated to the captain that the killing of those Indians would inevitably bring on a war, in which much innocent blood would be shed, and that the act in itself would be an atrocious murder, and a disgrace to his name forever. His good counsel was lost. The party went up the river. On being asked, at their return, what had become of the Indians, they coolly answered that "They had fallen overboard into the river!" Their canoe, on being examined, was found bloody and pierced with bullets. This was the first blood which was shed in this war, and terrible was the vengeance which followed.

In the evening of the same day, the party hearing that there was an encampment of Indians at the mouth of the Captina, went down the river to the place, attacked the Indians and killed several of them. In this affair one of Cresap's party was severely wounded.

The massacre at Captina, and that which took place at Baker's, about forty miles above Wheeling, a few days after that at Captina, were unquestionably the sole causes of the war of 1774. The last was perpetrated by thirty-two men, under the command of Daniel Greathouse. The whole number killed at this place and on the river opposite to it was twelve, besides several wounded. This horrid massacre was effected by a hypocritical stratagem which reflects the deepest dishonor on the memory of those who were agents in it.

The report of the murders committed on the Indians near Wheeling induced a belief that they would immediately commence hostilities, and this apprehension furnished the pretext for the murder above related. The ostensible object for raising the party under Greathouse was that of defending the family of Baker, whose house was opposite to a large encampment of Indians at the mouth of Big Yellow creek. The party were concealed in ambuscade, while their commander went over the river, under the mask of friendship, to the Indian camp, to ascertain their number; while there an Indian woman advised him to return home speedily, saying that the Indians were drinking and angry on account of the murder of their people down the river, and might do him some mischief. On his return to his party he reported that the Indians were too strong for an open attack. He returned to Baker's and requested him to give any Indians who might come over, in the course of the day, as much rum as they might call for, and get as many of them drunk as he possibly could. The plan succeeded. Several Indian men, with two women, came over the river to Baker's, who had previously been in the habit of selling rum to the Indians. The men drank freely and became intoxicated. In this state they were all killed by Greathouse and a few of his party. I say a few of his party; for it is but justice to state that not more than five or six of the whole number had any participation in the slaughter at the house. The rest protested against it as an atrocious murder. From their number being by far the majority, they might have prevented the deed; but alas! they did not. A little Indian girl alone was saved from the slaughter, by the humanity of some one of the party, whose name is not now known.

The Indians in the camps, hearing the firing at the house, sent a canoe with two men in it to inquire what had happened. These two Indians were both shot down as soon as they landed on the beach. A second and larger canoe was then manned with a number of Indians in arms; but in attempting to reach the shore, some distance below the house, were received by a well directed fire from the party, which killed the greater number of them and compelled the survivors to return. A great number of shots were exchanged across the river, but without damage to the white party, not one of whom was even wounded. The Indian men who were murdered were all scalped. The woman who gave the friendly advice to the commander of the party, when in the Indian camp, was amongst the slain at Baker's house.

The massacres of the Indians at Captina and Yellow creek comprehended the whole of the family of the famous but unfortunate Logan, who before these events had been a lover of the whites and a strenuous advocate for peace; but in the conflict which followed them, by way of revenge for the death of his people, he became a brave and sanguinary chief among the warriors.

The settlers along the frontiers, knowing that the Indians would make war upon them for the murder of their people, either moved off to the interior, or took up their residence in forts. The apprehension of war was soon realized. In a short time the Indians commenced hostilities along the whole extent of our frontiers.

Express was speedily sent to Williamsburg, the then seat of government of the colony of Virginia, communicating intelligence of the certainty of the commencement of an Indian war. The assembly was then in session. A plan for a campaign for the purpose of putting a speedy conclusion to the Indian hostilities was adopted between the Earl of Dunmore, the governor of the colony, and Gen. Lewis of Bottetourt county. Gen. Lewis was appointed to the command of the southern division of the forces to be employed on this occasion, with orders to raise a large body of volunteers and drafts, from the south-eastern counties of the colony, with all dispatch. These forces were to rendezvous at Camp Union in the Greenbriar country. The Earl of Dunmore was to raise another army in the northern countries of the colony, and in the settlements west of the mountains, and assemble them at Fort Pitt, and from thence descend the river to Point Pleasant, at the mouth of the Great Kanawha, the place appointed for the junction of the two armies, for the purpose of invading the Indian country and destroying as many of their villages as they could reach in the course of the season.

On the eleventh of September the forces under Gen. Lewis, amounting to eleven hundred men, commenced their march from Camp Union to Point Pleasant, a distance of one hundred and sixty miles. The tract of country between these two points was at that time a trackless desert. Capt. Matthew Arbuckle, the pilot, conducted the army by the nearest and best route to their place of destination. The flour and ammunition were wholly transported on pack horses, as the route was impassable for wheel carriages. After a painful march of nineteen days the army arrived, on the first of October, at Point Pleasant, where an encampment was made. Gen. Lewis was exceedingly disappointed at hearing no tidings of the Earl of Dunmore, who, according to previous arrangements, was to form a junction with him at this place. He immediately dispatched some scouts to go by land in the direction of Fort Pitt to obtain intelligence of the route which the earl had taken, and then return with the utmost dispatch. On the ninth three men, who had formerly been Indian traders, arrived in the camp, on express from the earl, to inform Lewis that he had changed his plan of operations, and intended to march to the Indian towns by the way of Hockhocking, and directing Gen. Lewis to commence his march immediately for the old Chillicothe town.

Very early in the morning of the tenth two young men set out from the camp to hunt, up the river. Having gone about three miles they fell upon a camp of the Indians, who were then in the act of preparing to march to attack the camp of Gen. Lewis. The Indians fired upon them and killed one of them. The other ran back to the camp with intelligence that the Indians, in great force, would immediately give battle.

Gen. Lewis instantly ordered out a detachment of the Botetourt troops under Col. Fleming and another of the Augusta troops under Col. Charles Lewis, remaining himself with the reserve for the defense of the camp. The detachment marched out in two lines and met the Indians in the same order about four hundred yards from the camp. The battle commenced a little after sunrise by a heavy firing from the Indians. At the onset our troops gave back some distance, until met by a reinforcement, on the arrival of which the Indians retreated a little way and formed a line behind logs and trees, reaching from the bank of the Ohio to that of the Kanawha. By this manœuvre our army and camp were completely invested, being inclosed between the two rivers, with the Indian line of battle in front, so that no chance of retreat was left. An incessant fire was kept up on both sides, with but little change of position until sundown, when the Indians retreated, and in the night recrossed the Ohio, and the next day commenced their march to their town on the Scioto.

Our loss in this destructive battle was seventy-five killed, and one hundred and forty wounded. Among the killed were Col. Charles Lewis, Col. Fields, Captains Buford, Murrey, Ward, Wilson and M'Clenachan; Lieutenants Allen, Goldsby and Dillon and several subaltern officers. Col. Lewis, a distinguished and meritorious officer, was mortally wounded by the first fire of the Indians, but walked into the camp and expired in his own tent.

The number of Indians engaged in the battle of the Point was never ascertained, nor yet the amount of their loss. On the morning after the engagement twenty-one were found on the battle ground; twelve more were afterwards found in different places where they had been concealed. A great number of their dead were said to have been thrown into the river during the engagement. Considering that the whole number of our men engaged in this conflict were riflemen, and from habit sharp shooters of the first order, it is presumable that the loss on the side of the Indians was at least equal to ours.

The Indians, during the battle, were commanded by the Cornstalk warrior, the king of the Shawanees. This son of the forest, in his plans of attack and retreat, and in all his manœuvres throughout the engagement, displayed the skill and bravery of the most consummate general. During the whole of the day he was heard from our lines, vociferating with the voice of Stentor, "Be strong, be strong." It is even said that he killed one of his men with his own hand for cowardice. The day after the battle, after burying the dead, entrenchments were thrown up round the camp, and a competent guard was appointed for the care and protection of the sick and wounded. On the day following Gen. Lewis commenced his march for the Shawanee's towns on the Scioto. This march was made through a trackless desert and attended with almost insuperable difficulties and privations.

In the meantime the Earl of Dunmore, having collected a force and provided boats at Fort Pitt, descended the river to Wheeling, where the army halted for a few days, and then proceeded down the river in about one hundred canoes, a few keel boats and pirogues, to the mouth of Hockhocking, and from thence overland until the army had got within eight miles of the Shawanee town Chillicothe, on the Scioto. Here the army halted and made a breast-work of fallen trees and entrenchments of such extent as to include about twelve acres of ground, with an inclosure in the centre containing about one acre, surrounded by entrenchments. This was the citadel which contained the marquees of the earl and his superior officers. Before the army had reached that place the Indian chiefs had sent several messengers to the earl asking peace. With this request he soon determined to comply, and therefore sent an express to Gen. Lewis with an order for his immediate retreat. This order Gen. Lewis disregarded and continued his march until his lordship in person visited his camp, was formally introduced to his officers and gave the order in person. The army of Gen. Lewis then commenced their retreat.

It was with the greatest reluctance and chagrin that the troops of Gen. Lewis returned from the enterprise in which they were engaged. The massacres of their relatives and friends at the Big Levels and Muddy creek, and above all their recent loss at the battle of the Point, had inspired these big knives, as the Indians called the Virginians, with an inveterate thirst for revenge, the gratification of which they supposed was shortly to take place in the total destruction of the Indians and their towns, along the Scioto and Sandusky rivers. The order of Dunmore was obeyed; but with every expression of regret and disappointment.

The earl and his officers having returned to his camp, a treaty with the Indians was opened the following day. In this treaty every precaution was used on the part of our people to prevent the Indians from ending it in the tragedy of a massacre. Only eighteen Indians, with their chiefs, were permitted to pass the outer gate of their fortified encampment, after having deposited their arms with the guard at the gate.

The treaty was opened by Cornstalk, the war chief of the Shawanees, in a lengthy speech in which he boldly charged the white people with having been the authors of the commencement of the war, in the massacres of the Indians at Captina and Yellow creek. This speech he delivered in so loud a tone of voice that he was heard all over the camp. The terms of the treaty were soon settled and the prisoners delivered up.

Logan, the Cayuga chief, assented to the treaty; but still indignant at the murder of his family, refused to attend with the other chiefs at the camp of Dunmore. According to the Indian mode in such cases, he sent his speech in a belt of wampum by an interpreter, to be read at the treaty.

Supposing that this work may fall into the hands of some readers who have not seen the speech of Logan, the author thinks it not amiss to insert this celebrated morsel of Indian eloquence in this place, with the observation that the authenticity of the speech is no longer a subject of doubt. The speech is as follows:

"I appeal to any white man to say if ever he entered Logan's cabin hungry, and he gave him not meat; if ever he came cold and naked, and he clothed him not. During the course of the last long and bloody war, Logan remained idle in his cabin, an advocate for peace. Such was my love for the whites that my countrymen pointed as they passed, and said, 'Logan is the friend of the white men.' I had even thought to have lived with you, but for the injuries of one man. Col. Cresap, the last spring, in cold blood, and unprovoked, murdered all the relations of Logan, not even sparing my women and children. There runs not a drop of my blood in the veins of any living creature. This called on me for revenge. I have sought it; I have killed many; I have fully glutted my vengeance. For my country I rejoice at the beams of peace; but do not harbor a thought that mine is the joy of fear. Logan never felt fear. He will not turn on his heel to save his life. Who is there to mourn for Logan? Not one!"

Thus ended, at the treaty of Camp Charlotte in the month of November, 1774, the disastrous war of Dunmore. It began in the wanton and unprovoked murders of the Indians at Captina and Yellow creek, and ended with an awful sacrifice of life and property to the demon of revenge. On our part we obtained at the treaty a cessation of hostilities and a surrender of prisoners, and nothing more.

---

[1] See appendix, "Logan, Michael Cresap and Simon Girty."

The plan of operations adopted by the Indians in the war of Dunmore shows very clearly that their chiefs were by no means deficient in the foresight and skill necessary for making the most prudent military arrangements for obtaining success and victory in their mode of warfare. At an early period they obtained intelligence of the plan of the campaign against them, concerted between the Earl of Dunmore and Gen. Lewis. With a view, therefore, to attack the forces of these commanders separately, they speedily collected their warriors, and by forced marches reached the Point before the expected arrival of the troops under Dunmore. Such was the privacy with which they conducted their march to Point Pleasant that Gen. Lewis knew nothing of the approach of the Indian army until a few minutes before the commencement of the battle, and it is every way probable that if Cornstalk, the Indian commander, had had a little larger force at the battle of the Point, the whole army of Gen. Lewis would have been cut off, as the wary savages had left them no chance of retreat. Had the army of Lewis been defeated, the army of Dunmore, consisting of but little more than one thousand men, would have shared the fate of those armies which, at different periods, have suffered defeats, in consequence of venturing too far into the Indian country, in numbers too small, and with munitions of war inadequate to sustain a contest with the united forces of a number of Indian nations.

It was the general belief among the officers of our army, at the time, that the Earl of Dunmore, while at Wheeling, received advice from his government of the probability of the approaching war between England and the colonies, and that afterwards all his measures with regard to the Indians had for their ultimate object an alliance with those ferocious warriors for aid of the mother country in their contest with us. This supposition accounts for his not forming a junction with the army of Lewis at Point Pleasant. This deviation from the original plan of the campaign jeopardized the army of Lewis and well nigh occasioned its total destruction. The conduct of the earl at the treaty shows a good understanding between him and the Indian chiefs. He did not suffer the army of Lewis to form a junction with his own, but sent them back before the treaty was concluded, thus risking the safety of his own forces, for at the time of the treaty the Indian warriors were about his camp, in force sufficient to have intercepted his retreat and destroyed his whole army.

CHAPTER XXVIII.

The Death of Cornstalk.

This was one of the most atrocious murders committed by the whites during the whole course of the war.

In the summer of 1777, when the confederacy of the Indian nations, under the influence of the British government, was formed and began to commit hostilities along our frontier settlements, Cornstalk and a young chief of the name of Redhawk and another Indian made a visit to the garrison at the Point, commanded at that time by Captain Arbuckle. Cornstalk stated to the captain that, with the exception of himself and the tribe to which he belonged, all the nations had joined the English, and that, unless protected by the whites, "They would have to run with the stream." Capt. Arbuckle thought proper to detain the Cornstalk chief and his two companions as hostages for the good conduct of the tribe to which they belonged. They had not been long in this situation before a son of Cornstalk's, concerned for the safety of his father, came to the opposite side of the river and hallooed; his father, knowing his voice, answered him. He was brought over the river. The father and son mutually embraced each other with the greatest tenderness. On the day following, two Indians who had concealed themselves in the weeds on the bank of the Kanawha, opposite the fort, killed a man of the name of Gilmore, as he was returning from hunting. As soon as the dead body was brought over the river there was a general cry among the men who were present:

"Let us kill the Indians in the fort."

They immediately ascended the bank of the river, with Capt. Hall at their head, to execute their hasty resolution. On their way they were met by Capt. Stuart and Capt. Arbuckle, who endeavored to dissuade them from killing the Indian hostages, saying that they certainly had no concern in the murder of Gilmore; but remonstrance was in vain. Pale as death with rage, they cocked their guns and threatened the captains with instant death if they should attempt to hinder them from executing their purpose.

When the murderers arrived at the house where the hostages were confined, Cornstalk rose up to meet them at the door, but instantly received seven bullets through his body; his son and his other two fellow hostages were instantly dispatched with bullets and tomahawks. Thus fell the Shawanee war chief, Cornstalk, who like Logan, his companion in arms, was conspicuous for intellectual talent, bravery and misfortune.

The biography of Cornstalk, as far as it is now known, goes to show that he was no way deficient in those mental endowments which constitute human greatness. On the evening preceding the battle of Point Pleasant he proposed going over the river to the camp of Gen. Lewis for the purpose of making peace. The majority in the council of warriors voted against the measure.

"Well," said Cornstalk, "since you have resolved on fighting, you shall fight, although it is likely we shall have hard work to-morrow; but if any man shall attempt to run away from the battle, I will kill him with my own hand," and accordingly fulfilled his threat, with regard to one cowardly fellow.

After the Indians had returned from the battle Cornstalk called a council at the Chillicothe town to consult what was to be done next. In this council he reminded the war chiefs of their folly in preventing him from making peace before the fatal battle of Point Pleasant, and asked:

"What shall we do now? The long-knives are coming upon us by two routes. Shall we turn out and fight them?"

All were silent. He then asked:

"Shall we kill our squaws and children, and then fight until we shall be all killed ourselves?"

To this no reply was made. He then rose up and struck his tomahawk in the war post in the middle of the council house, saying,

"Since you are not inclined to fight, I will go and make peace."

And accordingly did so. On the morning of the day of his death a council was held in the fort at the Point in which he was present. During the sitting of the council it is said that he seemed to have a presentiment of his approaching fate. In one of his speeches he remarked to the council:

"When I was young, every time I went to war I thought it likely that I might return no more; but I still lived. I am now in your hands, and you may kill me if you choose. I can die but once, and it is alike to me whether I die now or at another time."

When the men presented themselves before the door for the purpose of killing the Indians, Cornstalk's son manifested signs of fear, on observing which his father said:

"Don't be afraid, my son. The Great Spirit sent you here to die with me, and we must submit to his will. It is all for the best."

CHAPTER XXIX.

Wappatomica Campaign.

Under the command of Col. Angus M'Donald four hundred men were collected from the western part of Virginia by the order of the Earl of Dunmore, the then governor of Virginia. The place of rendezvous was Wheeling, some time in the month of June, 1774. They went down the river in boats and canoes to the mouth of Captina, from thence by the shortest route to the Wappatomica town, about sixteen miles below the present Coshocton. The pilots were Jonathan Zane, Thomas Nicholson and Tady Kelly. About six miles from the town the army were met by a party of Indians, to the number of forty or fifty, who gave a skirmish by the way of ambuscade in which two of our men were killed and eight or nine wounded. One Indian was killed and several wounded. It was supposed that several more of them were killed, but they were carried off. When the army came to the town it was found evacuated; the Indians had retreated to the opposite shore of the river, where they had formed an ambuscade, supposing the party would cross the river from the town. This was immediately discovered. The commanding officer then sent sentinels up and down the river, to give notice, in case the Indians should attempt to cross above or below the town. A private in company of Capt. Cresap, of the name of John Hargus, one of the sentinels below the town, displayed the skill of a backwoods sharpshooter; seeing an Indian behind a blind across the river, raising up his head, at times, to look over the river, Hargus charged his rifle with a second ball and taking deliberate aim passed both balls through the neck of the Indian. The Indians dragged off the body and buried it with the honors of war. It was found the next morning and scalped by Hargus.

Soon after the town was taken the Indians from the opposite shore sued for peace. The commander offered them peace on condition of their sending over their chiefs as hostages. Five of them came over the river and were put under guard as hostages. In the morning they were marched in front of the army over the river. When the party had reached the western bank of the Muskingum the Indians represented that they could not make peace without the presence of the chiefs of the other towns. On which one of the chiefs was released to bring in the others. He did not return in the appointed time. Another chief was permitted to go on the same errand, who in like manner did not return. The party then moved up the river to the next town, which was about a mile above the first and on the opposite shore. Here we had a slight skirmish with the Indians, in which one of them was killed and one of our men wounded. It was then discovered that, during all the time spent in the negotiation, the Indians were employed in removing their women and children, old people and effects, from the upper towns. The towns were burned and the corn cut up. The party then returned to the place from which they set out, bringing with them the three remaining chiefs who were sent to Williamsburg. They were released at the peace the succeeding fall.

The army were out of provisions before they left the towns and had to subsist on weeds, one ear of corn each day, with a very scanty supply of game. The corn was obtained at one of the Indian towns.

CHAPTER XXX.

Gen. McIntosh's Campaign.

In the spring of the year 1778, government having sent a small force of regular troops under the command of Gen. McIntosh, for the defense of the western frontier, the general, with the regulars and militia from Fort Pitt, descended the Ohio about thirty miles and built Fort McIntosh on the site of the present Beavertown. The fort was made of strong stockades, furnished bastions and mounted with one six pounder. This station was well selected as a point for a small military force, always in readiness to pursue, or intercept, the war parties of Indians who frequently made incursions into the settlements on the opposite side of the river, in its immediate neighborhood. The fort was well garrisoned and supplied with provisions during the summer.

Some time in the fall of the same year General McIntosh received an order from government to make a campaign against the Sandusky towns. This order he attempted to obey with one thousand men; but owing to the delay in making necessary outfits for the expedition the officers, on reaching Tuscarawa, thought it best to halt at that place, build and garrison a fort, and delay the farther prosecution of the campaign until the next spring. Accordingly they erected Fort Laurens [1] on the bank of the Tuscarawa. Some time after the completion of the fort,

[1] Fort Laurens was near where the present village of Bolivar is now, in Tuscarawas county, Ohio. (See "History of Tuscarawas Valley," by C. H. Mitchener; page 142.)

the general returned with the army to Fort Pitt, leaving Col. John Gibson, with a command of one hundred and fifty men, to protect the fort until spring. The Indians were soon acquainted with the existence of the fort, and soon convinced our people, by sad experience, of the bad policy of building and attempting to hold a fort so far in advance of our settlements and other forts.

The first annoyance the garrison received from the Indians was some time in the month of January. In the night time they caught most of the horses belonging to the fort, and taking them off some distance into the woods, they took off their bells and formed an ambuscade by the side of a path leading through the high grass of a prairie at a little distance from the fort. In the morning the Indians rattled the horse bells at the farther end of the line of the ambuscade. The plan succeeded; a fatigue of sixteen men went out for the horses and fell into the snare. Fourteen were killed on the spot, two were taken prisoners, one of whom was given up at the close of the war, the other was never afterwards heard of.

Gen. Benjamin Biggs, then a captain in the fort, being officer of the day, requested leave of the colonel to go out with the fatigue party which fell into the ambuscade.

"No," said the colonel, "this fatigue party does not belong to a captain's command. When I shall have occasion to employ one of that number I shall be thankful for your service; at present you must attend to your duty in the fort."

On what trivial circumstances do life and death sometimes depend!

In the evening of the day of the ambuscade the whole Indian army, in full war dress and painted, marched in single file through a prairie in view of the fort. Their number, as counted from one of the bastions, was 847. They then took up their encampment on an elevated piece of ground at a small distance from the fort, on the opposite side of the river. From this camp they frequently held conversations with the people of our garrison. In these conversations they seemed to deplore the long continuance of the war and hoped for peace; but were much exasperated at the Americans for attempting to penetrate so far into their country. This great body of Indians continued the investment of the fort as long as they could obtain subsistence, which was about six weeks.

An old Indian of the name of John Thompson, who was with the American army in the fort, frequently went out among the Indians during their stay at their encampment, with the mutual consent of both parties. A short time before the Indians left the place they sent word to Col. Gibson by the old Indian, that they were desirous of peace, and that if he would send them a barrel of flour they would send in their proposals the next day; but although the colonel complied with their request they marched off without fulfilling their engagement. The commander, supposing the whole number of the Indians had gone off, gave permission to Col. Clark, of the Pennsylvania line, to escort the invalids, to the number of eleven or twelve, to Fort M'Intosh. The whole number of this detachment was fifteen. The wary Indians had left a party behind for the purpose of doing mischief. These attacked this party of invalids and their escort about two miles from the fort and killed the whole of them with the exception of four, among whom was the captain, who ran back to the fort. On the same day a detachment went out from the fort, brought in the dead and buried them with the honors of war in front of the fort gate. In three or four days after this disaster a relief of seven hundred men, under Gen. M'Intosh, arrived at the fort with a supply of provisions, a great part of which was lost by an untoward accident. When the relief had reached within about one hundred yards of the fort, the garrison gave them a salute of a general discharge of musketry, at the report of which the pack horses took fright, broke loose, and scattered the provisions in every direction through the woods, so that the greater part of it could never be recovered again.

Among other transactions which took place about this time, was that of gathering up the remains of the fourteen men, who had fallen in the ambuscade during the winter, for interment, and which could not be done during the investment of the place by the Indians. They were found mostly devoured by the wolves.

The fatigue party dug a pit large enough to contain the remains of all of them, and after depositing them in the pit, merely covering them with a little earth, with a view to have revenge on the wolves for devouring their companions, they covered the pit with slender sticks, rotten wood and bits of bark, not of sufficient strength to bear the weight of a wolf. On the top of this covering they placed a piece of meat as bait for the wolves. The next morning seven of them were found in the pit. They were shot and the pit filled up.

For about two weeks before the relief arrived the garrison had been put on the short allowance of half a pound of sour flour and an equal weight of stinking meat for every two days. The greater part of the last week they had nothing to subsist on but such roots as they could find in the woods and prairies and raw hides. Two men lost their lives by eating wild parsnip roots by mistake. Four more nearly shared the same fate, but were saved by medical aid.

On the evening of the arrival of the relief two days' rations were issued to each man in the fort. These rations were intended as their allowance during their march to Fort McIntosh; but many of the men, supposing them to have been back rations, ate up the whole of their allowance before the next morning. In consequence of this imprudence, in eating immoderately after such extreme starvation from the want of provisions, about forty of the men became faint and sick during the first day's march. On the second day, however, the sufferers were met by a great number of their friends from the settlements to which they belonged, by whom they were amply supplied with provisions.

Maj. Vernon, who succeeded Col. Gibson in the command of Fort Laurens, continued its possession until the next fall, when the garrison, after being like their predecessors reduced almost to starvation, evacuated the place.

Thus ended the disastrous business of Fort Laurens, in which much fatigue and suffering were endured and many lives lost; but without any beneficial result to the country.

CHAPTER XXXI.

The Moravian Campaign.

This ever memorable campaign took place in the month of March 1782. The weather, during the greater part of the month of February, had been uncommonly fine, so that the war parties from Sandusky visited the settlements and committed depredations earlier than usual. The family of a William Wallace,[1] consisting of his wife and five or six children, were killed, and John Carpenter taken prisoner. These events took place in the latter part of February. The early period at which those fatal visitations of the Indians took place led to the conclusion that the murderers were either Moravians or that the warriors had had their winter quarters at their towns on the Muskingum. In either case, the Moravians being in fault, the safety of the frontier settlements required the destruction of their establishments at that place.

Accordingly, between eighty and ninety men were hastily collected together for the fatal enterprise. They rendezvoused and encamped the first night on the Mingo bottom, on the west side of the Ohio river. Each man furnished himself with his own arms, ammunition and provision. Many of them had horses. The second day's march brought them within one mile of the middle Moravian town, where they encamped for the night. In the morning the men were divided into two equal parties, one of which was to cross the river about a mile above the town, their videttes having reported that there were Indians on both sides of the river. The other party was divided into three divisions, one of which was to take a circuit in the woods, and reach

[1]This was Robert Wallace, not William. He resided where Samuel McConnell now lives, one mile east of Florence. Robert Wallace died in 1808, and was buried in the Florence grave yard; but no stone marks the spot.—(*Simpson.*)

the river, a little distance below the town, on the east side. Another division was to fall into the middle of the town, and the third at its upper end.

When the party designed to make the attack on the west side had reached the river, they found no craft to take them over; but something like a canoe was seen on the opposite bank. The river was high with some floating ice. A young man of the name of Sloughter swam the river and brought over, not a canoe, but a trough designed for holding sugar water. This trough could carry but two men at a time. In order to expedite their passage a number of men stripped off their clothes, put them into the trough, together with their guns, and swam by its sides, holding its edges with their hands. When about sixteen had crossed the river their two sentinels, who had been posted in advance, discovered an Indian whose name was Shabosh. One of them broke one of his arms by a shot. A shot from the other sentinel killed him. These heroes then scalped and tomahawked him. By this time about sixteen men had got over the river, and supposing that the firing of the guns which killed Shabosh [1] would lead to an instant discovery, they sent word to the party designed to attack the town on the east side of the river to move on instantly, which they did.

In the meantime, the small party which had crossed the river marched with all speed to the main town on the west side of the river. Here they found a large company of Indians gathering corn, which they had left in their fields the preceding fall, when they removed to Sandusky. On the arrival of the men at the town they professed peace and good will to the Morav-

---

[1] This Indian, John Shabosh, was killed and scalped by Charles Bilderback, who lived near the mouth of Short Creek, W. Va. Bilderback went with Col. Crawford on his campaign of defeat in May and June (1782) following, and returned home safely. But the Indians, knowing he had killed Shabosh, had a mortal hatred of him, and in 1789 they captured him and his wife and made their escape across the Ohio river with them. On reaching the Tuscarawas they intended to burn Bilderback on the spot where he had killed and scalped Shabosh, but a party of whites from the border, having followed on the trail, came close after them and prevented the burning. But the Indians killed him and cut him to pieces on the spot where he had killed Shabosh seven years before. Nine months later his wife was ransomed on the Miami, and got home in 1791. She married John Green, and afterwards removed to Fairfield county, Ohio, where she died in 1842, near Lancaster. It is said she was the mother of the first white child born in Fairfield county.—(*Simpson.*)

ians, and informed them that they had come to take them to Fort Pitt for their safety. The Indians surrendered, delivered up their arms and appeared highly delighted with the prospect of their removal, and began, with all speed, to prepare victuals for the white men, and for themselves, on their journey. A party of white men and Indians were immediately dispatched to Salem, a short distance from Gnadenhutten, where the Indians were gathering in their corn, to bring them into Gnadenhutten. The party soon arrived with the whole number of the Indians from Salem.

In the meantime the Indians at Gnadenhutten were confined in two houses some distance apart, and placed under guards, and when those from Salem arrived they were divided, and placed in the same houses with their brethren of Gnadenhutten.

The prisoners being thus secured, a council of war was held to decide on their fate. The officers, unwilling to take on themselves the whole responsibility of the awful decision, agreed to refer the question to the whole number of the men. The men were accordingly drawn up in a line. The commandant of the party, Col. David Williamson,[1] then put the question to them in form:

---

[1] Col. David Williamson located in Buffalo township, Washington county, at an early day, on what is now known as the McPherson farm, on Buffalo Creek, taking up several large tracts of land, and in 1787, five years after the Gnadenhutten massacre, he was elected sheriff of the county, despite his leadership of the bloody expedition against the Moravians. He married Polly Urie, of Hopewell township. They had four sons and four daughters. At the spring election of 1785, in Donegal township, Washington county, for two or more persons whose names were to be submitted to the Supreme Executive Council of the state, for appointment as justice of the peace of the township, and also to sit as a judge of the courts of record for seven years, the people cast 44 votes for David Williamson and 26 for William Johnston. It was the duty of the county prothonotary, Thomas Scott, to transmit the result of this election to the Supreme Council, and in doing so he wrote as follows about Williamson: "I wish through you to inform the Council that the Williamson elected is the same Col. Williamson who (killed) slaughtered the Moravian Indians. If this deed may be thought a defect in his character (which many of us think) it is not the only one; nor can I easily paint him better than (in the following familiar and homely phrases, to wit) by just telling Council that he is a foolish (gawky) impertinent and insolent boy, totally void of all the necessary qualifications for so important a trust." This letter seems to have influenced the Council against Williamson, for he was not appointed. Johnston was commissioned. But two years later, as stated, Williamson was elected sheriff, and re-elected in 1789.—(*Crumrine's "Courts of Justice, Bench and Bar, of Washington County."*)

Thomas Scott was the first prothonotary of Washington county. Col. Williamson was born near Carlisle, Pa., in 1752, son of John Williamson.

"Whether the Moravian Indians should be taken prisoners to Pittsburg or put to death, and requested that all those who were in favor of saving their lives should step out of the line, and form a second rank."

On this sixteen, some say eighteen, stepped out of the rank, and formed themselves into a second line; but alas! This line of mercy was far too short for that of vengeance.

The fate of the Moravians was then decided on, and they were told to prepare for death.

The prisoners, from the time they were placed in the guard house, foresaw their fate, and began their devotions of singing hymns, praying and exhorting each other to place a firm reliance on the mercy of the Saviour of men. When their fate was announced to them these devoted people embraced, kissed, and bedewing each others faces and bosoms with their mutual tears, asked pardon of the brothers and sisters for any offense they might have given them through life. Thus, at peace with God, and each other, on being asked by those who were impatient for the slaughter:

"Whether they were ready to die?"

They answered, "That they had commended their souls to God, and were ready to die."

The particulars of this dreadful catastrophe are too horrid to relate. Suffice it to say that in a few minutes these two slaughter-houses, as they were then called, exhibited in their ghastly interior the mangled, bleeding remains of these poor unfortunate people, of all ages and sexes, from the aged grey headed parents down to the helpless infant at its mother's breast, dishonored by the fatal wounds of the tomahawk, mallet, war club, spear and scalping knife.

Thus, O! Brainard and Zeisberger! Faithful missionaries who devoted your whole lives to incessant toil and sufferings in your endeavors to make the wilderness of paganism "rejoice and blossom as the rose" in faith and piety to God! thus perished

---

He came west of the mountains when a boy, and then induced his father to come also. In 1777, when 25 years old, he was a captain of militia. He was 30 years of age when he led the expedition against the Moravians. In 1785 he was a colonel. He died in 1814 in poverty. His body was interred in the old burial ground on North Main street, Washington, Pa., but no stone marks the spot.

your faithful followers by the murderous hands of the more than savage white men. Faithful pastors! your spirits are again associated with those of your flock, where the wicked cease from troubling and the weary are at rest!

The number of the slain, as reported by the men on their return from the campaign, was eighty-seven or eighty-nine; but the Moravian account, which no doubt is correct, makes the number ninety-six. Of these, sixty-two were grown persons, one-third of whom were women, the remaining thirty-four were children. All these, with a few exceptions, were killed in the house. Shabosh was killed about a mile above the town, on the west side of the river. His wife was killed while endeavoring to conceal herself in a bunch of bushes at the water's edge, on the arrival of the men at the town, on the east side of the river. A man at the same time was shot in a canoe, while attempting to make his escape from the east to the west side of the river. Two others were shot while attempting to escape by swimming the river.

A few men, who were supposed to be warriors, were tied and taken some distance from the slaughter houses to be tomahawked. One of these had like to have made his escape at the expense of the life of one of the murderers. The rope by which he was led was of some length. The two men who were conducting him to death fell into a dispute who should have the scalp. The Indian, while marching with a kind of dancing motion and singing his death song, drew a knife from a scabbard suspended round his neck, cut the rope and aimed at stabbing one of the men; but the jerk of the rope occasioned the men to look around. The Indian then fled towards the woods, and while running dextrously untied the rope from his wrists. He was instantly pursued by several men who fired at him, one of whom wounded him in the arm. After a few shots the firing was forbidden, for fear the men might kill each other as they were running in a straggling manner. A young man then mounted on a horse and pursued the Indian, who, when overtaken, struck the horse on the head with a club. The rider sprang from the horse, on which the Indian seized, threw him down and drew his tomahawk to kill him. At that instant one of the party got near enough to shoot the Indian, which he did merely in time to save the life of his companion.

Of the whole number of the Indians at Gnadenhutten and Salem, only two made their escape. These were two lads of fourteen or fifteen years of age. One of them, after being knocked down and scalped, but not killed, had the presence of mind to lie still among the dead until the dusk of the evening, when he silently crept out of the door and made his escape. The other lad slipped through a trap door into the cellar of one of the slaughter-houses, from which he made his escape through a small cellar window. These two lads were fortunate in getting together in the woods the same night. Another lad, somewhat larger, in attempting to pass through the same window, it is supposed stuck fast and was burnt alive.

The Indians of the upper town were apprised of their danger in due time to make their escape, two of them having found the mangled body of Shabosh. Providentially they all made their escape, although they might have been easily overtaken by the party if they had undertaken their pursuit. A division of the men were ordered to go to Shonbrun; but finding the place deserted, they took what plunder they could find, and returned to their companions without looking farther after the Indians. After the work of death was finished and the plunder secured, all the buildings in the town were set on fire and the slaughter houses among the rest. The dead bodies were thus consumed to ashes. A rapid retreat to the settlements finished the campaign.

Such were the principal events of this horrid affair. A massacre of innocent, unoffending people, dishonorable not only to our country, but human nature itself.

Before making any remarks on the causes which led to these disgraceful events under consideration, it may be proper to notice the manner in which the enterprise was conducted as furnishing evidence that the murder of the Moravians was intended, and that no resistance from them was anticipated. In a military point of view the Moravian campaign was conducted in the very worst manner imaginable. It was undertaken at so early a period that a deep fall of snow, a thing very common in the early part of March in former times, would have defeated the enterprise. When the army came to the river, instead of constructing a sufficient number of rafts to transport the requisite number over the river at once, they commenced crossing in a sugar trough, which could carry only two men at a time, thus jeopardizing the safety of those who first went over. The two sentinels who shot Shabosh, according to military law ought to have been executed on the spot for having fired without orders, thereby giving premature notice of the approach of our men. The truth is, nearly the whole number of the army ought to have been transported over the river, for after all their forces employed, and precautions used in getting possession of the town on the east side of the river, there were but one man and one squaw found in it, all the others being on the other side. This circumstance they ought to have known beforehand, and acted accordingly. The Indians on the west side of the river amounted to about eighty, and among them above thirty men, besides a number of young lads, all possessed of guns and well accustomed to the use of them; yet this large number was attacked by about sixteen men. If they had really anticipated resistance they deserved to lose their lives for their rashness. It is presumable, however, that having full confidence in the pacific principles of the Moravians, they did not expect resistance; but calculated on blood and plunder without having a shot fired at them. If this was really the case, the author leaves it to justice to find, if it can, a name for the transaction.

One can hardly help reflecting with regret that these Moravians did not for the moment lay aside their pacific principles and do themselves justice. With a mere show of defense, or at most a few shots, they might have captured and disarmed these few men, and held them as hostages for the safety of their people and property until they could have removed them out of their way. This they might have done on the easiest terms, as the remainder of the army could not have crossed the river without their permission, as there was but one canoe at the place, and the river too high to be forded. But, alas, these truly Christian people suffered themselves to be betrayed by hypocritical professions of friendship until "they were led as sheep to the slaughter!" Over this horrid deed humanity must shed tears of commiseration as long as the record of it shall remain.

Let not the reader suppose that I have presented him with a mere imaginary possibility of defense on the part of the Moravians. This defense would have been an easy task. Our people did not go on that campaign with a view of fighting. There may have been some brave men among them; but they were far from being all such. For my part I cannot suppose for a moment that any white man who can harbor a thought of using his arms for the killing of women and children, in any case, can be a brave man. No! he is a murderer.

The history of the Moravian settlements on the Muskingum and the peculiar circumstances of their inhabitants during the revolutionary contest between Great Britain and America deserve a place here.

In the year 1772 the Moravian villages were commenced by emigrations from Friedenhutten on the Big Beaver and from Wyalusing and Sheshequon on the Susquehanna. In a short time they rose to considerable extent and prosperity, containing upwards of four hundred people. During the summer of Dunmore's war they were much annoyed by war parties of the Indians, and disturbed by perpetual rumors of the ill intentions of the white people of the frontier settlements towards them; yet their labors, schools and religious exercise, went on without interruption.

In the revolutionary war, which began in 1775, the situation of the Moravian settlements was truly deplorable. The English had associated with their own means of warfare against the Americans the "scalping knife and tomahawk" of the merciless Indians. These allies of England committed the most horrid depredations along the whole extent of our defenseless frontier. From early in the spring until late in the fall the early settlers of the western parts of Virginia and Pennsylvania had to submit to the severest hardships and privations. Cooped up in little stockade forts, they worked their little fields in parties under arms, guarded by sentinels, and were doomed from day to day to witness, or hear reports, of the murders or captivity of their people, the burning of their houses and the plunder of their property.

The war with the English fleets and armies, on the other side of the mountains, was of such a character as to engage the whole attention and resources of our government, so that, poor as the first settlers of this county were, they had to bear almost the whole burden of the war during the revolutionary contest. They chose their own officers, furnished their own means and conducted the war in their own way. Thus circumstanced, "they became a law unto themselves," and on certain occasions perpetrated acts which the government was compelled to disapprove. This lawless temper of our people was never fully dissipated until the conclusion of the whiskey rebellion in 1794.

The Moravian villages were situated between the settlements of the whites and the town of the warriors, about sixty miles from the former, and not much farther from the latter. On this account they were denominated "the half way houses of the warriors." Thus placed between two rival powers engaged in furious warfare, the preservation of their neutrality was no easy task, perhaps impossible. If it requires the same physical force to preserve a neutral station among belligerent nations, that it does to prosecute a war, as is unquestionably the case, this pacific people had no chance for the preservation of theirs. The very goodness of their hearts, their aversion to the shedding of human blood, brought them into difficulties with both parties. When they sent their runners to Fort Pitt to inform us of the approach of the war parties, or received, fed, secreted and sent home prisoners who had made their escape from the savages, they made breaches of their neutrality as to the belligerent Indians. Their furnishing the warriors with a resting place and provisions was contrary to their neutral engagements to us; but their local situation rendered those accommodations to the warriors unavoidable on their part; as the warriors possessed both the will and the means to compel them to give them whatever they wanted from them.

The peaceable Indians first fell under suspicion with the Indian warriors and the English commandant at Detroit, to whom it was reported that their teachers were in close confedcracy with the American congress, for preventing not only their own people, but also the Delawares and some other nations, from associating their arms with those of the British for carrying on the war against the American colonies. The frequent failures of the war expeditions of the Indians was attributed to the Moravians, who often sent runners to Fort Pitt to give notice of their approach. This charge against them was certainly not without foundation. In the spring of the year 1781 the war chief of the Delawares fully apprised the missionaries and their followers of their danger both from the whites and Indians, and requested them to remove to a place of safety from both. This request was not complied with. The almost prophetic predictions of this chief were literally fulfilled.

In the fall of the year 1781 the settlements of the Moravians were broken up by upwards of three hundred warriors, the missionaries taken prisoners, after being robbed of almost everything. The Indians were left to shift for themselves in the barren plains of Sandusky, where most of their horses and cattle perished from famine, during the winter. The missionaries were taken prisoners to Detroit; but after an examination by the governor permitted to return to their beloved people again. In the latter part of February a party of about one hundred and fifty of the Moravian Indians returned to their deserted villages on the Muskingum to procure corn to keep their families and cattle from starving. These, to the amount of ninety-six, fell into the hands of Williamson and his party and were murdered.

The causes which led to the murder of the Moravians are now to be detailed.

The pressure of the Indian war along the whole of the western frontier, for several years preceding the event under consideration, had been dreadfully severe. From early in the spring until the commencement of winter, from day to day, murders were committed in every direction by the Indians. The people lived in forts which were in the highest degree uncomfortable. The men were harrassed continually with the duties of going on scouts and campaigns. There was scarcely a family of the first settlers who did not, at some time or other, lose more or less of their number by the merciless Indians. Their cattle were killed, their cabins burned and their horses carried off. These losses were severely felt by a people so poor as we were at that time. Thus circumstanced our people were exasperated to madness by the extent and severity of the war. The unavailing endeavors of the American congress to prevent the Indians from taking up the hatchet against either side in the revolutionary contest contributed much to increase the general indignation against them, at the same time these pacific endeavors of our government divided the Indians amongst themselves, on the question of war or peace with the whites. The Moravians, part of the Delawares, and some others, faithfully endeavored to preserve peace; but in vain. The Indian maxim was "He that is not for us is against us." Hence the Moravian missionaries and their followers were several times on the point of being murdered by the warriors. This would have been done had it not been for the prudent conduct of some of the war chiefs.

On the other hand, the local situation of the Moravian villages excited the jealousy of the white people. If they took no direct agency in the war yet they were, as they were then called, "half way houses" between us and the warriors, at which the latter could stop, rest, refresh themselves and traffic off their plunder. Whether these aids thus given to our enemies were contrary to the laws of neutrality between belligerents is a question which I willingly leave to the decision of civilians. On the part of the Moravians they were unavoidable. If they did not give or sell provisions to the warriors they would take them by force. The fault was in their situation not in themselves.

The longer the war continued the more our people complained of the situation of these Moravian villages. It was said that it was owing to their being so near us that the warriors commenced their depredations so early in the spring, and continued them until so late in the fall.

In the latter end of the year 1781 the militia of the frontier came to a determination to break up the Moravian villages on the Muskingum. For this purpose a detachment of our men went out under the command of Col. David Williamson,[1] for the purpose of inducing the Indians with their teachers to move farther off, or bring them prisoners to Fort Pitt. When they arrived at the villages they found but few Indians, the greater number of them having removed to Sandusky. These few were well treated, taken to Fort Pitt and delivered to the commandant of that station, who after a short detention sent them home again. This procedure gave great offense to the people of the country, who thought that the Indians ought to have been killed. Col. Williamson who, before this little campaign, had been a very popular man, on account of his activity and bravery in war, now became the subject of severe animadversions on account of his lenity to the Moravian Indians. In justice to the memory of Col. Williamson I have to say that, although at that time very young, I was personally acquainted with him, and from my recollection of his conversation I saw with confidence that he was a brave man but not cruel. He would meet an enemy in battle, and fight like a soldier; but not murder a prisoner. Had he possessed the authority of a superior officer in a regular army, I do not believe that a single Moravian Indian would have lost his life; but he possessed no such authority. He was only a militia officer, who could advise but not command. His only fault was that of too easy a compliance with popular opinion and

[1] The Rev. John Heckewelder, the historian of the Moravians, states that this campaign in the fall of 1781 was commanded by Capt. Biggs. This was not the case. It was commanded by Col. David Williamson, the same who commanded the fatal campaign the succeeding spring. (D.)

popular prejudice. On this account his memory has been loaded with unmerited reproach.

Several reports unfavorable to the Moravians had been in circulation for some time before the campaign against them. One was that the night after they were liberated at Fort Pitt, they crossed the river and killed or made prisoners of a family of the name of Monteur. A family on Buffalo creek had been mostly killed in the summer or fall of 1781, and it was said by one of them who, after being made prisoner, made his escape, that the leader of the party of Indians who did the mischief was a Moravian. These, with other reports of similar import, served as a pretext for their destruction, although no doubt they were utterly false.

Should it be asked what sort of people composed the band of murderers of these unfortunate people, I answer. They were not miscreants or vagabonds; many of them were men of the first standing in the country. Many of them were men who had recently lost relations by the hand of the savages; several of the latter class found articles which had been plundered from their own houses, or those of their relations, in the houses of the Moravians. One man,[1] it is said, found the clothes of his

---

[1] Robert Wallace was the man here spoken of who found his wife's clothes. Her name was Mary Wallace. She was taken near Florence, Pa., in the fall of 1781, and was killed near Hookstown, Beaver county. Her bones were found in 1783 by some hunters, and were interred by her husband at Cross Creek in 1785.—(*Simpson.*)

Hassler's "Old Westmoreland" gives the following version of the Wallace tragedy:

"The outrage against Robert Wallace was one of the events which inspired the frontiersmen's massacre of the Moravians at Gnadenhutten. On Sunday, Feb. 10, 1782, a band of 40 Indians visited the home of Wallace, on Raccoon creek, in Washington county, while Wallace was away, burned his cabin, killed his cattle and hogs, and carried away his wife and three children, a boy of 10, one of three, Robert, and a baby. When Robert Wallace started with Col. David Williamson's force on their mission of reprisal at Gnadenhutten he found, near the Ohio river, impaled upon the sharpened trunk of a sapling, the torn and naked body of his wife. Nearby was the mutilated corpse of his infant. His two other sons had been carried off into captivity. The dead were buried on the border of the forest, and Williamson swept on with his 150 angry followers to their frightful revenge on the banks of the Muskingum."

Wm. M. Farrar's monograph on this episode wholly discredits the story of the finding of the bodies of Mrs. Wallace and her baby having any influence in shaping or expediting the Moravian raid. He says the trail of the savages who committed this deed was 25 or 30 miles further north than the one followed by the raiders; that the bodies of mother and child had been carefully hidden, so as not to aid pursuit, and remained concealed until found years afterward; that at the date of the massacre Robert Wallace did not know his wife was dead, but supposed her to be a prisoner of the Indians; and he did not learn otherwise until three years afterward. Ascertaining about where the mother and child had been killed, he searched and found the remains and buried them at Cross Creek graveyard, as stated by Simpson.

wife and children who had been murdered by the Indians but a few days before. They were still bloody; yet there was no unequivocal evidence that these people had any direct agency in the war. Whatever of our property was found with them had been left by the warriors in exchange for the provisions which they took from them. When attacked by our people, although they might have defended themselves, they did not. They never fired a single shot. They were prisoners and had been promised protection. Every dictate of justice and humanity required that their lives should be spared. The complaint of their villages being "half way houses for the warriors" was at an end, as they had been removed to Sandusky the fall before. It was therefore an atrocious and unqualified murder. But by whom committed? By a majority of the campaign? For the honor of my country I hope I may safely answer this question in the negative. It was one of those convulsions of the moral state of society in which the voice of the justice and humanity of a majority is silenced by the clamor and violence of a lawless minority. Very few of our men imbrued their hands in the blood of the Moravians. Even those who had not voted for saving their lives retired from the scene of slaughter with horror and disgust. Why then did they not give their votes in their favor? The fear of public indignation restrained them from doing so. They thought well; but had not heroism enough to express their opinion. Those who did so deserve honorable mention for their intrepidity. So far as it may hereafter be in my power, this honor shall be done them. While the names of the murderers shall not stain the pages of history, from my pen at least.[1]

[1] The names of some of the men who were at Gnadenhütten, March 8, 1782, with Colonel Williamson are: Joseph Vance, John McWilliams, Charles Campbell, Robert Marshall, Thomas Marshall, Thomas Cherry, James Ross, Moses Patterson, David Kerr, John Graham, Samuel Merchant, Robert Wallace, Judge James Taylor, Solomon Vaile, David Gault, Solomon Urie (died in 1830).—(*Simpson.*)

Another member of the expedition was Obadiah Holmes, Jr. His grand nephew, Col. J. T. Holmes, a prominent attorney at law of Columbus, O., and a careful student of early frontier history, writing to the publishers of this edition touching the motive of the leaders and members of the Moravian expedition says:

"I was amazed, at the beginning of 1900, when my attention was first forcibly turned to the subject of the Moravian massacre, and when I took it up for consideration, to learn that there was no muster roll of Williamson's command to be found. I was not content, however, to accept the first assurance which came to me to that effect. Crumrine's history of Washington County says there was a list in some attic, or in the custody of some family, in that county. I spent considerable time and labor trying to locate it, or some other, but failed to obtain the smallest trace of it, although I thought I had exceptional facilities for obtaining a list, if one existed.

"One of my grandfather's brothers, Obadiah Holmes, Jr. (1760-1834), was on both the Moravian and Sandusky campaigns. He voted against the killing, and lived an honored Christian life from first to last among men. He and Colonel Williamson stood together on the bank of the Muskingum River at Gnadenhutten, between the prison houses and the stream, after the vote, and after the massacre began, and as they so stood my great uncle interposed his person to save the life of an Indian boy who was pursued by one of the maddened majority, whose menaces were successfully defied. My great uncle protected this little fellow, and took him home with him. The boy lived with the family on the homestead, two miles below Catfish Camp, on the south bank of Chartiers Creek, or with some of its members, for approximately ten years next following. Then the wanderlust came over him and he disappeared, presumably returning to his own people.

"I have often queried and debated, on my private record, why Dr. Doddridge did not leave us in print, or in manuscript, more particulars, which he must have had, and which he must have known were most liable to perish; this especially in connection with the Logan family incident, the Fort Henry sieges and the two campaigns mentioned. There were reasons, no doubt, for all the omissions.

"I have followed author after author, some of them plainly without a moment's original research, denouncing the Gnadenhutten expedition as unauthorized, unorganized, a mob, and the men as border ruffians, the scum of society, cutthroats, cowards, murderers, assassins, demons, and so on and on until, with the mass of actual facts in hand, I was a little tired at this climax. The truth will not justify an indiscriminate condemnation of the participants in the Moravian campaign.

"You have asked who planned this campaign, and where Colonel Williamson was elected leader? I was born among those hills, about sixteen miles from the site of Carpenter's block house, which is at the mouth of Indian Short Creek—just above it—on the the Ohio side. It is credible tradition that the expedition, the actual campaign, was first proposed in a small company of frontiersmen gathered and talking in an informal way at Carpenter's block house in the latter part of February or the beginning of March, 1782. The calls of the suffering borderers on the government for relief had been insistent and pathetic in the preceding months. This is of record, made at the time. Out of those calls, or by reason of them, came the authority for the expedition and the expedition itself.

"The rendezvous, and the place of Colonel Williamson's election, was at Mingo Bottom. There were two Mingoes in those days: First, the famous Mingo Spring in Ohio, a little way below Steubenville, if not now taken into the city; and, second, a long valley on the Virginia side, running back from the Ohio River, across from the lower end of Steubenville. This latter was Mingo Bottom. The former was Mingo Spring. In time they were confused, except that the Bottom was not called the Spring, while the latter has succeeded to the fame of both. Very few know of the tradition, even, that there were two.

"Col. Wm. Crawford started on the Sandusky expedition from Mingo Spring three months after Gnadenhutten; and, by the way, Colonel Williamson was elected second in command at the Spring and conducted the retreat after the defeat at Sandusky Plains. The Williamson force encountered a great deal of trouble at starting for Gnadenhutten in March, 1782, in making the crossing of the Ohio River from the Bottom to the Spring. The stream was full of floating cakes of ice, making the work excessively chilly and discouraging. The old Moravian trail from Mingo passed within four miles of my birthplace and early home, and one of the Indian trails going east broke off from it near where Cadiz now stands; and, three miles down Middle Fork, passed within a mile of that home. It followed Indian Short Creek from the forks, where Adena is located, down to the Ohio at Carpenter's.

"One member of the expedition, I have ascertained, killed sixteen of the Moravian Indians, as he claimed, and then desisted only because his arm was wearied to a standstill; and he sat down and cried because he found in it no satisfaction for his murdered wife and children. Another afterward boasted of the number he had slain; and this man had the misfortunate some time later—I think later than the Sandusky campaign—to be captured by the Indians and to undergo the most exquisite tortures they could inflict in putting him to death.

"Obadiah Holmes, Jr., was one of the volunteers on each of the expeditions. He died in Pittsburgh, at the home of his son, Dr. Shepley Ross Holmes, in June, 1834, and is buried at Woodville, about ten miles out of the city, beside his wife, Jane Richardson. The descendants of Obadiah Holmes, Jr.—he had ten daughters and three sons—permeate Pittsburgh society. Obadiah Holmes, Jr. was one of the sixteen members of the Moravian expedition who voted against the massacre. He distinguished himself as a young man of courage and self-sacrifice on each campaign. His descendants are sons and daughters of the American Revolution by virtue of the commission which he bore at the close of the war. There was never, at any time, in his case or conduct anything of which any one need be or ever has been ashamed."

In a paper on the Moravian massacre by Wm. M. Farrar, read in 1891 at the sixth annual meeting of the Ohio Archeological and Historical Society, the author says: "The expedition was neither infantry nor cavalry, mounted nor dismounted, but a mixed crowd made up in part from that reckless and irresponsible element usually found along the borders of civilization; boys from eighteen to twenty years of age, who joined the expedition from love of adventure; and partly of such well-known characters as Capt. Sam Brady, of West Liberty, Virginia, and at least one of the Wetzels, from near Wheeling, who, from their experience and well known bravery as frontiersmen, are said to have exercised very great influence in deciding the fate of the Indians. * * * Col. David Williamson was the one member of the expedition who, by reason of the position he filled, could not hide from public censure, and hence his undue share of it."

Farrar quotes a tradition that Joseph Vance, proprietor of Vance's Fort, had told Robert Lyle, in 1792, that the scheme of the raid originated at Vance's Fort, in the fall of 1781, with the men of some twenty-five or thirty families then forting there for protection from the Indians. These men believed the Moravian villages to be sheltering places for plundering bands of savages. The intention was to make the raid that fall, but it was nullified unexpectedly by the department sending out Colonel Williamson with two companies of soldiers to remove the Muskingum Moravians to Fort Pitt. Williamson found, however, that an expedition from Detroit had taken the missionaries and their converts to Sandusky. But in the following spring the spirit of destruction flamed up again, and the purpose of extermination was ruthlessly carried out. Even the families of many of the participants in the raid were ignorant of their connection with it.

CHAPTER XXXII.

The Indian Summer.

As connected with the history of the Indian wars of the western country it may not be amiss to give an explanation of the term *Indian summer.* This expression, like many others, has continued in general use notwithstanding its original import has been forgotten. A backwoodsman seldom hears this expression without feeling a chill of horror, because it brings to his mind the painful recollection of its original application. Such is the force of the faculty of association in human nature.

The reader must here be reminded that, during the long continued Indian wars sustained by the first settlers of the western country, they enjoyed no peace excepting in the winter season, when, owing to the severity of the weather, the Indians were unable to make their excursions into the settlements. The onset of winter was therefore hailed as a jubilee by the early inhabitants of the country who, throughout the spring and the early part of the fall, had been cooped up in their little uncomfortable forts, and subjected to all the distresses of the Indian war. At the approach of winter, therefore, all the farmers, excepting the owner of the fort, removed to their cabins on their farms, with the joyful feeling of a tenant of a prison on recovering his release from confinement. All was bustle and hilarity, in preparing for winter, by gathering in the corn, digging potatoes, fattening hogs and repairing the cabins. To our forefathers, the gloomy months of winter were more pleasant than the zephyrs of spring and the flowers of May.

It however sometimes happened that after the apparent onset of winter the weather became warm, the smoky time commenced and lasted for a considerable number of days. This was the Indian summer, because it afforded the Indians another opportunity of visiting the settlements with their destructive warfare. The melting of the snow saddened every countenance and the general warmth of the sun chilled every heart with horror. The apprehension of another visit from the Indians, and of being driven back to the detested fort, was painful in the highest degree and the distressing apprehension was frequently realized.

Toward the latter part of February we commonly had a fine spell of open warm weather, during which the snow melted away. This was denominated the *Pawwawing days,* from the supposition that the Indians were then holding their war councils, for planning off their spring campaigns into the settlements. Sad experience taught us that in this conjecture we were not often mistaken.

Sometimes it happened that the Indians ventured to make their excursions too late in the fall, or too early in the spring for their own convenience.

A man of the name of John Carpenter[1] was taken early in the month of March, in the neighborhood of this place. There had been several warm days, but the night preceding his capture there was a heavy fall of snow. His two horses, which they took with him, nearly perished in swimming the Ohio. The Indians, as well as himself, suffered severely with the cold before they reached the Moravian towns on the Muskingum. In the morning after the first day's journey beyond the Moravian towns, the Indians sent out Carpenter to bring in the horses which had been turned out in the evening, after being hobbled. The horses had made a circuit and fallen into the trail by which they came the preceding day, and were making their way homeward. When he overtook the horses and had taken off their fetters, as he said, he had to make a most awful decision. He had a chance and barely a chance, to make his escape, with a certainty of death should he attempt it without success; on the other hand the horrible prospect of being tortured to death by fire presented itself, as he was the first prisoner taken that spring; of course the general custom of the Indians, of burning the first prisoner every

---

[1] John Carpenter afterwards built the fort at the mouth of Short Creek, on the Ohio side. In 1800 he removed to what is now Coshocton county, Ohio, where he is buried—he and his wife.—(*Simpson.*)

spring, doomed him to the flames. After spending a few minutes in making his decision he resolved on attempting an escape, and effected it by way of Forts Laurens, M'Intosh and Pittsburg. If I recollect rightly, he brought both his horses home with him.

This happened in the year 1782. The capture of Mr. Carpenter and the murder of two families about the same time, that is to say, in the two or three first days of March, contributed materially to the Moravian campaign, and the murder of that unfortunate people.

CHAPTER XXXIII.

Crawford's Campaign.

This, in one point of view at least, is to be considered as a second Moravian campaign, as one of its objects was that of finishing the work of murder and plunder with the Christian Indians at their new establishment on the Sandusky. The next object was that of destroying the Wyandot towns on the same river. It was the resolution of all those concerned in this expedition not to spare the life of any Indians that might fall into their hands, whether friends or foes. It will be seen in the sequel that the result of this campaign was widely different from that of the Moravian campaign the preceding March.

It would seem that the long continuance of the Indian war had debased a considerable portion of our population to the savage state of our nature. Having lost so many relatives by the Indians, and witnessed their horrid murders and other depredations on so extensive a scale, they became subjects of that indiscriminating thirst for revenge which is such a prominent feature in the savage character, and having had a taste of blood and plunder, without risk or loss on their part, they resolved to go on and kill every Indian they could find, whether friend or foe.

Preparations for this campaign commenced soon after the return of the Moravian campaign in the month of March, and as it was intended to make what was called at that time *a dash,* that is an enterprise conducted with secrecy and dispatch, the men were all mounted on the best horses they could procure. They furnished themselves with all their outfits, except some ammunition which was furnished by the lieutenant colonel of Washington county.

On the 25th of May, 1782, 480 men mustered at the old Mingo towns, on the western side of the Ohio river.[1] They were all volunteers from the immediate neighborhood of the Ohio, with the exception of one company from Ten Mile in Washington county. Here an election was held for the office of commander-in-chief for the expedition. The candidates were Col. Williamson and Col. Crawford. The latter was the successful candidate. When notified of his appointment, it is said that he accepted it with apparent reluctance.

The army marched along *Williamson's trail,* as it was then called, until they arrived at the upper Moravian town, in the fields belonging to which there was still plenty of corn on the stalks, with which their horses were plentifully fed during the night of their encampment there.

Shortly after the army halted at this place two Indians were discovered by three men, who had walked some distance out of the camp. Three shots were fired at one of them, but without hurting him. As soon as the news of the discovery of Indians had reached the camp more than one-half of the men rushed out, without command, and in the most tumultuous manner, to see what happened. From that time Col. Crawford felt a presentiment of the defeat which followed.

The truth is, that notwithstanding the secrecy and dispatch of the enterprise, the Indians were beforehand with our people. They saw the rendezvous on the Mingo Bottom, knew their number and destination. They visited every encampment immediately on their leaving it, and saw from their writing on the

[1] Butterfield says Westmoreland county sent 130 men, Washington county 320, and Ohio county, Virginia, 20, as nearly as could be ascertained.

trees and scraps of paper that " No quarter was to be given to any Indian, whether man, woman or child." Nothing material happened during their march until the sixth of June, when their guides conducted them to the site of the Moravian villages, on one of the upper branches of the Sandusky river; but here, instead of meeting with Indians and plunder, they met with nothing but vestiges of desolation. The place was covered with high grass and the remains of a few huts alone announced that the place had been the residence of the people whom they intended to destroy; but who had moved off to Scioto some time before.

In this dilemma what was to be done? The officers held a council in which it was determined to march one day longer in the direction of upper Sandusky, and if they should not reach the town in the course of the day, to make a retreat with all speed.

The march was commenced the next morning through the plains of Sandusky and continued until about two o'clock, when the advance guard was attacked and driven in by the Indians, who were discovered in large numbers in the high grass with which the place was covered. The Indian army was at that moment about entering a piece of woods, almost entirely surrounded by plains; but in this they were disappointed by a rapid movement of our men. The battle then commenced by a heavy fire from both sides. From a partial possession of the woods which they had gained at the onset of the battle, the Indians were soon dislodged. They then attempted to gain a small skirt of wood on our right flank, but were prevented from doing so by the vigilance and bravery of Maj. Leet,[1] who commanded the right wing of the army at that time. The firing was incessant and heavy until dark, when it ceased. Both armies lay on their arms during the night. Both adopted the policy of kindling large fires along the line of battle, and then retiring some distance in the rear of them, to prevent being surprised by a night attack. During the conflict of the afternoon three of our men were killed and several wounded.

---

[1] Major Daniel Leet died at Sewickley Bottom, June 18, 1830.

In the morning our army occupied the battle ground of the preceding day. The Indians made no attack during the day, until late in the evening, but were seen in large bodies traversing the plains in various directions. Some of them appeared to be employed in carrying off their dead and wounded.

In the morning of this day a council of the officers was held, in which a retreat was resolved on as the only means of saving their army, the Indians appearing to increase in number every hour. During the sitting of this council Col. Williamson proposed taking one hundred and fifty volunteers and marching directly to upper Sandusky. This proposition the commander-in-chief prudently rejected, saying:

"I have no doubt but that you would reach the town, but you would find nothing there but empty wigwams, and having taken off so many of our best men you would leave the rest to be destroyed by the host of Indians with which we are now surrounded, and on your return they would attack and destroy you. They care nothing about defending their towns. They are worth nothing. Their squaws, children and property, have been removed from them long since. Our lives and baggage are what they want, and if they can get us divided they will soon have them. We must stay together and do the best we can."

During this day preparations were made for a retreat by burying the dead, burning fires over their graves to prevent discovery, and preparing means for carrying off the wounded. The retreat was to commence in the course of the night. The Indians. however, became apprised of the intended retreat, and about sundown attacked the army with great force and fury in every direction excepting that of Sandusky.

When the line of march was formed by the commander-in-chief and the retreat commenced, our guides prudently took the direction of Sandusky, which afforded the only opening in the Indian lines, and the only chance of concealment. After marching about a mile in this direction the army wheeled about to the left, and by a circuitous route gained the trail by which they came before day. They continued their march the whole of the next day, with a trifling annoyance from the Indians, who fired a few distant shots at the rear guard, which slightly wounded two or three men. At night they built fires, took their suppers, secured the horses and resigned themselves to repose, without placing a single sentinel or vidette for safety. In this careless situation they might have been surprised and cut off by the Indians who, however, gave them no disturbance during the night, nor afterwards during the whole of their retreat. The number of those composing the main body in the retreat was supposed to be about three hundred.

Most unfortunately, when a retreat was resolved on, a difference of opinion prevailed concerning the best mode of effecting it. The greater number thought best to keep in a body and retreat as fast as possible, while a considerable number thought it safest to break off in small parties, and make their way home in different directions, avoiding the route by which they came. Accordingly many attempted to do so, calculating that the whole body of the Indians would follow the main army. In this they were entirely mistaken. The Indians paid but little attention to the main body of the army, but pursued the small parties with such activity that but very few of those who composed them made their escape.

The only successful party who were detached from the main army was that of about forty men under the command of Captain Williamson, who, pretty late in the night of the retreat, broke through the Indian lines under a severe fire, and with some loss, and overtook the main army on the morning of the second day of the retreat.

For several days after the retreat of our army the Indians were spread over the whole country, from Sandusky to the Muskingum, in pursuit of the straggling parties, most of whom were killed on the spot. They even pursued them almost to the banks of the Ohio. A man of the name of Mills was killed two miles to the eastward of the site of St. Clairsville, in the direction of Wheeling from that place. The number killed in this way must have been very great; the precise amount, however, was never fairly ascertained.

At the commencement of the retreat Col. Crawford placed himself at the head of the army and continued there until they had gone about a quarter of a mile, when, missing his son John Crawford,[1] his son-in-law Major Harrison, and his nephews Major Rose[2] and William Crawford, he halted and called for them as the line passed, but without finding them. After the army had passed him he was unable to overtake it, owing to the weariness of his horse. Falling in company with Doctor Knight[3] and two others they traveled all night, first north, and then to the east, to avoid the pursuit of the Indians. They directed their course during the night by the north star. On the next day they fell in with Captain John Biggs and Lieutenant Ashley, the latter of whom was severely wounded. There were two others in company with Biggs and Ashley. They encamped together the succeeding night. On the next day, while on their march, they were attacked by a party of Indians who made Colonel Crawford and Doctor Knight prisoners. The other four made their escape, but Captain Biggs and Lieutenant Ashley were killed the next day.

Colonel Crawford and Dr. Knight were immediately taken to an Indian encampment at a short distance from the place where they were captured. Here they found nine fellow prisoners and seventeen Indians. On the next day they were marched to the old Wyandot town, and on the next morning were paraded to set off,

---

[1] John Crawford got home. He died in Adams county, Ohio, in 1816. (Butterfield's History, pages 295-6).

[2] Major John Rose was a native of Russia. His real name was Gustavus H. de Rosenthal, of Livonia, Russia, a baron of the empire. He was not a nephew of Col. Crawford. He was elected secretary of the Council of Censors of Pennsylvania in 1783, but resigned in 1784. He was an aide on the staff of General Irvine, commandant at Fort Pitt. The identity of Rose was never disclosed until 1784, after his return to Russia, when, on Feb. 21, he wrote a letter to Gen. Irvine, to whom he had become greatly attached, stating that he had left his native country because he had killed in a duel within the precincts of the royal palace in St. Petersburg a man whom he had seen strike his aged uncle. Fearful of the Czar's displeasure, not on account of the killing, but because of the violation of the sanctity of the palace, Rose fled to England, and learning there of the war in America he came to this country. Time and absence mitigated his offense. After his return home he was appointed grand marshal of Livonia. He died in 1830.

[3] Dr. John Knight was surgeon of the Seventh Virginia Regiment. Both he and Rose were virtually assigned to service by Gen. Irvine in the command of Col. Crawford. Rose acted as adjutant.—(*Simpson.*)

as they were told, to go to the new town. But alas! a very different destination awaited these captives. Nine of the prisoners were marched off some distance before the colonel and the doctor, who were conducted by Pipe [1] and Wingemond, two Delaware chiefs. Four of the prisoners were tomahawked and scalped on the way at different places.

Preparations had been made for the execution of Colonel Crawford by setting a post about fifteen feet high in the ground, and making a large fire of hickory poles about six yards from it. About half a mile from the place of execution the remaining five of the nine prisoners were tomahawked and scalped by a number of squaws and boys. When arrived at the fire the colonel was stripped and ordered to sit down. He was then severely beaten with sticks and afterwards tied to the post by a rope of such length as to allow him to walk two or three times round it, and then back again. This done, they began the torture by discharging a great number of loads of powder upon him, from head to foot, after which they began to apply the burning ends of the hickory poles, the squaws in the meantime throwing coals and hot ashes on his body, so that in a little time he had nothing but coals to walk on. In the midst of his sufferings he begged of the noted Simon Girty [2] to take pity on him and shoot him. Girty tauntingly answered:

"You see I have no gun, I cannot shoot," and laughed heartily at the scene.

After suffering about three hours he became faint and fell down on his face; an Indian then scalped him, and an old squaw threw a quantity of burning coals on the place from which the scalp was taken. After this he rose and walked round the post a little, but did not live much longer. After he expired his body was thrown into the fire and consumed to ashes. Colonel Crawford's son [3] and son-in-law were executed at the Shawnees' town.

---

[1] Pipe died on the Maumee river in 1794. It is not known when or where Wingemond died.— (*Simpson*).

[2] See Appendix: "Logan, Michael Cresap and Simon Girty."

[3] This statement of the execution of Crawford's son conflicts with Butterfield's statement.

Dr. Knight was doomed to be burned at a town about forty miles distant from Sandusky, and committed to the care of a young Indian to be taken there. The first day they traveled about twenty-five miles, and encamped for the night. In the morning the gnats being very troublesome, the doctor requested the Indian to untie him, that he might help him to make a fire to keep them off. With this request the Indian complied. While the Indian was on his knees and elbows, blowing the fire, the doctor caught up a piece of a tent pole which had been burned in two, about eighteen inches long, with which he struck the Indian on the head with all his might, so as to knock him forward into the fire. The stick however broke, so that the Indian, although severely hurt, was not killed, but immediately sprang up; on this the doctor caught up the Indian's gun to shoot him, but drew back the cock with so much violence that he broke the main spring. The Indian ran off with an hideous yelling. Dr. Knight[1] then made the best of his way home, which he reached in twenty-one days, almost famished to death. The gun being of no use, after carrying it a day or two he left it behind. On his journey he subsisted on roots, a few young birds, and berries.

A Mr. Slover,[2] who had been a prisoner among the Indians and was one of the pilots of the army, was also taken prisoner, to one of the Shawanee towns on the Scioto. After being there a few days, and as he thought in favor of the Indians, a council of the chiefs was held in which it was resolved that Slover should be burned. The fires were kindled and he was blackened and tied to a stake, in an uncovered end of the council house. Just as they were about commencing the torture there came on suddenly a heavy thunder gust with a great fall of rain which put out the fires. After the rain was over the Indians concluded that it was then too late to commence and finish the torture that day, and therefore postponed it till the next day. Slover was then loosed

---

[1] Dr. Knight moved to Shelbyville, Ky., where he died March 12, 1838. (Butterfield's history, page 374.)

[2] John Slover, a wilderness guide, left Fayette county, Pa., and went to Kentucky some years after he got home from this campaign. It is not known when he died.—(*Simpson.*)

from the stake, conducted to an empty house, to a log of which he was fastened with a buffalo tug fastened round his neck, his arms were pinioned behind him with a cord. Until late in the night the Indians sat up smoking and talking. They frequently asked Slover how he would like to eat fire the next day. At length one of them laid down and went to sleep, the other continued smoking and talking with Slover. Sometime after midnight he also laid down and went to sleep. Slover then resolved to make an effort to get loose if possible, and soon extricated one of his hands from the cord and then fell to work with the tug round his neck; but without effect. He had not been long engaged in these efforts before one of the Indians got up and smoked his pipe awhile. During this time Slover kept very still for fear of an examination. The Indian lying down, the prisoner renewed his efforts, but for some time without effect. He resigned himself to his fate. After resting for awhile he resolved to make another and a last effort, and as he related, put his hand to the tug, and without difficulty slipped it over his head. The day was just then breaking. He sprang over a fence into a cornfield, but had proceeded but a little distance in the field before he came across a squaw and several children lying asleep under a mulberry tree. He then changed his course for part of the commons of the town, on which he saw some horses feeding. Passing over the fence from the field he found a piece of an old quilt. This he took with him. It was the only covering he had. He then untied the cord from the other arm, which by this time was very much swelled. Having selected, as he thought, the best horse on the commons, he tied the cord to his lower jaw, mounted him and rode off at full speed. The horse gave out about ten o'clock, so that he had to leave him. He then traveled on foot with a stick in one hand, with which he put up the weeds behind him, for fear of being tracked by the Indians. In the other hand he carried a bunch of bushes to brush the gnats and mosquitoes from his naked body. Being perfectly acquainted with the route he reached the river Ohio in a short time, almost famished with hunger and exhausted with fatigue.

Thus ended this disastrous campaign. It was the last one which took place in this section of the country during the revolutionary contest of the Americans with the mother country. It was undertaken with the very worst of views, those of murder and plunder. It was conducted without sufficient means to encounter, with any prospect of success, the large force of Indians opposed to ours in the plains of Sandusky. It was conducted without that subordination and discipline so requisite to insure success in any hazardous enterprise, and it ended in a total discomfiture. Never did an enterprise more completely fail of attaining its object. Never, on any occasion, had the ferocious savages more ample revenge for the murder of their pacific friends than that which they obtained on this occasion.

Should it be asked what consideration led so great a number of people into this desperate enterprise? Why, with so small a force, and such slender means, they pushed on so far as the plains of Sandusky? The answer is, that many believed that the Moravian Indians, taking no part in the war, and having given offense to the warriors on several occasions, their belligerent friends would not take up arms in their behalf. In this conjecture they were sadly mistaken. They did defend them with all the force at their command, and no wonder, for, notwithstanding their Christian and pacific principles, the warriors still regarded the Moravians as their relations, whom it was their duty to defend.

The reflections which naturally arise out of the history of the Indian war in the western country, during our revolutionary contest with Great Britain, are not calculated to do honor to human nature, even in its civilized state. On our side, indeed, as to our infant government, the case is not so bad. Our congress faithfully endeavored to prevent the Indians from taking part in the war on either side. The English government, on the other hand, made allies of as many of the Indian nations as they could, and they imposed no restraint on their savage mode of warfare. On the contrary the commandants at their posts along our western frontier received and paid the Indians for scalps and prisoners. Thus the skin of a white man's, or even a woman's head served, in the hands of the Indian, as current coin, which he exchanged for arms and ammunition, for the farther prosecution of his barbarous warfare, and clothing to cover his half naked body. Were not these rewards the price of blood? Of blood shed in a cruel manner on an extensive scale; but without advantage to that government which employed the savages in their warfare against their relatives and fellow Christians, and paid for their murders by the piece.

The enlightened historian must view the whole of the Indian war, from the commencement of the revolutionary contest, in no other light than a succession of the most wanton murders of all ages, from helpless infancy to decrepid old age, and of both sexes; without object and without effect.

On our side it is true that the pressure of the war along our Atlantic border was such that our government could not furnish the means for making a conquest of the Indian nations at war against us. The people of the western country, poor as they were at that time, and unaided by government, could not subdue them. Our campaigns, hastily undertaken, without sufficient force and means, and illy executed, resulted in nothing beneficial. On the other hand, the Indians, with the aid their allies could give them in the western country, were not able to make a conquest of the settlements on this side of the mountains. On the contrary our settlements, and the forts belonging to them, became stronger and stronger from year to year during the whole continuance of the wars. It was therefore a war of mutual but unavailing slaughter, devastation and revenge, over whose record humanity still drops a tear of regret, but that tear cannot efface its disgraceful history.

CHAPTER XXXIV.

ATTACK ON RICE'S FORT.

This fort consisted of some cabins and a small block house, and was, in dangerous times, the residence and place of refuge for twelve families of its immediate neighborhood. It was situated on Buffalo creek, about twelve or fifteen miles from its junction with the river Ohio.

Previously to the attack on this fort, which took place in the month of September, 1782, several of the few men belonging to the fort had gone to Hagerstown to exchange their peltry and furs for salt, iron and ammunition, as was the usual custom of those times. They had gone on this journey somewhat earlier that season than usual, because there had been *a still time*. That is no recent alarms of the Indians.

A few days before the attack on this fort about 300 Indians had made their last attack on Wheeling fort. On the third night of the investment of Wheeling the Indian chiefs held a council, in which it was determined that the siege of Wheeling should be raised, two hundred of the warriors return home, and the remaining hundred of picked men make a dash into the country and strike a heavy blow somewhere before their return. It was their determination to take a fort somewhere and massacre all its people, in revenge for their defeat at Wheeling.

News of the plan adopted by the Indians was given by two white men who had been made prisoners when lads, raised among the Indians, and taken to war with them. These men deserted from them soon after their council at the close of the siege of Wheeling.[1] The notice was indeed but short, but it reached Rice's fort about half an hour before the commencement of the attack. The intelligence was brought by Mr. Jacob Miller who received

[1] One of these deserters was Christian Fast, who had been captured in Col. Langheim's expedition in 1781. Fast was from what is now Fayette county, Pa. He died in Orange township, Ashland county, Ohio, in 1849, aged 85 years, leaving nine sons and four daughters.—(*Simpson.*)

it at Dr. Moore's, in the neighborhood of Washington. Making all speed home he fortunately arrived in time to assist in the defense of the place. On receiving this news the people of the fort felt assured that the blow was intended for them and in this conjecture they were not mistaken. But little time was allowed them for preparation. The Indians had surrounded the place before they were discovered; but they were still at some distance. When discovered the alarm was given, on which every man ran to his cabin for his gun and took refuge in the block house. The Indians, answering the alarm with a war whoop from their whole line, commenced firing and running towards the fort from every direction. It was evidently their intention to take the place by assault; but the fire of the Indians was answered by that of six brave and skillful sharpshooters. This unexpected reception prevented the intended assault and made the Indians take refuge behind logs, stumps and trees. The firing continued with little intermission for about four hours. In the intervals of the firing the Indians frequently called out to the people of the fort:

"Give up, give up, too many Indian. Indian too big. No kill."

They were answered with defiance. "Come on you cowards; we are ready for you. Show us your yellow hides and we will make holes in them for you."

During the evening many of the Indians, at some distance from the fort, amused themselves by shooting the horses, cattle, hogs and sheep, until the bottom was strewed with their dead bodies.

About ten o'clock at night the Indians set fire to a barn about thirty yards from the fort. The barn was large and full of grain and hay. The flame was frightful and at first it seemed to endanger the burning of the fort, but the barn stood on lower ground than the fort. The night was calm, with the exception of a slight breeze up the creek. This carried the flame and burning splinters in a different direction, so that the burning of the barn, which at first was regarded as a dangerous if not fatal occurrence, proved in the issue the means of throwing a strong light to a great distance in every direction, so that the Indians durst not approach the fort to set fire to the cabins, which they might have done, at little risk, under the cover of darkness. After the barn was set on fire the Indians collected on the side of the fort opposite the barn, so as to have the advantage of the light, and kept a pretty constant fire, which was as steadily answered by that of the fort, until about two o'clock, when the Indians left the place and made a hasty retreat.

Thus was this little place defended by a Spartan band of six men against one hundred chosen warriors, exasperated to madness by their failure at Wheeling fort. Their names shall be inscribed in the list of the heroes. of our early times. They were Jacob Miller, George Lefler, Peter Fullenweider, Daniel Rice, George Felebaum and Jacob Lefler, jr. George Felebaum was shot in the forehead, through a port hole, at the second fire of the Indians and instantly expired, so that in reality the defense of the place was made by only five men.

The loss of the Indians was four, three of whom were killed at the first fire from the fort, the other was killed about sun down. There can be no doubt but that a number more were killed and wounded in the engagement, but concealed or carried off.

A large division of these Indians on their retreat passed within a little distance of my father's fort. In following their trail, a few days afterwards, I found a large poultice of chewed sassafras leaves. This is the dressing which the Indians usually apply to recent gun shot wounds. The poultice which I found had become too old and dry, was removed and replaced with a new one.

Examples of personal bravery and hair breadth escapes are always acceptable to readers of history. An instance of both of these happened during the attack on this fort, which may be worth recording.

Abraham Rice, one of the principal men belonging to the fort of that name, on hearing the report of the deserters from the Indians mounted a very strong, active mare and rode in all haste to another fort, about three and a half miles from his own, for further news, if any could be had, concerning the presence of a body of Indians in the neighborhood. Just as he reached the place he heard the report of the guns at his own fort. He instantly returned as fast as possible until he arrived within sight of the fort. Finding that it still held out, he determined to reach it and assist in its defense, or perish in the attempt. In doing this, he had to cross the creek, the fort being some distance from it on the opposite bank. He saw no Indians until his mare sprang down the bank of the creek, at which instant about fourteen of them jumped up from among the weeds and bushes and discharged their guns at him. One bullet wounded him in the fleshy part of the right arm above the elbow. By this time several more of the Indians came up and shot at him. A second ball wounded him in the thigh a little above the knee, but without breaking the bone; the ball then passed transversely through the neck of the mare; she however sprang up the bank of the creek, fell to her knees and stumbled along about a rod before she recovered; during this time several Indians came running up to tomahawk him. He made his escape after having about thirty shots fired at him from a very short distance. After riding about four miles he reached Lamb's fort much exhausted with the loss of blood. After getting his wounds dressed and resting a while he set off late in the evening with twelve men, determined if possible to reach the fort under cover of the night. When they got within about two hundred yards of it they halted. The firing at the fort still continued; ten of the men, thinking the enterprise too hazardous, refused to go any farther and retreated. Rice and two other men crept silently along towards the fort, but had not proceeded far before they came close upon an Indian in his concealment. He gave the alarm yell, which was instantly passed round the lines with the utmost regularity. This occasioned the Indians to make their last effort to take the place and make their retreat, under cover of the night. Rice and his two companions returned in safety to Lamb's fort.

About ten o'clock next morning sixty men collected at Rice's fort for the relief of the place. They pursued the Indians who kept in a body for about two miles. The Indians had then divided into small parties and took over the hills in different directions, so that they could be tracked no farther. The pursuit was of course given up.

A small division of the Indians had not proceeded far after their separation before they discovered four men coming from a neighboring fort in the direction of that which they had left. The Indians waylaid the path and shot two of them dead on the spot. The others fled. One of them being swift of foot soon made his escape. The other, being a poor runner, was pursued by an Indian who after a smart chase came close to him. The man then wheeled round and snapped his gun at the Indian. This he repeated several times. The Indian then threw his tomahawk at his head but missed him; he then caught hold of the ends of his belt which was tied behind in a bow knot. In this again the Indian was disappointed, for the knot came loose so that he got the belt but not the man, who wheeled round and tried his gun again. It happened to go off and laid the Indian dead at his feet.

CHAPTER XXXV.

Expected Attack on my Father's Fort.

When we received advice at my father's fort of the attack on Rice's blockhouse, which was but a few miles distant, we sent word to all those families who were out on their farms to come immediately to the fort. It became nearly dark before the two runners had time to give the alarm to the family of a Mr. Charles Stuart who lived about three-quarters of a mile from the fort. They returned in great haste, saying that Stuart's house was burned down, and that they had seen two fires between that and the fort, at which the Indians were encamped. There was, therefore, no doubt that an attack would be made on our fort early in the morning.

In order to give the reader a correct idea of the military tactics of our early times I will give, in detail, the whole progress of the preparations which were made for the expected attack and, as nearly as I can, I will give the commands of Capt. Teter,[1] our officer, in his own words.

In the first place he collected all our men together, and related the battles and skirmishes he had been in, and really they were not few in number. He was in Braddock's defeat, Grant's defeat, the taking of Fort Pitt, and nearly all the battles which took place between the English and the French and the Indians, from Braddock's defeat until the capture of that place by Gen. Forbes. He reminded us, "That in case the Indians should succeed we need expect no mercy, that every man, woman and child would be killed on the spot. They have been defeated at one fort and now they are mad enough. If they should succeed in taking ours all their vengeance will fall on our heads. We must fight for ourselves and one another, and for our wives and children, brothers and sisters. We must make the best preparations we can. A little after day break we shall hear the crack of the guns."

He then made a requisition of all the powder and lead in the fort. The ammunition was accurately divided amongst all the men, and the amount supposed to be fully sufficient. When this was done, "Now," says the captain, "when you run your bullets, cut off the necks very close, and scrape them, so as to make them a little less, and get patches one hundred finer than those you commonly use, and have them well oiled, for if a rifle happens to be choked in the time of battle there is one gun and one man lost for the rest of the battle. You will have no time to unbreach a gun and get a plug to drive out a bullet. Have the locks well oiled, and your flints sharp, so as not to miss fire."

Such were his orders to the men. He then said to the women:

---

[1] See Appendix: "The Teter and Manchester Families."

"These yellow fellows are very handy at setting fire to houses, and water is a very good thing to put out fire. You must fill every vessel with water. Our fort is not well stockaded, and these ugly fellows may rush into the middle of it and attempt to set fire to our cabins in twenty places at once."

They fell to work, and did as he had ordered.

The men having put their rifles in order, "Now," says he, "let every man gather in his axes, mattocks and hoes, and place them inside of his door, for the Indians may make a dash at them with their tomahawks to cut them down, and an axe in that case might hit when a gun would miss fire."

Like a good commander our captain, not content with giving orders, went from house to house to see that everything was right.

The ladies of the present day will suppose that our women were frightened half to death, with the near prospect of such an attack of the Indians; on the contrary, I do not know that I ever saw a merrier set of women in my life. They went on with their work of carrying water and cutting bullet patches for the men apparently without the least emotion of fear, and I have every reason to believe that they would have been pleased with the crack of the guns in the morning.

During all this time we had no sentinels placed around the fort, so confident was our captain that the attack would not be made before day break.

I was at that time thirteen or fourteen years of age, but ranked as a fort soldier. After getting my gun and all things else in order I went up into the garret loft of my father's house, and laid down about the middle of the floor, with my shot pouch on and my gun by my side, expecting to be waked up by the report of the guns at day break, to take my station at the port hole assigned me, which was in the second story of the house. I did not awake till about sun rise, when the alarm was all over. The family which we supposed had been killed had come into the fort about day break. Instead of the house being burnt it was only a large old log on fire, near the house, which had been seen by our expresses. If they had seen anything like fire, between that and the fort, it must have been fox fire. Such is the creative power of imagination when under the influence of fear.

CHAPTER XXXVI.

Coshocton Campaign.

This campaign took place in the summer of 1780, and was directed against the Indian villages at the forks of the Muskingum. The place of rendezvous was Wheeling. The number of regulars and militia about eight hundred. From Wheeling they made a rapid march, by the nearest route, to the place of their destination. When the army reached the river a little below Salem, the lower Moravian town, Colonel Broadhead sent an express to the missionary of that place, the Rev. John Heckewelder, informing him of his arrival in his neighborhood with his army, requesting a small supply of provisions and a visit from him in his camp. When the missionary arrived at the camp the general informed him of the object of the expedition he was engaged in, and enquired of him whether any of the Christian Indians were hunting, or engaged in business, in the direction of his march. On being answered in the negative, he stated that nothing would give him greater pain than to hear that any of the Moravian Indians had been molested by the troops, as these Indians had always, from the commencement of the war, conducted themselves in a manner that did them honor.

A part of the militia had resolved on going up the river to destroy the Moravian villages, but were prevented from executing their project by General Broadhead, and Colonel Shepherd of Wheeling.

At White Eyes' Plain, a few miles from Coshocton, an Indian prisoner was taken. Soon afterwards two more Indians were discovered, one of whom was wounded, but he, as well as the other, made his escape.

The commander, knowing that these two Indians would make the utmost dispatch in going to the town to give notice of the approach of the army, ordered a rapid march, in the midst of a heavy fall of rain, to reach the town before them and take it by surprise. The plan succeeded. The army reached the place in three divisions. The right and left wings approached the river a little above and below the town, while the center marched directly upon it. The whole number of the Indians in the village on the east side of the river, together with ten or twelve from a little village some distance above, were made prisoners without firing a single shot. The river having risen to a great height, owing to the recent fall of rain, the army could not cross it. Owing to this the villages with their inhabitants, on the west side of the river, escaped destruction.

Among the prisoners sixteen warriors were pointed out by Pekillon, a friendly Delaware chief, who was with the army of Broadhead.

A little after dark a council of war was held to determine on the fate of the warriors in custody. They were doomed to death and by the order of the commander they were bound, taken a little distance below the town, and dispatched with tomahawks and spears and scalped.

Early the next morning an Indian presented himself on the opposite bank of the river and asked for the big captain. Broadhead presented himself and asked the Indian what he wanted. To which he replied:

"I want peace."

"Send over some of your chiefs," said Broadhead.

"May be you kill," said the Indian.

He was answered, "They shall not be killed."

One of the chiefs, a well looking man, came over the river and entered into conversation with the commander in the street; but while engaged in conversation a man of the name of Wetzel came up behind him with a tomahawk concealed in the bosom of his hunting shirt and struck him on the back of his head. He fell and instantly expired.

About eleven or twelve o'clock the army commenced its retreat from Coshocton. Gen. Broadhead committed the care of the prisoners to the militia. They were about twenty in number. After marching about half a mile the men commenced killing them. In a short time they were all dispatched, except a few women and children who were spared and taken to Fort Pitt, and after some time exchanged for an equal number of their prisoners.[1]

CHAPTER XXXVII.

Captivity of Mrs. Brown.

On the 27th day of March, 1789, about 10 o'clock in the forenoon, as she was spinning in her house, her black woman who had stepped out to gather sugar water screamed out, "Here are Indians." She jumped up, ran to the window and then to the door, where she was met by one of the Indians presenting his gun. She caught hold of the muzzle and turning it aside begged him not to kill, but take her prisoner. The other Indian in the meantime caught the negro woman and her boy, about four years old, and brought them into the house. They then opened a chest and took out a small box and some articles of clothing, and without doing any further damage, or setting fire to the house, set off with herself and son about two years and a half old, the black woman and her two children, the oldest four years and the youngest one year old. After going about one and a half mile, they halted and held a consultation, as she supposed, about killing

---

[1] The destruction of Coshocton, according to the story related in "Old Westmoreland," resulted from the action of an Indian council there in February, 1781, voting to join the hostile league of savage western tribes against the colonies. The league permitted bands of warriors to go out on bloody raids against the Penna. and Virginia borders. Col. Brodhead determined to attack Coshocton and punish the Delawares for their perfidy. This he did. (See pages 128-9, "Old Westmoreland.") This book does not agree with Doddridge's account of the destruction of Coshocton. It says: "Doddridge's book well describes conditions of pioneer life in Western Pennsylvania, but as to historical events it is totally unreliable. At the time Brodhead destroyed Coshocton, Doddridge was about 12 years old, and he did not write his "Notes" until 40 years afterward. His only sources of information were the exaggerated yarns told by ignorant frontiersmen beside the log cabin fires into the ears of the wondering boy."

the children. This she understood to be the subject by their gestures and frequently pointing at the children. To one of the Indians who could speak English she held out her little boy and begged him not to kill him, as he would make a fine little Indian after a while. The Indian made a motion to her to walk on with her child. The other Indian then struck the negro boy with the pipe end of his tomahawk, which knocked him down, and then dispatched him by a blow with the edge across the back of the neck and then scalped him.

About four o'clock in the evening they reached the river, about a mile above Wellsburg, and carried a canoe, which had been thrown up in some drift wood, into the river. They got into this canoe and worked it down to the mouth of Rush run, a distance of about five miles. They pulled up the canoe into the mouth of the run, as far as they could, then went up the run about a mile and encamped for the night. The Indians gave the prisoners all their own clothes for covering and added one of their own blankets. A while before daylight the Indians got up and put another blanket over them.

About sun rise they began their march up a very steep hill, and about two o'clock halted on Short creek, about twenty miles from the place from whence they had set out in the morning. The place where they halted had been an encampment shortly before, as well as a place of deposit for the plunder which they had recently taken from the house of a Mr. Vanmeter, whose family had been killed. The plunder was deposited in a sycamore tree. They tapped some sugar trees when there before. Here they kindled a fire and put on a brass kettle, with a turkey which they had killed on the way, to boil in sugar water.

Mr. Glass,[1] the first husband of Mrs. Brown, was working with an hired man in a field, about a quarter of a mile from the house, when his wife and family were taken, but knew nothing of the event until two o'clock. After searching about the place and going to several houses in quest of his family, he went to

---

[1] Mrs. Glass, after the death of Mr. Glass, married John Brown. One daughter was born, Jane, who became on March 12, 1811, the wife of Bishop Alexander Campbell, founder of the Disciple church. They were married by Rev. James Hughes, of Lower Buffalo.—(*Simpson.*)

Mr. Wells's fort, and collected ten men besides himself, and the same night lodged in a cabin on the bottom on which the town now stands.

Next morning they discovered the place from which the Indians had taken the canoe from the drift, and their tracks at the place of their embarkation. Mr. Glass could distinguish the track of his wife by the print of the high heel of her shoe. They crossed over the river and went down on the other side until they came to the mouth of Rush run; but discovering no tracks of the Indians most of the men concluded that they would go to the mouth of the Muskingum by water, and therefore wished to turn back. Mr. Glass begged of them to go as far as the mouth of Short creek, which was only two or three miles farther. To this they agreed. When they got to the mouth of Rush run they found the canoe of the Indians. This was identified by a proof which goes to show the presence of mind of Mrs. Brown. While going down the river one of the Indians threw into the water several papers which he had taken out of Mr. Glass's trunk; some of these she picked up out of the water, and under pretense of giving them to the child dropped them into the bottom of the canoe. These left no doubt. The trail of the Indians and their prisoners up the run to their camp, and then up the river hill, was soon discovered. The trail at that time, owing to the softness of the ground and the height of the weeds, was easily followed.

About an hour after the Indians had halted Mr. Glass and his men came within sight of the smoke of their camp. The object then was to save the lives of the prisoners by attacking the Indians so unexpectedly as not to allow them time to kill them. With this view they crept as slily as they could till they got within something more than one hundred yards from the camp. Fortunately Mrs. Brown's little son had gone to a sugar tree to get some water, but not being able to get it out of the bark trough his mother had stepped out of the camp to get it for him. The negro woman was sitting some distance from the two Indians who were looking attentively at a scarlet jacket which they had taken some time before. On a sudden they dropped the jacket and turned their eyes towards the men, who, supposing they were discovered, immediately discharged several guns and rushed up on them at full speed with an Indian yell. One of the Indians, it was supposed, was wounded the first fire, as he fell and dropped his gun and shot pouch. After running about one hundred yards a second shot was fired after him by Maj. M'Guire,[1] which brought him to his hands and knees; but there was no time for pursuit, as the Indians had informed Mrs. Brown that there was another encampment close by. They therefore returned home with all speed, and reached the Beach Bottom fort that night.

The other Indian, at the first fire, ran a little distance beyond Mrs. Brown, so that she was in a right line between him and the white men; here he halted for a little to put on his shot pouch which Mr. Glass, for the moment, mistook for an attempt to kill his wife with a tomahawk. This artful manœuvre, no doubt, saved the life of the savage, as his pursuers durst not shoot at him without risking the life of Mrs. Brown.

CHAPTER XXXVIII.

Escape of Lewis Wetsel.

The following narrative goes to show how much may be effected by the skill, bravery and physical activity of a single individual in the partizan warfare carried on against the Indians on the western frontier.

Lewis Wetsel[1] was the son of John Wetsel, a German, who

[1] Major Francis McGuire died Sept. 18, 1820, aged 66 years, and was buried one-half mile west of Independence, Pa., near Dr. Parkinson's residence. Barbara, his wife, died Dec. 29, 1835, aged 81 years.—(*Simpson.*)

[1] The Wetsel family, John and his five sons, Martin, George, John, Jacob and Lewis, with two daughters, Susan and Christiana, settled in 1772 at the mouth of Wheeling Creek, in the West Virginia panhandle. All the men were hunters and Indian fighters, but Lewis was the most reckless and daring. He made the fighting of Indians a business, not a summer recreation. He died in the summer of 1808, aged 44 years, while visiting Philip Sikes, a relative, 20 miles in the interior from Natchez, Miss. Lewis Wetsel's rifle and pipe belonged, in 1890, to the late Judge G. L. Cranmer, of Wheeling, known as "Wheeling's Historian." On the pipe was inscribed in rude characters, "Lewis Wetsel, 1801."

settled on Big Wheeling, about fourteen miles from the river. He was amongst the first adventurers into that part of the country. His education, like that of his contemporaries, was that of the hunter and warrior. When a boy he adopted the practice of loading and firing his rifle as he ran. This was a means of making him so destructive to the Indians afterwards. When about thirteen years old he was taken prisoner by the Indians, together with his brother Jacob, about eleven years years old. Before he was taken he received a slight wound in the breast from a bullet, which carried off a small piece of his breast bone. The second night after they were taken the Indians encamped at the big lick, twenty miles from the river, on the waters of M'Mahan's creek. The boys were not confined. After the Indians had fallen asleep Lewis whispered to his brother Jacob that he must get up and go back home with him. Jacob at first objected but afterwards got up and went along with him. When they had got about one hundred yards from the camp they sat down on a log.

"Well," said Lewis, "we can't go home barefooted. I will go back and get a pair of moccasins for each of us," and accordingly did so, and returned.

After sitting a little longer, "Now," says he, "I will go back and get father's gun, and then we'll start."

This he effected. They had not traveled far on the trail by which they came before they heard the Indians coming after them. It was a moonlight night. When the Indians came pretty nigh them they stepped aside into the bushes, let them pass, then fell into their rear and traveled on. On the return of the Indians they did the same. They were then pursued by two Indians on horse back, whom they dodged in the same way. The next day they reached Wheeling in safety, crossing from the Indian shore to Wheeling island on a raft of their own making. By this time Lewis had become almost spent from his wound.

In the year 1782, after Crawford's defeat, Lewis went with a Thomas Mills, who had been in the campaign, to get his horse, which he had left near the place where St. Clairsville now stands. At the Indian springs, two miles from St. Clairsville, on the

Wheeling road, they were met by about forty Indians, who were in pursuit of the stragglers from the campaign. The Indians and white men discovered each other about the same moment.

Lewis fired first and killed an Indian; the fire from the Indians wounded Mills in the heel; he was soon overtaken and killed. Four of the Indians then singled out, dropped their guns, and pursued Wetsel. Wetsel loaded his rifle as he ran. After running about half a mile, one of the Indians having got within eight or ten steps of him, Wetsel wheeled round and shot him down, ran and loaded his gun as before. After going about three-quarters of a mile farther a second Indian came so close to him that when he turned to fire the Indian caught the muzzle of his gun, and as he expressed it " He and the Indian had a severe wring." He however succeeded in bringing the muzzle to the Indian's breast and killed him on the spot. By this time he, as well as the Indians, were pretty well tired; the pursuit was continued by the two remaining Indians. Wetsel, as before, loaded his gun and stopped several times during this latter chase; when he did so the Indians tree'd themselves. After going something more than a mile Wetsel took advantage of a little open piece of ground over which the Indians were passing, a short distance behind him, to make a sudden stop for the purpose of shooting the foremost, who got behind a little sapling which was too small to cover his body. Wetsel shot and broke his thigh. The wound, in the issue, proved fatal. The last of the Indians then gave a little yell and said, " No catch dat man, gun always loaded," and gave up the chase, glad, no doubt, to get off with his life.

It is said that Lewis Wetsel, in the course of the Indian wars in this part of the country, killed twenty-seven Indians, besides a number more along the frontier settlements of Kentucky.

CHAPTER XXXIX.

The Struggle of Adam Poe.[1]

In the summer of 1782 a party of seven Wyandots made an incursion into a settlement some distance below Fort Pitt, and several miles from the Ohio river. Here finding an old man alone in a cabin they killed him, packed up what plunder they could find and commenced their retreat. Amongst their party was a celebrated Wyandot chief who, in addition to his fame as a warrior and counsellor, was as to his size and strength a real giant.

The news of the visit of the Indians soon spread through the neighborhood, and a party of eight good riflemen was collected, in a few hours, for the purpose of pursuing the Indians. In this party were two brothers of the names of Adam and Andrew Poe. They were both famous for courage, size and activity. This little party commenced the pursuit of the Indians with a determination, if possible, not to suffer them to escape, as they usually did on such occasions by making a speedy flight to the river, crossing it, and then dividing into small parties, to meet at a distant point, in a given time.

The pursuit was continued the greater part of the night after the Indians had done the mischief. In the morning the party found themselves on the trail of the Indians, which led to the river. When arrived within a little distance of the river Adam Poe, fearing an ambuscade, left the party, who followed

---

[1] This was Andrew Poe's struggle, not Adam's, says McKnight's "Our Western Border," which contains an account of this fight written by Simpson R. Poe, of Ravenna, Ohio. grandson of Andrew. It does not differ materially from the Doddridge story. But Dr. Doddridge got the two Poes mixed. The larger of the two Indians was named Big Foot. Andrew Poe was first of the two brothers to settle west of the mountains, about 1763. Both were natives of Frederick county, Maryland. Andrew was born Sept. 30, 1742, and Adam six years later. After acquiring some means by working in Pittsburgh, Andrew bought a farm on Harmon's Creek, in Washington county, about 12 miles back from the Ohio, where half a dozen years later he was joined by Adam, who also bought a farm there. Adam Poe died Sept. 23, 1838, and was buried three miles north of Massillon, Stark county, Ohio. Andrew Poe died in 1823 and is buried at Mill Creek, Beaver county, Pa.

directly on the trail, to creep along the brink of the river bank, under cover of the weeds and bushes, to fall on the rear of the Indians, should he find them in ambuscade. He had not gone far before he saw the Indian raft at the water's edge. Not seeing any Indians he stepped softly down the bank with his rifle cocked. When about half way down he discovered the large Wyandot chief and a small Indian within a few steps of him. They were standing with their guns cocked, and looking in the direction of our party, who by this time had gone some distance lower down the bottom. Poe took aim at the large chief, but his rifle missed fire. The Indians hearing the snap of the gun lock, instantly turned round and discovered Poe, who, being too near them to retreat, dropped his gun and instantly sprang from the bank upon them, and seizing the large Indian by the cloths on his breast, and at the same time embracing the neck of the small one, threw them both down on the ground, himself being uppermost. The smaller Indian soon extricated himself, ran to the raft, got his tomahawk, and attempted to dispatch Poe, the large Indian holding him fast in his arms with all his might, the better to enable his fellow to effect his purpose. Poe, however, so well watched the motions of the Indian that when in the act of aiming his blow at his head, by a vigorous and well directed kick with one of his feet he staggered the savage and knocked the tomahawk out of his hand. This failure on the part of the small Indian was reproved by an exclamation of contempt from the large one.

In a moment the Indian caught up his tomahawk again, approached more cautiously, brandishing his tomahawk and making a number of feigned blows in defiance and derision. Poe, however, still on his guard, averted the real blow from his head, by throwing up his arm and receiving it on his wrist on which he was severely wounded; but not so as to lose entirely the use of his hand.

In this perilous moment Poe, by a violent effort, broke loose from the Indian, snatched up one of the Indian's guns and shot the small Indian through the breast as he ran up the third time to tomahawk him.

The large Indian was now on his feet, and grasping Poe by a shoulder and leg threw him down on the bank. Poe instantly disengaged himself and got on his feet. The Indian then seized him again and a new struggle ensued, which, owing to the slippery state of the bank, ended in the fall of both combatants into the water. In this situation it was the object of each to drown the other. Their efforts to effect their purpose were continued for some time with alternate success, sometimes one being under the water and sometimes the other. Poe at length seized the tuft of hair on the scalp of the Indian, with which he held his head under the water until he supposed him drowned. Relaxing his hold too soon, Poe instantly found his gigantic antagonist on his feet again, and ready for another combat. In this they were carried into the water beyond their depth. In this situation they were compelled to loose their hold on each other and swim for mutual safety. Both sought the shore to seize a gun and end the contest with bullets. The Indian being the best swimmer reached the land first. Poe, seeing this, immediately turned back into the water to escape, if possible, being shot, by diving. Fortunately the Indian caught up the rifle with which Poe had killed the other warrior.

At this juncture Andrew Poe, missing his brother from the party, and supposing from the report of the gun which he shot, that he was either killed or engaged in conflict with the Indians, hastened to the spot. On seeing him Adam called out to him to "Kill the big Indian on shore." But Andrew's gun, like that of the Indian, was empty. The contest was now between the white man and the Indian, who should load and fire first. Very fortunately for Poe, the Indian, in loading, drew the ramrod from the thimbles of the stock of the gun with so much violence that it slipped out of his hand and fell a little distance from him; he quickly caught it up and rammed down his bullet. This little delay gave Poe the advantage. He shot the Indian as he was raising his gun to take aim at him. As soon as Andrew had shot the Indian he jumped into the river to assist his wounded brother to shore; but Adam, thinking more of the honor of carrying the big Indian's scalp home, as a trophy of victory, than of his own safety, urged Andrew to go back and prevent the struggling savage from rolling himself into the river and escaping. Andrew's solicitude for the life of his brother prevented him from complying with this request.

In the meantime the Indian, jealous of the honor of his scalp, even in the agonies of death, succeeded in reaching the river and getting into the current, so that his body was never obtained.

An unfortunate occurrence took place during this conflict. Just as Andrew arrived at the top of the bank, for the relief of his brother, one of the party who had followed close behind him, seeing Adam in the river and mistaking him for a wounded Indian, shot at him and wounded him in the shoulder. He, however, recovered from his wounds. During the contest between Adam Poe and the Indians the party had overtaken the remaining six of them. A desperate conflict ensued, in which five of the Indians were killed. Our loss was three men killed and Adam Poe severely wounded.

Thus ended this Spartan conflict, with the loss of three valiant men on our part and with that of the whole of the Indian party with the exception of one warrior.[1] Never, on any occasion, was there a greater display of desperate bravery, and seldom did a conflict take place which, in the issue, proved fatal to so great a proportion of those engaged in it.

---

[1] One of the men slain was John Cherry. This fight occurred at the mouth of Tomlinson Run. Seven Wyandots, three of whom were sons of Dunquat, the Wyandot half-king—one of these three being Scotosh—were on a foray south of the Ohio. They took Philip Jackson, while at work in his flax field on Harman's creek, in Washington county. The Indians knew him to be a carpenter, and designed using him to build houses for them. But his capture was seen by his son, who fled nine miles to Fort Cherry, on Little Raccoon creek, and told there what had happened. A rescue party set out next morning. It consisted of John Jack, John Cherry, Adam Poe, Andrew Poe, Wm. Castleman, William Rankin and James Whitacre. They rode in a gallop direct to the mouth of Tomlinson's Run, above which, at the top of the hill, they tied their horses, and descended cautiously to the river bank. At the mouth of the stream were five Indians with their prisoners preparing to cross the Ohio. John Cherry fired the first shot at them, and was himself killed by the return fire. Four of these five Indians were killed, and Jackson was rescued without injury. It was here and at this time that Andrew Poe had his famous encounter in the water with two Indians—two of these seven who at the moment happened to be some distance from the other five. Andrew Poe killed one and his brother Adam the other. Scotosh was the only one of the seven Indians who escaped. "John Cherry was," says Hassler's "Old Westmoreland," "a man of great popularity, and a natural leader on the frontier." "His body was carried home on a horse and buried in the old Cherry graveyard in Mt. Pleasant township," says Simpson.

The fatal issue of this little campaign, on the side of the Indians, occasioned an universal mourning among the Wyandot nation. The big Indian, with his four brothers, all of whom were killed at the same place, were amongst the most distinguished chiefs and warriors of their nation. The big Indian was magnanimous as well as brave. He, more than any other individual, contributed by his example and influence to the good character of the Wyandots for lenity towards their prisoners. He would not suffer them to be killed or ill treated. This mercy to captives was an honorable distinction in the character of the Wyandots, and was well understood by our first settlers, who, in case of captivity, thought it a fortunate circumstance to fall into their hands.

It is consoling to the historian to find instances of those endowments of mind which constitute human greatness even among savages. Their original stamina of those endowments, or what it called *genius,* are but thinly scattered over the earth, and there can be but little doubt that the lower grades of society possess their equal proportion of the basis of moral greatness; or, in other words, there is as much of *native genius,* in proportion to numbers, among savages, as there is among civilized people. The difference between these two extremes of society is merely the difference of education. This view of human nature, philosophically correct, is well calculated to increase the benevolence, even of the good Samaritan himself, and encourage his endeavors for the instruction of the most ignorant and the reformation of the most barbarous.

Had the aborigines of our country been possessed of science to enable them to commit to the faithful page of history the events of their intercourse with us, since the discovery and settlement of their native land by the Europeans, what would be the contents of this history? Not such as it is from the hands of our historians, who have presented nought but the worst features of the Indian character, as exhibited in the course of their wars against the invaders of their country, while the wrongs inflicted on them by civilized men have occupied but a very small portion of the record. Their sufferings, their private virtues, their bravery and magnanimity in war, all individual instances of greatness of mind, heroism, and clemency to captives, in the midst of the cruelties of their barbarous warfare, must soon be buried with themselves in the tomb of their national existence.

CHAPTER XL.

The Affair of the Johnsons.

The following narrative goes to show that the long continuance of the Indian war had inspired even the young lads of our country not only with all the bravery but even the subtlety of the Indians themselves.

In the fall of the year 1793 two boys of the name of John and Henry Johnson, the first thirteen and latter eleven years old, whose parents lived in Carpenter's station, a little distance above the mouth of Short creek, on the west side of the Ohio river, were sent out in the evening to hunt the cows. At the foot of the river hill, at the back of the bottom, they sat down under a hickory tree to crack nuts. After some time they saw two men coming towards them, one of whom had a bridle in his hand; being dressed like white men they mistook them for their father and an uncle in search of horses. When they discovered their mistake and attempted to run off the Indians, pointing their guns at them, told them to stop or they would kill them. They halted and were taken prisoners.

The Indians, being in pursuit of horses, conducted the boys by a circuitous route over the Short creek hills in search of them, until, late in the evening, they halted at a spring in a hollow place about three miles from the fort. Here they kindled a small fire, cooked and ate some victuals, and prepared to repose for the night.

Henry, the oldest of the boys, during the ramble had affected the greatest satisfaction at having been taken prisoner. He said his father was a hard master, who kept him always at hard work, and allowed him no play; but that for his part he wished to live in the woods and be a hunter. This deportment soon brought him into intimacy with one of the Indians, who could speak very good English. The Indian frequently asked the boys if they knew of any good horses running in the woods. Sometime before they halted one of the Indians gave the largest of the boys a little bag, which he supposed contained money, and made him carry it.

When night came on the fire was covered up, the boys pinioned and made to lay down together. The Indians then placed their hoppis straps[1] over them, and laid down, one on each side of them, on the ends of the straps.

Pretty late in the night the Indians fell asleep, and one of them becoming cold caught hold of John in his arms and turned him over on the outside. In this situation the boy, who had kept awake, found means to get his hands loose; he then whispered to his brother, made him get up, and untied his arms. This done, Henry thought of nothing but running off as fast as possible; but when about to start John caught hold of him, saying:

"We must kill these Indians before we go."

After some hesitation Henry agreed to make the attempt. John then took one of the rifles of the Indians and placed it on a log with the muzzle close to the head of one of them. He then cocked the gun and placed his little brother at the breach with his finger on the trigger, with instructions to pull it as soon as he should strike the other Indian. He then took one of the Indian's tomahawks and standing a-straddle of the other Indian struck him with it. The blow, however, fell on the back of the neck and to one side, so as not to be fatal. The Indian then attempted to spring up; but the little fellow repeated his blows with such force and rapidity on the skull that as he expressed it:

"The Indian laid still and began to quiver."

---

[1] A hoppis-strap was probably the tump-line strap, or burden band, carried by all Indian hunters and travelers in the early days. It was both used to carry burdens and fasten prisoners. Some think it the equivalent of bobble-strap, as which it may have been used as necessity required. Straps of any kind serve many purposes.

At the moment of the first stroke given by the elder brother with the tomahawk the younger one pulled the trigger and shot away a considerable portion of the Indian's lower jaw. This Indian, a moment after receiving the shot, began to flounce about and yell in the most frightful manner. The boys then made the best of their way to the fort and reached it a little before day break. On getting near the fort they found the people all up and in great agitation on their account. On hearing a woman exclaim, "Poor little fellows, they are killed, or taken prisoners," the oldest one answered, "No! mother, we are here yet."

Having brought nothing away with them from the Indian Camp, their relation of what had taken place between them and the Indians was not fully credited. A small party was soon made up to go and ascertain the truth or falsehood of their report. This party the boys conducted to the spot by the shortest route. On arriving at the place they found the Indian whom the eldest brother had tomahawked lying dead in the camp. The other had crawled away and taken his gun and shot pouch with him. After scalping the Indian the party returned to the fort, and the same day a larger party went out to look after the wounded Indian, who had crawled some distance from the camp and concealed himself in the top of a fallen tree, where, notwithstanding the severity of his wound, with a Spartan bravery he determined to sell his life as dearly as possible, and having fixed his gun for the purpose, on the approach of the men to a proper distance, he took aim at one of them and pulled the trigger, but his gun missed fire. On hearing the snap of the lock one of the men exclaimed:

"I should not like to be killed by a dead Indian."

The party concluding that the Indian would die at any rate thought best to retreat and return and look for him after some time. On returning, however, he could not be found, having crawled away and concealed himself in some other place. His skeleton and gun were found some time afterwards.

The Indians who were killed were great warriors and very wealthy. The bag which was supposed to contain money it was conjectured was got by one of the party who went out first in the morning. On hearing the report of the boys he slipped off by himself and reached the place before the party arrived. For some time afterwards he appeared to have a greater plenty of money than his neighbors.

The Indians themselves did honor to the bravery of these two boys. After their treaty with Gen. Wayne, a friend of the Indians who were killed made inquiry of a man from Short creek what had become of the boys who killed the Indians? He was answered that they lived at the same place with their parents. The Indian replied, "You have not done right. You should make kings of those boys."

APPENDIX

APPENDIX.

MEMOIR OF THE REV. DR. JOSEPH DODDRIDGE.

By NARCISSA DODDRIDGE.[1]

The author of " Doddridge's Notes," the Rev. Dr. Joseph Doddridge, was the eldest son of John Doddridge of Maryland, of English descent, and of Mary, daughter of Col. Richard Wells, of the same state. He was born Oct. 14, 1769, in Friend's Cove, a valley situated a few miles south of the town of Bedford, in Bedford county, Pennsylvania. His father hav-

---

[1] Miss Narcissa Doddridge, author of this memoir, died in January, 1874, two years prior to publication of the second edition of these " Notes."

NARCISSA DODDRIDGE.

She was the eldest daughter of John and Mary Wells Doddridge, and was born at Wellsburg, Brooke Co., Virginia, April 7th, 1796.

She is remembered as a woman of superior intellect and strength of character, with a quiet, thoughtful nature. She looked upon life seriously, even as a child. Never marrying, she gave her life to the service of humanity, particularly to her family and those nearest her. The beauty of her generous personality made a lasting impression upon all who knew her.

Virginia in the beginning of the nineteenth century demanded much of its women, many of whose names have been recorded in history. Narcissa Doddridge realized the needs of the times, and exerted her efforts to make life more worth living in the colony of new settlers in the new world. The pioneers of that period had limited means of support, and required assistance and direction from those of wider experience in the unknown country. This noble woman seemed to grasp the situation by reason of her large vision, and although never aggressive, or self assertive, she radiated a memorable influence for good in the community in which she lived.

Dr. Doddridge and his daughter were closely united in affection. In his declining years she devoted herself to care of him with the utmost tenderness and loyalty. She inherited marked literary ability and fine personal characteristics from her distinguished father.

Her years passed in the fulfillment of opportunities at hand while her varied talents and ambitions lay dormant under the exactions of domestic routine. Her friends were well aware that she was fitted for position in a wider social circle and a higher sphere of life, and those who had the privilege of intimacy regarded her as a woman of unusual gifts and at the same time a friend gracious and loyal, with warm affections. She was interested in the progress of her age, and the cause of temperance had in her an ardent advocate, who never neglected an opportunity in its behalf. Her valued work in this direction can only be alluded to here, while her name deserves to be spoken reverently by all who labor in and sympathize with this great service for mankind.

In later years Miss Doddridge resided in Wellsburg, Virginia, in the old homestead that her father had bequeathed to her. After a long illness, she died, January 30th, 1874, and was buried beside her father in the Brooke Cemetery.

ing lost his estate in Bedford county, by neglecting to complete his title to a settlement right, in the spring of 1773 removed to the western part of Washington county, Pennsylvania, settling a short distance east of the line which divides that state from Virginia.[1]

Thus in the fourth year of his age the subject of this memoir became a resident of the western country, then an immense wilderness, and the greater part of it in the possession of its native inhabitants, the Indians. The opportunities afforded by his early and continued association with the pioneer settlers, assisted by a habit of close observation, a tenacious memory, and the interest he took in gathering up incidents indicative of the times and illustrative of the character of those among whom he lived, preeminently qualified him for giving an impartial and correct description of the country at its first settlement, as well as a truthful account of the manners, customs and wars of those who with himself labored to transform into fruitfulness and beauty its interminable forests.

From the picture which he has presented of the society in which he was reared we may justly conclude that his facilities for obtaining an education were very limited, and that to his own energy and perseverance he was mainly indebted for whatever intellectual culture he possessed. His views of life, its purposes and its duties, were just and liberal, drawn as they were from the Bible, general experience and observation. Regarding man as accountable to his creator for the due improvement and practical exercise of the talents committed to him, he endeavored by a life of active usefulness and uniform Christian effort to discharge his obligations to God and his fellow men.

Leaving his mother before he was eight years of age, his father sent him to Maryland to school, where he remained some years. After his return, until he attained the age of eighteen years, he was mostly occupied in labors on the farm. His father, a strict disciplinarian in the training and govern-

[1] See "The Doddridge Family," elsewhere.

ment of his family, was a member of the Wesleyan Methodist society, then in its infancy, and differing but little in its doctrines and public ritual from the Church of England, to which he had been attached in his native state. He was a man of intelligence and remarkable for firmness and decision of character, qualities which, as they were always exerted in favor of morality and religion, rendered his influence in the neighborhood in which he resided decidedly healthful and salutary. Shortly after identifying himself with the settlers in Washington county, he erected on his own premises a house for public worship, designed also for educational purposes. This memento of his piety and the interest he took in the moral and intellectual improvement of those around him is yet standing, though in a dilapidated condition, still retaining its original cognomen, Doddridge's Chapel. [1]

All the children of Mr. Doddridge's first marriage, viz: Joseph, Philip, Ann and Ruth, were at an early day brought under the influence of religious truth, and became members of the adopted church of their father. Joseph, the subject of this notice, according to the reminiscences furnished the writer by the Hon. Thomas Scott, late of Chillicothe, Ohio, labored several years as an itinerant in the Wesleyan Society. Mr. Scott, who was at the period referred to a traveling preacher of the Methodist church, says:

" My acquaintance with the Rev. J. Doddridge commenced at the house of Rev. John J. Jacob in Hampshire county, Va., in July, 1788. He was then in company with Rev. Francis Asbury by whom he was held in high esteem. At a conference held at Uniontown, Pa., a short time previous, he had been received as a traveling preacher in the Wesleyan connection, was then on his way to the Holston circuit, and subsequently labored on the West River and Pittsburg circuits."

---

[1] The date of construction of this chapel is unknown. It passed finally into possession of the Methodist Episcopal denomination, and was by them used for holding services. Later the African Methodist Episcopals used it. Then it was taken down and the logs removed to the adjoining McConnell farm. The burial ground adjoining the site of this old meeting house is still enclosed, but there have been no interments in it for many years.—(*Crumrine.*)

At the request of the Rev. Mr. Asbury he studied the German language with a view to preaching in German settlements. His knowledge of this language, which was thorough, he found very useful to him in after life. In April, 1791, he was recalled from his field of labor to attend the death bed of his father, who had previously appointed him executor of his estate.[1] The duties thus devolving upon him, together with the unprotected situation of his step-mother and the younger members of the family, which required his personal supervision, rendered it necessary for him to relinquish his duties as an itinerant preacher of the Methodist church, which, as his subsequent history will show, were never again resumed.

After arranging the business entrusted to him by his deceased father, finding some available means at his disposal, he resolved to qualify himself more thoroughly for the responsible calling which he had chosen, by devoting a portion of time to the acquisition of learning, more particularly to perfecting himself in a knowledge of languages; his education thus far having been prosecuted under disadvantageous circumstances. Accordingly he entered Jefferson Academy at Canonsburg, Pa. His brother Philip, who had been from childhood associated with him in efforts to acquire knowledge, both laboring by day in field or forest, and at night poring over books at the family hearth stone, became a student in the academy at the same time. Philip, who subsequently became very eminent as a jurist and a statesman, died in 1832 at Washington, D. C., while he was a member of congress.

The following extract from a letter written by a Presbyterian clergyman, the Rev. Robert Patterson,[2] late of Pittsburgh, shows the estimation in which the brothers were held in the institution at Canonsburg.

---

[1] The will of his father, John Doddridge, dated May 14, 1791, is witnessed by Josiah Reeves, Philip Doddridge, and David (X, his mark) Harriman.—(*Simpson.*)

[2] Rev. Robert Patterson lived when a boy where William Dunlap now lives in Cross Creek township. He was a son of Rev. Joseph Patterson. He died in 1854, aged 81 years.

Green Tree P. O., near Pittsburg, June, 1850.

It affords me pleasure to comply with your request respecting my early acquaintance with the Rev. Dr. Doddridge for whose memory I cherish the most profound regard. From 1791 until 1794 I was a student in Jefferson academy. During a portion of this time Dr. Doddridge was there. We were room mates, boarding in the family of Rev. Mr. Mercer. David Johnson, the principal, and the students generally, as is usual in literary institutions, soon determined the grade of his intellect, his moral character and his personal worth; and none, during my connection with the academy, stood higher than he in the estimation of those who knew him. Being his senior in years and science it was sometimes my privilege to give him explanations and help him through knotty passages in his lessons, in doing which I soon discovered that it was not necessary to tell him the same thing twice, so retentive and comprehensive was his mind. His brother Philip was a student with him at the same time. Both of them were remarkable for original genius, intellectual strength, and close investigation of any subject that came before them. These qualities, combined with ingenuous, amiable dispositions and uprightness of deportment, endeared them to all who had the pleasure of knowing them.

It was probably about this time that the subject of this memoir resolved to take orders in the Protestant Episcopal church. This determination was not, we presume, the result of any diminution of his regard for the society with which he had been previously connected; for through life he manifested a warm attachment to that people, treated their ministers with the greatest courtesy and hospitality, and was ever ready to testify to their zealous and self-denying labors in the cause of their Lord and Master. In the absence of any direct information as to the cause of his withdrawal we have grounds to conclude that as his mind became more matured, and his reading more extended, his confidence in the Episcopacy of that body was lessened. We are, furthermore, well assured that his judgment and preferences were decidedly in favor of a precomposed ritual of public worship. The labors subsequently performed by Dr. Doddridge as a member of the Episcopal church were so extensive and valuable, and his devotion to that church so zealous, that we consider it proper to give our readers all the information upon the subject now attainable.

We therefore, in connection with this subject, give his views on these points as expressed in a letter written in 1822 to the Rev. John Waterman, a talented and highly respectable clergyman of the Methodist church. The letter was written in reply to one from Mr. Waterman, inviting him to attend a camp-meeting shortly to be held in the neighborhood of one of his parishes, and hinting that if he did not do so he should conclude that he was deterred from so doing by the fear of offending a clerical brother who was supposed to hold extreme views on the subject of the apostolic succession of the bishops.

DEAR BROTHER: Your letter inviting me to attend your camp-meeting is before me. I should be pleased to meet with you one day at least. But even this is uncertain. You live by the altar, I do not. I must depend on my medical profession for a support. You are aware that the time of a physician is not at his own disposal. * * * * * I certainly would not do anything that would bring me into collision with a clerical brother, but not from a feeling of fear. I value consistency of character. * * * * * The first Christian service I ever heard was that of the Church of England in Maryland.

When I was a minister in your society a prayer book was put into my hands with an order to use it every Sunday, Wednesday, Friday and Holyday; also on baptismal and sacramental occasions, which I did. So I may say, that in the main the forms of worship I now use have been those of my whole life, and I think I shall end as I began. If you have left the venerable church of your ancestors, and built an Episcopacy on the priesthood; if you have laid aside the prayer-book, and become presbyterial in your forms of worship, the faults, if any, are not mine. I am truly sorry that these events have happened. Glad should I be if we were still one people.

As to the apostolic succession of the bishops, to which you refer, it is a subject to which I have not devoted much attention, and probably never shall. The subject for reasons which I have mentioned to you is not agreeable to me; yet I respect the claim and feel satisfied that my ordination has descended through so valid and respectable a channel. From this claim, however, I will not conclude against the efficacy of the ministry in other hands. It is enough for me to know and feel that other societies are Christian too. Therefore. I will not curse whom God hath not cursed; and I am willing to join in worship with them, so far as I can do so consistently with the duties which I owe to the church of which I am a member. * * * *

* * * *

In March, 1792, being then a resident of Pennsylvania, Dr. Doddridge was admitted to the order of deacons in the Episcopal church, in Philadelphia, by the Right Rev. Bishop White. By the same prelate and in the same city he was in March, 1800, ordained a priest, having in the interval between his ordinations removed to Virginia. His reasons for preferring at this time to continue under the jurisdiction of Bishop White are thus given in a letter to Bishop Moore of Virginia in 1819.

When I received deacon's orders I lived in Pennsylvania, but previous to being admitted to the priesthood, I removed to Virginia. I stated the circumstance to Bishop White, at the time, urging that the residence of the bishop of Virginia was so far from my own that I could not hold the requisite correspondence with him without great inconvenience, and also that from what I had learned concerning our church in that state, I did not think that my uniting with its convention would be in any way satisfactory to myself, or beneficial to others; the church in Virginia having at that period little more than a nominal existence. Therefore I preferred remaining in fact, though not canonically, under his jurisdiction. The bishop was satisfied with my reasons and accordingly all my communications have been made to him.

To the doctrines and formularies of the Protestant Episcopal church Dr. Doddridge was devotedly attached, regarding them as promotive of piety and edification. And, although for nearly twenty-five years he occupied the cheerless position of an advance guard in her ministry, yet he faltered not in his labors. The convention which organized the diocese of Ohio was held at Columbus in 1818. For twenty years prior to that date Dr. Doddridge had been preaching frequently at various places in Eastern Ohio, and there formed a number of congregations which afterwards became members of the diocese of Ohio.

EARLY CHURCHES IN NORTH WESTERN VIRGINIA AND OHIO.

We shall now give a brief notice of the congregations formed by Dr. Doddridge during the early years of his ministry in the Episcopal church, and our authority for the same. We do not find among his papers any indicating that he entered into written agreements with his parishioners to perform clerical duties continuously from the year 1800. He attended to such duties continuously from the year 1792, but probably, prior to 1800, all his receipts were from voluntary contributions, which we may conclude did not amount to much, from the fact that a few years after his entrance into the ministry he was under the necessity of combining with his clerical profession that of medicine in order to obtain a support.

His lovely and amiable wife, when speaking of this early period of her married life, would playfully say that before her husband commenced the practice of medicine he was too poor to buy himself a second suit of clothes, and when Saturday afternoon intervened he was obliged to remain incognito while she adjusted his habiliments for his appearance in the pulpit on Sunday. The labor of the laundress as well as the skill of the seamstress were frequently called into requisition on these occasions, knee breeches and long stockings being then in vogue.

Dr. Doddridge's subscription papers for the year 1800, and for some years thereafter, show that in his country parishes the remuneration promised him for clerical services was to be paid in cash, or wheat delivered in some merchant mill, or such other produce as might be agreed upon by the parties.

In Virginia he seems to have found many who desired to walk in the "old paths" by worshipping God in the way of their fathers. As a matter of interest to their descendants, we shall give the names of the supporters of the church in several of these parishes built up in the wilderness, as they stand in the subscription book of their pastor for the year 1800. From these lists may be gleaned some knowledge of the number of their descendants who still adhere to the faith of their forefathers. They will also show that the number of those in the western regions who felt a decided preference for the Episcopal church at that early day was by no means small.

In the notes furnished the writer by Judge Scott he says: "In the year 1793 Rev. J. Doddridge had three parishes in Virginia, viz: West Liberty in Ohio county, St. John's and St. Paul's in Brooke county."

St. John's Church.

St. John's parish, which is still in existence, was doubtless the first one organized by Dr. Doddridge in North Western Virginia. As early as 1793 it was provided with a small log church, since replaced by a handsome brick edifice. This parish continued under the charge of its first pastor for nearly thirty years, when declining health compelled him to sever a relation around which clustered many endearing and fondly cherished associations of his youthful and maturer years.

The names of subscribers in this parish in the year 1800, are as follows:

George Atkinson,
Absalom Wells,
Archibald Ellson,
John Davis,
Charles M'Key,
Charles Elliot,
William Atkinson,
John Strong,
George Swearengen,
William Davis,
Richard Wells,
Asel Owings,
Andrew Maneally,
Thomas Nicholson,
John Myers,
John Foster,
Abel Johnson,
William Baxter,
James White,
George Wells,
George Mahon,
Simon Elliot jun.,
Simon Elliot,
Daniel Swearengen,
Anthony Wilcoxen,
Andrew Morehead,
Alex. Morrow,
George Elliot,
William Lowther,
William Adams,
James Britt,
John Crawford,
John Ellson,
Peter Hay,
George Richardson,
Andrew Lackey,
Hugh Lingen,
John Hendricks,
Richard T. Ellson,
Israel Swearengen,
Richard Ellson, "
Thomas Crawford,
Jane Morrow.

Church at West Liberty.

In the summer of 1792 Dr. Doddridge collected a congregation at West Liberty, the seat of justice for Ohio county, Va. Hon. T. Scott says in his reminiscences of Dr. Doddridge that in this place Episcopal services were held in the Court House. This parish was much weakened by the removal of many of its members to Wheeling when the county seat was removed to that place. Dr. Doddridge, however, still held services in West Liberty every third Sunday in the year 1800. The supporters of the church in that year were:

Moses Chapline,	Nathan Harding,	Isaac Taylor,
Benjamin Biggs,	Charles Tibergein,	Thomas Beck,
Andrew Fout,	Ebzy Swearengen,	Thomas Wyman,
Silas Hedges,	William Griffith,	Stephen G. Francis,
John Wilson,	Christian Foster,	William Dement,
Walter Skinner,	Lyman Fouts,	Zaccheus Biggs,
Abraham Roland,	Ticy Cooper,	Benijah Dement,
Thomas Dickerson,	James Wilson,	William Cully,
John Cully,	Jacob Zoll,	George G. Dement,
Nicholas Rogers,	John Abrams,	John Willius, sen.,
Samuel Beck,	John Kirk,	William Willius.
	Amount subscribed $98.	

West Liberty, like many other places in the western country in the early part of the present century, presented a fine opening for Episcopal missionary labor, in the absence of which the field has been successfully cultivated by others, and at the present period there is probably not an Episcopalian in the place. It may not be amiss in this connection to call attention to the fact that the ritual of the Episcopal church was exceedingly popular among the rude pioneers of the west. The book of Common Prayer has always been found suited to all classes and conditions of mankind.

St. Paul's Church in Brooke County, Va.

We have no means of positively ascertaining when this primitive structure was erected. We presume, however, that it was prior to 1793, as Judge Scott in his reminiscences speaks of it as one of the churches of which Dr. Doddridge had charge in that year. It was located about five miles east of Charleston and the Ohio river. The building was of logs, and surrounded by noble forest trees, amid which in subsequent years might be seen the "narrow houses" of many of those who had worshipped within its walls. The list of names in this parish for the year 1800 is small, containing only the following:

Aaron Robinson,	William Hendling,	James Robinson,
Israel Robinson,	John Harris,	Peter Mooney.
Peter Ross,	Benedict Wells,	

At a later period St. Paul's was principally sustained by the late George Hammond, Esq., and some of his relatives and friends, among whom we find the names of Gist, Hood, Crawford, Wells and others.

Church in Steubenville, Ohio.

To David Moody, one of the early settlers of Steubenville, the writer is indebted for the following items of information respecting the introduction of the Episcopal church in that place. He says: "The Rev. Dr. Doddridge was the first Christian minister who preached in our little village. As early as 1796 he held monthly services in it, his congregation meeting in a frame building which stood on the south side of Market and Water streets. In 1798 the first court house for the county was built, in which an upper room was reserved for religious purposes, free to all denominations. In this room the Episcopalians met for worship. With some intervals this early missionary of the church continued to officiate in Steubenville until Dr. Moore took charge of the parish in 1820."

Trinity Church at Charlestown, now Wellsburg.

At Charlestown, now Wellsburg, Brooke co., Va., the residence of Rev. J. Doddridge, Episcopal services in 1800 were held in Brooke Academy. This town was at an early period of its settlement a stopping place for immigrants from beyond the Alleghenies, some of whom became permanent citizens. From the number of names attached to the subscription paper of Dr. Doddridge for the year 1800 it is inferred that the congregation was then large. There is now a neat church edifice in the place, and notwithstanding numerous removals a few families remain who are warmly attached to the church. The subscribers for 1800 were as follows:

Philip Doddridge,	A. Green,	Oliver Brown,
Nicholas P. Tillinghast,	John T. Windsor,	Sebastian Derr,
Patience Vilettle,	Alex. Caldwell,	Josias Reeves,
Elizabeth Taylor,	Robt. T. Moore,	James Darrow,
Silas Bent,	James H. White,	William Thorp,
John Connel,	Robt. H. Johnson,	Henry Prather,
Thomas Hinds,	Charles Prather,	James Clark,
Wm. McConnell,	Nicholas Murray,	John Fling,
John Bly,	Samuel Talman,	Thomas Oram.

In December, 1800, Dr. Doddridge entered into an agreement with a number of individuals living west of the Ohio, to perform the duties of an Episcopal clergyman every third Saturday at the house of the widow McGuire. The subscription book, which is dated December 1, 1800, contains the following names:

George Mahan,	Benj. Doyle,	William McConnell,
William Whitcraft,	Joseph Williams,	John Scott,
Eli Kelly,	John Long,	George Ritchey,
George Halliwell,	Mary McGuire,	Moses Hanlon.
William McColnall,	John McKnight,	
John McConnell,	Frederick Allbright,	

The little congregation was, we conclude, the germ of the present parish of St. James on Cross creek, Jefferson co., Ohio, as among the above names we find four of those attached to the petition signed by that parish on the 1st of Dec., 1816, to be sent to the general convention in 1817, asking leave of that body to form a diocese in the western country. These names are George Mahan, Wm. McConnell, John McConnell and Benj. Doyle.

We are not acquainted with the gradations by which the congregation at the widow McGuire's expanded into the parish of St. James, nor how long services were held at her house; but from the pastor's papers we find that from 1814 until his resignation in 1823, he remained rector of the parish of St. James, the Rev. Intrepid Morse then assuming charge of it in connection with that of St. Paul's at Steubenville. That the services of Dr. Doddridge were efficient at St. James's church is shown by the fact that when the diocese of Ohio was organized in 1818 he reported fifty-two communicants, and over one hundred baptisms within two years.

At Wheeling, Grave Creek, and some other points, were many families from Maryland and Eastern Virginia, who having been brought up in the Church of England, now in their wilderness homes longed to unite in prayer and praise to God in the language of her incomparable liturgy. These people Dr. Doddridge visited as often as his other engagements would permit, not unfrequently holding service in the open air, the stately forest trees being their only surroundings and shelter from sun and shower.

> "Ah, why
> Should we, in the world's riper years, neglect
> God's ancient sanctuaries, and adore
> Only among the crowd, and under roofs
> That our frail hands have raised?"

From several records before us it appears that the few Episcopal clergymen in the west at an early period continued for many years to keep up a church organization, and intimate relations among their people and with each other. These meetings were probably appointed for prayer, consultation and the mutual edification of ministers and people, and seem to have been held semi-annually. The secretary designates them as conventions.

* * * * *

A similar memorandum states that at a meeting of the Protestant Episcopal clergy held in St. Thomas's Church in Washington country in 1810 it was resolved, That Rev. Dr. Doddridge do open a correspondence with the Rt. Rev. Bishop White of Philadelphia for the purpose of obtaining through him permission from the general convention to form a diocese in the western country. From another source we learn that the object of the memorialists at this time was to unite the western counties of Pennsylvania, Western Virginia and the state of Ohio in one diocese.

Dr. Doddridge was an indefatigable laborer and while buoyed up by the hope that his efforts for promoting the interests of the Episcopal church in the western country would be seconded by the zeal and ministrations of missionary brethren from beyond the Alleghenies, he exerted himself to visit and cheer desponding members of the same faith at widely distant points. But alas! they were doomed to bitter disappointment. Their appeals were vain. No missionaries came, and those who ardently desired for themselves and families the formula of the church to which they had been attached in earlier days and more favored localities, were compelled to join other communions or live and die without the ordinances of the gospel.

After his removal to Virginia in 1800 Dr. Doddridge extended his missionary operations into the north western territory. His reasons for so doing are thus given in a letter to the bishop of Virginia.

With a view to the attainment of an Episcopacy in this country as early as possible, my clerical labors have of late years been mostly in the state of Ohio, conceiving that that object would be more speedily accomplished by forming congregations in a state in which there was no bishop, than by doing the same thing in the western parts of Pennsylvania and Virginia in each of which states there is a diocesan.

St. Thomas's church in St. Clairsville, Belmont county, Ohio, was brought into existence in 1813 by the removal of some of Dr. Doddridge's former parishioners to that place, to whom he made occasional visits. Some years later, however, he held monthly services there, and also at Morristown, ten miles distant, where he had organized a congregation. The parish of St. Thomas was represented in the first annual convention of the diocese of Ohio by John Carter as a lay delegate. In the same convention St. Peter's church at Morristown was represented by Walter Thrall as a lay delegate. About the same period Dr. Doddridge began preaching at Zanesville, Ohio, and soon organized a parish there of which he was rector in 1818. This parish was represented in the first convention by John Matthews as lay delegate. Ten churches were represented in the first annual convention of the diocese of Ohio, of which four had been organized by the missionary labors of Dr. Doddridge, and this while he had charge of several parishes in Virginia, and was extensively engaged in the practice of medicine.

In many of the places which he visited in his various missionary excursions he left the nucleus of congregations which, for the want of subsequent spiritual nurture, never expanded into active life. If a proper supply of missionaries could have been had, there might now be ten Episcopal churches in Ohio where there is one. As a minister of the cross Dr. Doddridge was untiring in his exertions, his services on such occasions generally averaging two per day and often more.

Dr. Doddridge's correspondence with his clerical brethren was extensive, and we regret that our limits will admit of but a small portion of it. We select from numerous others a letter to Bishop White, as possessing special historical interest, inasmuch as it gives a synopsis of the religious aspect of the country, his reasons for desiring an Episcopal organization, at an early period of its settlement, and his efforts to effect that object.

This letter is dated Wellsburg, Dec. 14, 1818. It expresses grief over the decision of Bishop White and the standing committee that no missionaries could be sent to the west, but admits dissipation of uneasiness over the prospect of failure to obtain an episcopacy in the west. Then Dr. Doddridge proceeds to frankly explain to the bishop the religious state of the western country, and to set forth the laxity of the Episcopal authorities in missionary work, saying:

To the Presbyterians alone we are indebted for almost the whole of our literature. They began their labors at an early period of the settlement of the country, and have extended their ecclesiastical and educational establishments so as to keep pace with the extension of our population; with a Godly care which does them honor.

Were it not for the herculean labors of the Methodist society, many of our remote settlements would have been at this day almost in a state of barbarism. There is scarcely a single settlement in the whole extent of the western country which has not been blessed with the ministry of this people. To this ministry the public morality and piety are immensely indebted.

With the Anabaptists I am but little acquainted, but have been informed that their establishments are respectable. The settlements and meeting-houses of the Friends in the state of Ohio are numerous and in a flourishing condition.

The Roman Catholic clergy, without making any ostentatious parade, are traversing every part of the country, carrying the ministry to almost every family of their people.

All these communities, as to every thing belonging to apostolic zeal for the salvation of men, have certainly gone far beyond ourselves. They have not waited for a request from their people for spiritual help; but have gone into the "hedges and highways," or to use a more appropriate phraseology into the "bush and woods" to seek for them: and their labors have been for the most part marked with a degree of disinterestedness which entitles their clergy to highest credit. * * * * *

It is to be regretted that the Calvinists in this country are cleft into many divisions and that they are as Jews and Samaritans towards each other.

I formerly indulged the hope that the Methodist society would, sooner or later, in obedience to the order of their spiritual father, adopt the use of the service book which he gave them, and that with the increase of their number and wealth, they would found literary institutions, so as to associate science with their zeal in the public ministry of the gospel. This hope may yet be realized.

One serious objection, in my opinion, applies to all the religious denominations in this country—the want of established forms of public worship. My zeal for their introduction will not be considered a zeal without knowledge, when it is remembered that, until the Reformation, the Christian world knew no other, and that even the present exceptions to the practice in this respect are on a very limited scale. The public reading of the scriptures and the participation of the people in the public offices of devotion, are certainly matters of the highest importance to the edification, faith and piety of all.

To some extent the aspect of the religious profession in the western country, as to its intrinsic character, is by no means such as I think it ought to be. In many instances, it is not that of the steady exercise of faith, hope and charity, exemplified by a constant succession of good deeds; but that of a certain routine of supernatural feelings in which science, faith, and moral virtue, have little to do. Private instruction, and it is to be feared private devotion, also, have been partially laid aside for public profession and the exhibition of enthusiastic raptures, which certainly have for their ultimate object the making of proselytes. In some parts, a profession of supernatural feelings of a particular stamp and configuration in conformity to the respective models furnished by different societies constitute the larger amount of the claims of the applicant to church membership and the ministry.

What a misfortune that a test purporting to be of so much importance, and yet so equivocal and delusive, so favorable to hypocrisy, should have been so extensively adopted by societies in which there is certainly much of real piety.

As a patriot, as well as an Episcopalian, I wished for that system of Christian doctrine, those forms of worship, and that form of ecclesiastical government, which bear the impress of the primitive ages, and which, of course, are best for this world as for the next. For the spiritual benefit of the many thousands of our Israel here I was most anxious for the organization of the Episcopal church in this country at an early period of its settlement.

All my endeavors to obtain these objects were unsuccessful. From year to year I have witnessed the plunder of our people to increase the number and build the churches of societies, in my view, less valuable than their own.

How often have these people said to me in the bitterness of their hearts, "must we live and die without baptism for our children, and without the sacrament for ourselves?"

The great states of Kentucky and Tennessee have been, for the most part, settled by the descendants of members of the Church of England. Not one in a thousand of these people have, to this day, ever heard the voice of a clergyman of their own church, but they have heard those of every other denomination. Hence it results that by far the greater number of these people are lost to us forever.

The course I have pursued for the attainment of an Episcopacy in this country is partially known to you. The treatment of which I spoke to the Rev. Mr. Johnson—alluded to in your letter, shall be frankly stated, and I trust for the last time. As I have never asked for promotion in the church nor received any emolument from it these subjects of complaint are of little importance to myself. In proportion as they bear the aspect of negligence on the part of the fathers of the church to the spiritual interests of our people in these immense regions, they have been subjects of deep regret to me, and but little so on any other account.

When, in 1810, the few Episcopal clergymen in this country made application through you, to the general convention, to be associated together in a separate diocese, we confidently expected that, as our situation so evidently required the arrangement, it would be made. We never received the slightest information respecting the fate of our petition until the arrival of a clergyman at my house from Philadelphia, whose name I do not now recollect—in 1812, about eighteen months after the session of the general convention in which the subject had been agitated. The issue of the business blasted our hopes. From that time our intercourse with each other became less frequent than it ever had been before; our ecclesiastical affairs fell into a state of languor, and one of our clergymen, wearied with disappointment, and seeing no prospect of any event favorable to the prosperity of the church, relinquished the ministry.

I kept my station, cheerless as it was, without hope of doing anything beyond keeping together a few of my parishioners during my own life time, after which, as I supposed, they and their descendants must attach themselves to such societies as they might think best.

Such was the gloomy and unpleasant prospect before me. How often, during these years of hopeless despondency and discouragement, have I said to myself, Is there not a single clergyman of my profession, of a zealous and faithful spirit, who would accept the holy and honorable office of a chorea episcopus for my country, and find his reward in the exalted pleasures of an approving conscience in gathering in the lost sheep of our Israel, and planting churches in this new world? Is there not one of our bishops possessed of zeal and hardihood enough to induce him to cross the Allegheny mountains and engage in this laudable work? Year after year answered these questions in the negative.

You may judge how strange it appeared to me to see the annual statements of the contributions of my Atlantic brethren to Bible societies and other institutions for propagating the gospel in foreign countries, while no concern was expressed or measures adopted for the spiritual relief of their own people, in their own country, who were perishing for lack of knowledge.

Meantime other ecclesiastical societies here were blessed with the presence and ministrations of their Episcopal fathers, while, to this day, this country has never been favored with the presence of a bishop of our church.[1]

---

[1] In the year 1824, Bishop White made an attempt to visit the western country, but an accident on the road prevented his coming farther than Pittsburg.

We claim, and as I hope justly, the apostolic succession, but where, I ask, is our apostolic zeal for the salvation of mankind? While the Roman Catholic missionaries for the society de propaganda, as well as those of other denominations, are traversing the most inhospitable climes, encountering every difficulty, privation and danger for the laudable purpose of making converts to the Christian faith, will the spiritual fathers of our church never leave the temples erected by the piety of their fore-fathers to visit and administer to the spiritual wants of their destitute people even in their own country?

I beseech you, my friend and brother, not to consider any thing in this letter as dictated by a spirit of asperity, or the chagrin of disappointment. The statements I make proceed from the anguish of my heart, and truth compels me to say, that fortunately for the Christian world, but to the disgrace of our community, such an instance of the utter neglect of the spiritual interests of so many people, so near at hand, and for so long a continuance, is without a parallel in the whole history of the Christian church.

When, about three years ago, I heard through indirect channels, some favorable reports concerning the prospects and the extension of the Episcopal church in the eastern states, I determined to make one more effort, for the purpose of ascertaining the practicability of planting churches to the westward. Accordingly, in the autumn of 1815, I made a missionary tour in the interior of the state of Ohio, going as far as Chillicothe, where I held divine service twice. I also officiated both going and returning in nearly all the intermediate towns between that place and my place of residence. The prospect which this service presented was not discouraging. In almost every place I found skeletons of Episcopal congregations.

The year following, in Oct., 1816, according to an agreement made with the Rev. James Kilbourn, at my house a few weeks previous, I went to Worthington, Ohio. During the tour I officiated eighteen times. The proceedings of our meeting at that place are known to you. The communications which I made to you and Bishop Hobart at that time concerning them were never answered.

Last week I made a tour of six days in the southern parts of Belmont and Monroe counties, Ohio, during which I officiated seven times and formed one congregation—in the latter county—in which I baptized thirty children, and had it not been that a mistake of one day occurred in the appointment, I was informed that the baptisms would have exceeded one hundred. Many of these people had been my parishioners previous to removing to their present localities, and, together with their neighbors, had delayed the baptism of their children, in the hope of receiving that rite from a clergyman of their own church. This occurrence affected me deeply. * * * * *

Your brother in Christ,
JOS. DODDRIDGE.

Among the papers of Dr. Doddridge we find the copy of a letter of six pages addressed to the Rt. Rev. Bishop Hobart, written in Wellsburg in Dec., 1816, soon after the meeting at Worthington, above alluded to as remaining unanswered. In this letter he gives the bishop much information respecting the state of religion in the western country, the openings presented for Episcopalian missionaries and the anxiety of the people for their services, etc., etc. He also speaks of the meeting at Worthington, giving their proceedings in detail, and in conclusion, "begs his Rt. Rev. brother speedily and freely to communicate to him his remarks on the course they had taken," adding, "If in any thing we have done amiss, or omitted to do any thing we ought to have done, pray let us know it."

The important meeting at Worthington, Ohio, referred to in the preceding letter has heretofore been wholly ignored in the written history of the Protestant Episcopal church in Ohio. In it were initiated the measures which finally resulted in the formation of the diocese of Ohio, and the elevation to the episcopate of that eminent man Philander Chase, to whose active zeal and devotion to the cause of Christ, and Christian education, the diocese was indebted in a great measure for its early prosperity, and the establishment of one of its noblest institutions, Kenyon college.

* * *

We are indebted to Gen. G. H. Griswold of Worthington, Ohio, for the following memoranda relative to this convention.

Worthington, Ohio, June 17, 1861.

Relative to the convention or meeting of Episcopalians in Ohio, in 1816, for the purpose of taking measures to organize a diocese, electing a bishop, etc., I can answer; That such a meeting was held at this place on the 21st and 22d days of October of that year, which was attended by Rev. Dr. Joseph Doddridge of Virginia and Rev. James Kilbourn, at that time I believe the only Episcopal clergymen in the west; also by a number of lay delegates of whom I can name but the following; Ezra Griswold and David Prince, who represented the parish at this place, a Mr. Cunningham[1] from near Steubenville, and a Mr. Palmer. The two latter made their quarters at our house.

This convention, originating with the clergymen before named, was, as I understand, the first ever held in Ohio, and from which has arisen whatever of success and importance our church has attained. As I have no copy of the proceedings of that convention I cannot inform you what was therein done beyond the adoption of a circular, an appeal to the church east for help, and some order for further action, or subsequent conventions.

Dr. Doddridge held services and preached three times at this place, forenoon, afternoon and evening on Sunday, 20th Oct., and went to Columbus and preached in the evening of Tuesday 22d; myself and a Mr. Goodrich were in attendance, at Columbus, from this place.

Dr. Doddridge was, as I well recollect, very popular with the people, and very generally mentioned as probably the future bishop.

The foregoing facts I got mostly from the records of this parish, some old books of my father, and my own private diary kept at the time. My residence has been continuous at this place since 1803.

Miss N. Doddridge.

Yours truly,

G. H. GRISWOLD.

[1] Mr. Cunningham was a delegate from the parish of St. James in Jefferson co., Ohio, but may have represented the parish at Steubenville also. —Ed.

This preliminary convention issued a circular addressed to the bishops and clergy of the Protestant Episcopal church east of the Alleghenies, setting forth in feeling terms the destitution of the church in the west, and concluding with the very appropriate scriptural invocation, "Come over into Macedonia and help us."

Shortly after this circular was issued, petitions, numerously signed, from the several parishes in Ohio and Virginia, asking leave to form a diocese in the western country were sent to Bishops White and Hobart to be laid before the general convention at its setting in New York, in the spring of the year 1817. Dr. Doddridge received no direct information of the action of the convention upon these petitions until August, when a letter reached him from Rev. Roger Searle.

This letter, dated Plymouth, Conn., Aug. 4, 1817, said:

"With a view to the organization of the church in the state of Ohio, a convention is duly appointed to convene at Columbus, 5th of January next, and you will have perceived, from the journal of its proceedings, that the provisions of the late general convention are such as to have met your wishes, as made known by you to the house of bishops and to the bishops and others separately."

Another letter from Rev. Searle, dated at Zanesville, Dec. 1., 1817, replying to a communication from Dr. Doddridge, dated Nov. 24th, says:

"I sincerely regret that you did not receive a copy of the journal of the proceedings of the late general convention. I cannot for a moment entertain the idea that this neglect was a matter of design on the part of the bishops and clergy whose immediate duty it might have been to forward it to you, with other communications regarding the church generally in this western country. I should, indeed, have sent you one myself without delay, had I not thought you would receive several copies through Bishops White, Hobart and others. But, my dear friend, I herewith send you one per mail," etc.

Dr. Doddridge could not but feel deeply wounded by this omission to make him acquainted as early as possible with the proceedings of a convention in which it was known that he felt the deepest interest. He knew how pressing was the need for the organization of a diocese in the west, and that in consequence of the failure of the effort made in 1810 to obtain an Episcopate in the western country, several of the clergy, though still faithful to the church, discouraged and hopeless of ever seeing their dearest wishes realized, made no exertions to extend her borders by forming new congregations. Dr. Doddridge, however, had never remitted his efforts, and although the measures recommended to the general convention were, with a few modifications, adopted, his name was not mentioned in the convention, no direct reference was made to the labors he had performed, and worst of all no official or unofficial notice of its action was ever sent to him. This discourteous treatment of him by the ecclesiastical authorities of his church certainly justifies the severe terms in which he refers to this subject in his Notes.

In accordance with the action of the general convention the preliminary convention for organizing the diocese of Ohio met at Columbus on the 5th of January, 1818. Owing to the want of timely notice, but one of the four parishes organized by Dr. Doddridge in Ohio was represented in that body. On the evening of the second day John Matthews, from St. James's church, Zanesville, appeared and took his seat. In the report on the state of the church made to the convention by Rev. Philander Chase he stated that in Zanesville he found a very respectable congregation of Episcopalians, duly organized under the pious and praiseworthy exertions of the Rev. Mr. Doddridge. The preliminary convention having organized the diocese by the adoption of a constitution and the appointment of a standing committee, adjourned to meet at Worthington, Ohio, on the 5th of June, 1818.

The prospect of having, at length, a bishop for the west filled the heart of Dr. Doddridge with great joy. He attended the first annual convention at Worthington accompanied by delegates from the four parishes he had organized in Ohio. The lay delegates were admitted without question, but the right of Dr. Doddridge to a seat was doubted, and a committee of five members appointed to examine and report whether, according to the true interpretation of the canons, he could be admitted a member of the convention. The committee after due deliberation made the report that, " according to the existing canons and resolutions of the last general convention, Dr. Doddridge, in his present relative situation, cannot be admitted to a seat as a member of this convention "; also " that he lose no time in taking such measures as, under the existing canons of the church, are essential to constitute him a member of this convention, so that the diocese may more fully profit by his labors;" further, that Dr. Doddridge " be requested to take a seat in this convention as an honorary member during the remainder of the session."

* * *

Dr. Doddridge appeared in convention and took his seat with the clergy. This strict enforcement of a technical construction of the canons did not at all please him. He thought the circumstances of his case were such as to make it unnecessary to raise the question. In a letter to a clerical brother written soon after the event he says: " When at the convention at Worthington, it seemed to me that I was doomed to drink the last dregs of the cup of humiliation. Almost the first thing that took place after I entered was a lengthy discussion on the question of my right to a seat in the convention." It must be remembered in this connection that there were only four clergy in the convention aside from Dr. Doddridge, and that of the four two, viz: Rev. Philander Chase and Rev. James Kilbourn, sat for St. John's church, Worthington, while Dr. Doddridge represented four flourishing parishes. Moreover the very existence of the convention itself was owing to measures initiated by him.

The convention at Worthington on the 4th of June, 1818, elected Rev. Philander Chase bishop of the diocese of Ohio. Dr. Doddridge not being entitled to vote, but sitting as an honorary member in convention, expressed his entire satisfaction and hearty concurrence in the election of a bishop which had been made. On the next day Dr. Doddridge, by request, made his report of the state of the church.

* * *

After the adjournment of the first annual convention of the diocese of Ohio, Dr. Doddridge continued his ministration to his Ohio congregations with as much regularity as possible. In the spring of 1819 he had the satisfaction of being relieved of his charge of the parish at Zanesville by the Rev. Intrepid Morse, an able and zealous minister. The second annual convention of the diocese of Ohio met at Worthington on the second day of June, 1819. Dr. Doddridge did not attend this convention, interesting as the first one presided over by a bishop, not yet being entitled to a seat in it.

The address of the bishop on this occasion was one of rare interest as containing a vivid picture of the manner of preaching the gospel in those early times. It contained many references to Dr. Doddridge illustrating the character and value of the work he performed.

* * *

The hardships under which the early missionary work was carried on required a zeal and faith equal to that of the apostolic age of the church. The valuable character of the work performed by Dr. Doddridge is shown by the fact that the churches were scattered over a territory extensive enough for a modern diocese, in a region almost entirely destitute of the gospel.

Some years after Dr. Doddridge had taken orders in the Protestant Episcopal church, which, within the bounds of his labors furnished him but a meagre support, he found it necessary, in order to meet the wants of an increasing family, to combine with his clerical profession one that would be more lucrative in the region in which he lived. He chose that of medicine, completing his course of preparation in Philadelphia, under Dr. Benjamin Rush.

Several years previous to this time he had entered into a matrimonial connection with Jemima, orphan daughter of Capt. John Bukey, who had at an early period of the settlement west, emigrated from New Jersey, locating on a farm on Short creek, in Ohio county, Virginia. Mr. Bukey died some years after his arrival in the country, leaving a wife, three sons and four daughters; the youngest of whom, at the age of sixteen, became the wife of Dr. Doddridge.[1] Mary, the eldest, married Major John M'Colloch, of Short Creek, Virginia. Marcie united her destiny with that of Colonel Harman Greathouse, late of Kentucky. Two of the sons, John and Hezekiah, at an early age, were employed as spies under Captain Samuel Brady, of Indian war notoriety. The youngest, Rudolph, while yet a youth, settled in Shelby county, Kentucky.

In the department of medicine Dr. Doddridge was eminently successful and deservedly popular, and to the avails of an extensive but laborious practice he was indebted for the means to rear and educate a large family of children.

That he occupied a high position in the estimation of his brethren of the medical fraternity, who had opportunities for knowing him well, is unquestionable. One evidence of this fact is a certificate under the seal of the Medico-Surgical Society of East Ohio—instituted in 1821—announcing to him that "said society, being well convinced of his abilities and scientific skill, had made him an honorary member of their association." The secretary of the society, in a note enclosing the document, says:

> I do not know, dear brother, that the accompanying certificate will be acceptable to thee, yet it may, at some future day, serve to remind thee of the high esteem in which thee was held by such of thy medical brethren as had the best opportunity of judging of thy professional and moral worth.
>
> Truly thy friend,
>
> ANDERSON JUDKINS.

While Dr. Doddridge was pursuing his medical studies in Philadelphia in the year 1800 he became acquainted with some scientific characters, and as we learn from a printed communication over the signature of Reuben Haines, corresponding secretary, he was, "on the 1st day of 12th month, 1812, duly elected a corresponding member of the Academy of Natural Sciences," in that city.

---

[1] Jemima Bukey was born April 5, 1777.—(*Simpson.*)

He was at an early day initiated into the mysteries of masonry, regarding the institution in its fundamental principles as imposing on the initiated the obligation practically to illustrate in their lives the virtues of faith, hope, charity and fraternity, and as being secondary to the Christian religion in its meliorating influences upon the human family.

He was W. M. of the lodge at Wellsburg, Virginia, and perhaps of a pioneer lodge at Mingo Towns,[1] holding a warrant from the grand lodge of Pennsylvania, which charter was recalled in 1806, having been extinct some years.

His conversational powers were of a high order. He was easy of access, fond of innocent anecdotes and possessed in an eminent degree the tact for adapting his subjects and language to the peculiar tastes and capacities of those with whom he conversed.

Ordinarily he was fond of the society of ladies and children, saying that men in general were so engrossed with business matters, in which he took but little interest, that they could not be induced, for any length of time, to converse on any other subject; but the former he could understand and sympathize with, and they could mutually interest each other.

He never departed from that unaffected cordiality of manner, simplicity of dress, style of living, and generous hospitality which characterized the pioneer society in which he had been brought up, and which, in these respects, he considered much superior to the code of manners and etiquette of modern days.

In his intercourse with his neighbors he was cheerful and social, in his habits industrious, temperate and domestic. To the gratification of the palate he was indifferent, discountenancing both by example and precept the indulgence or cultivation of a fastidious appetite.

When in health he always rose at four o'clock, devoting the morning hours to meditation and literature. To those who trimmed the midnight lamp and indulged the morning slum-

[1] The Mingo Towns were situated on the Ohio river, three miles below the site of the present city of Steubenville.

ber, he would say in the elegant phraseology of Scripture, why do you purchase light, when the good providence of Him who said, " Let there be light and there was light," gives you that blessing " without money and without price."

His benevolence was proverbial, and like that of the good Samaritan, was exemplified in acts of kindness to the poor and afflicted, to whose relief he liberally contributed of his limited means; on some occasions—known to the writer—using his own house as a hospital for the sick, who were destitute of friends as well as of funds—where they gratuitously received the benefit of his medical skill together with such other appliances as their comfort and necessities required, until restored to health.

His philanthropic feelings induced him in various ways to endeavor to provide employment for the poorer class of laborers around him, in doing which, as he possessed no skill in the management of financial matters, and little discrimination in his judgment of human character, he very nearly impoverished himself.

In horticulture and the culture of bees he found an interesting and agreeable relaxation in his intervals of professional labor. His garden and orchard, both of which were well cultivated, added greatly to his home pleasures. The morning carols of feathered songsters among the leafy bowers were to him sweetest music; and he was often out betimes, as he said, mentally to unite with them in offering the matin song of praise to the giver of all mercies. He would not allow one of these winged tenants to be injured on his grounds, telling his children, who sometimes objected to the birds having the nicest cherries and other fruits, that " the same good Being who provided food and clothing for them, provided also for the little birds, and if He sent them to his premises for that provision, they must not be molested." And they were not.

In experimenting with bees, he deviated from the mode then prevailing—that of destroying them in order to procure their honey. And his success proved that his views respecting the economy and habits of these interesting insects were not incorrect.

In 1813 he published a *Treatise on the Culture of Bees* in which he gives a minute description of his apiary, and details his plan of treatment of the bees, which was that of colonizing them instead of killing them to procure the fruit of their labors.

* * *

The fatigue and exposure to which Dr. Doddridge was subjected in his practice of the healing art, unavoidable in a new and sparsely settled country, in the lapse of years, gradually undermined his constitution—not naturally robust—and engendered a disease which was at times attended with much acute suffering and nervous irritability.

When laboring under its paroxysms his distress was greatly augmented by mental depression, despondency, and a morbid sensitiveness; characteristics entirely foreign to him when in health, being then uniformly cheerful, self-reliant and hopeful.

His published writings in addition to those already mentioned, were " Logan, the Last of the Race of Shikellimus," a dramatic piece, sermons on special subjects, and orations delivered at masonic festivals, and other occasions. In 1825 he commenced the *Russian Spy*, a series of letters containing strictures on America, and an Indian novel, neither of which were completed.

During the winter of 1824 he arranged and prepared his manuscript of the Notes, etc., etc., for the press, but owing to ill health he could not give the necessary attention to the correction of proof-sheets, consequently many errors were overlooked, and on the whole the issue proved to its author an unprofitable investment of time and money.

Early in the fall he started eastward, having in view a two-fold object, that of improving his health by travel and the disposition of some of his books.

The letter which follows contains a brief review of his journey:

Bedford, Sept. 24, 1824.

MY DEAR WIFE: We are here. Our progress has been slow; but I have enjoyed the journey, and think my health is somewhat improved.

The mountain scenery through which we passed is varied, some beautiful, some grand and sublime beyond description. Whilst gazing with delight upon these displays of the Creator's power and goodness, my pleasure was suddenly checked by the reflection that those faculties by means of which I now hold communion with the beautiful in nature must soon be closed in death. But thanks be to Him who made all things, I can look forward by faith to a world where beauty, peace and purity are eternal, where none shall know sickness and weariness, such as I now feel.

At Brownsville and Uniontown I was invited to officiate, which I did, at the latter place baptizing two children. Have preached once in this place also. Thus without expecting it I have become a missionary.

Before arriving here, I intended, if possible, to find the house in which I first drank coffee, in 1777—and in the event of finding it, to invite a few friends to take a cup with me in the same room. Remembering the name of the landlord, Nagel, and being able to give a tolerable description of the house, I found upon enquiring that Dillon's Hotel, where we put up, now occupies the site of Nagel's house.

Yesterday I went out to see the famous Bedford springs, about two miles from the town. The site, owing to the surrounding mountains, is highly romantic. The buildings of this watering-place consist of baths, boarding-houses, and dormitories. The great Hall for amusements presents many fanciful and gorgeous decorations. On a low piece of ground, some distance from the Hall, on a pedestal of rock, stands a naiad, a large, half naked female figure, with a Grecian face and costume, holding in her left hand a huge concha, from the top of which the water of the spring is thrown upward to the height of ten or twelve feet; but poor girl, her fine white drapery is turning yellow, from the action of the sulphate of iron contained in the water which is constantly falling on it.

The spring issues from the western side of the Cove mountain, at the height and nearly twenty feet above the creek which runs at its base. It is large, and rises with great force through apertures in immense rocks, which still retain their primitive situation and aspect. A few rods higher up is another, but a smaller spring. The water of the principal spring is conducted into a large reservoir, supplying a long range of baths, which are filled at pleasure, by raising a small flood-gate. The water in the baths is reached by a flight of steps. I had not, however, the courage to make the descent. The side of the mountain from which the spring issues is cut into serpentine walks, for the convenience and benefit of pedestrians who wish to take exercise and inhale the mountain air.

I have been examining the oldest records here, for names of my family, but can only find that of my grand-father Joseph Doddridge, who is mentioned as foreman of a grand jury in 1777.

Being within ten miles of the place of my nativity, I wished to learn something concerning my father's title to the land on which he lived in Friend's Cove, but could find nothing, as his title, whatever it was, originated when this was a part of Cumberland county. I am informed here that the land is now owned by a Mr. Cissner, and that my father was unjustly deprived of it, but by whom I have not learned.

The Court House here was built in the reign of George III. The edifice is of stone, and is, without exception, the most misshapen, sombre-looking building I ever saw. I do not think the Bastile itself could have presented a more forbidding and gloomy aspect. I seated myself for a moment on the bench of justice, and after taking a survey of the antiquated, ill-shapen jury-boxes and council-table, gladly made my escape from the forum of my forefathers.

JOS. DODDRIDGE.

Soon after his return from Bedford Dr. Doddridge received a letter from Bishop Chase, just landed in America after his first visit to England to solicit funds to assist him in carrying out his enlarged views relative to the missionary and educational interests of his infant diocese—announcing his return, and appointing the 3rd day of November for the meeting at Chillicothe of the diocesan convention.

Taking with him a little son of eleven years, as traveling companion, he proceeded, by easy stages, to the convention, and while there, at the request of St. James's parish, at Zanesville, he accepted a missionary appointment to that church.

In consequence of the impaired state of his health, he had some time previous relinquished the charge of his parishes in Virginia and Ohio; and, from the same cause, he had been compelled to discontinue the practice of medicine in his vicinity, where attention to its duties involved the necessity of his being on horseback much of the time and exposure to every change of weather.

By restricting his labors to the parish at Zanesville, with proper care, he fondly hoped to regain a portion of his former health and vigor. But He in whose hand are all our "times" ordered otherwise. When winter set in he had a severe attack of pneumonia, which, together with his asthmatic disease, brought him to the verge of the grave, and a tedious convalescence ensued before he recovered sufficient strength to again resume his parochial duties.

During the continuance of his sufferings and confinement from debility, he acknowledged that he had much cause of gratitude to God, the oft repeated kindnesses of friends who did all they could to alleviate his sufferings and cheer him in his solitary confinement. But, notwithstanding these kind offices, how many hours of loneliness and despondency must have intervened, was known only to God and himself. After recovering some strength he thus wrote to a friend:

> My life is fast ebbing away. It has been spent for others, and now, instead of enjoying those accommodations and that repose which my infirmities require. I am alone, in exile from my dear family. But I must not murmur. God's will be done. In due time rest will be mine through the undeserved mercy of Him in whom I trust.

To his other afflictions this winter was added the loss of his little son, Reeves, who had accompanied him to Chillicothe, and whom he had left there at school. This sad bereavement deeply affected him, yet he endeavored to exercise a cheerful acquiescence in the will of Him who orders all things wisely.

* * *

Below is another extract from the reminiscences of Hon. T. Scott:

> In person Dr. Doddridge was tall but not thin, dark hair, fair complexion, blue eyes, which were full of expression, and his whole appearance imposing. When preaching there was nothing in his manner that savored of pedantry or rusticity, yet he did not possess that graceful action and delivery which are often met with in speakers in every other respect his inferiors. These apparent defects were, however, amply compensated by the earnestness with which he addressed his hearers, the purity of his style and language and the substance of his discourses.

During the remainder of his life he was unable to labor in a professional way; he still, however, found some relief in travel which, in his debilitated state, was necessarily slow.

In the course of the summer he spent some weeks with a sister in Chillicothe, after which he visited his son in Bloomingburg, Ohio. But finding that he gained no strength, hopeless of any favorable change in regard to his health, preferring in the bosom of his family to await the summons which should release him from suffering and from earth, he returned home, as he emphatically said, " To die."

When in full possession of his mental powers he spoke of death with great composure. Relying solely on the merits of Christ for salvation, he felt no fear, but seemed anxious to depart and be with God.

His protracted sufferings terminated on the 9th of November, 1826, in the fifty-eighth year of his age, at his home in Wellsburg, Brooke county, Virginia.[1]

Of the twelve children of the subject of this Memoir, four preceded him to the spirit-land; his wife and four others have since joined him there. One son, Joseph, and three daughters. Susan A., widow of Capt. Robert Larimore, of Chillicothe. Matilda D., wife of Mr. John Winters of New York, and the writer, are all that remain of the cheerful group which once surrounded his humble hearth-stone.

THE DODDRIDGE FAMILY.

John Doddridge emigrated from England and settled in the colony of New Jersey. He was a descendant of Sir John Doddridge, of Shepperton, England. This Sir John was father of the celebrated English divine, Philip Doddridge, author of a number of books and of many beautiful poems and hymns, one of the most notable of the latter being, "Oh, God of Bethel, by Whose Hand!" etc.

John Doddridge, the emigrant, had two children, Anne and Joseph. The latter married Mary Biggs. He died in Bedford county, Pa., February 14, 1779, leaving six daughters and two sons, viz: Sarah, Hannah, Elizabeth, Susan, Mary, Anne, Philip and John.

The last named John Doddridge was born in Maryland, March 30, 1745. He married Mary Wells, daughter of Col. Richard Wells, of Baltimore, Md., on December 23, 1767. She was born in Baltimore, September 19, 1748. About the year 1768 they removed to Friends Cove, a few miles south of Bedford, Bedford county, Pa., and left there for Washington county, Pa., in 1773. Their children were Joseph, born Oct. 14, 1769; Anne, born Nov. 3, 1770; Philip, born May 17, 1773, became very prominent in legal and political life; Susannah, born May 6, 1775, died in infancy; Ruth, born Aug. 30, 1776.

Mary Wells Doddridge, wife of John, died Nov. 30, 1776. John Doddridge died April 20, 1791. He had married a second time on Jan. 23, 1778, with Elizabeth Schrimplin, born Oct. 26, 1761. Their children were Josias, born Oct. 28, 1778; Eleanor, born Oct. 26, 1780; Abner, born Feb. 4, 1783, died in infancy; Benjamin, born March 30, 1784; Enoch, born July 4, 1786; John, born May 6, 1789. The interment of John Doddridge took place on his own farm, but in 1824 the body was disinterred and taken to Wellsburg.

John Doddridge was the first settler in Independence township, Washington county, Pa., in 1773, coming from Bedford county, and taking up on a Virginia certificate 437 acres of land on Cross Creek which was surveyed to him on April 6, 1786, under the title of "Extravagance." James Simpson's notes say that the first farm upon which the Doddridge family settled was where William Leggett resides, on Cross Creek, and that afterwards they removed to the farm where Milton Murdoch now lives, in the same township, where they built Doddridge's fort of which Capt. Samuel Teter, a relative of the Doddridge family, had command when the Indians were troublesome.

Most of the land owned by John Doddridge now belongs to Rev. Wm. Brown, of Canonsburg.

The marriage of Joseph Doddridge, first born of John Doddridge and Mary Wells, and author of "Doddridge's Notes," to Jemima Bukey, took place in Sept., 1783. Their children in order of birth were:

1—Philip Bukey Doddridge; born in Wellsburg Feb. 20, 1795; died in Columbus, Ohio, Sept. 9, 1860.

2—Narcissa Doddridge; born in Wellsburg, April 7, 1796; died Jan. 30, 1874.

3—Hezekiah Dunn Doddridge, born July 8, 1799; died in infancy.

4—Eliza Matilda Doddridge, born in Wellsburg June 10, 1800; died Feb. 1, 1819.

5—Harriet Tabitha Doddridge, wife of Major William Duval, of Fort Smith, Ark., born Aug. 14, 1802; died Jan. 20, 1841.

6—Joseph John Gantt Doddridge, born May 27, 1806; died in Woodstock, Ill., Feb. 16, 1889.

7—Bazaleel Wells Doddridge, born March 27, 1809; died in infancy.

8—Susan Amelia Doddridge, born in Wellsburg, April 4, 1811; died in Mt. Vernon, Ohio, Sept. 25, 1882.

9—Robert Reeves Doddridge, born in Wellsburg, Dec. 8, 1813; died in Chillicothe, Ohio, Dec. 12, 1825.

10—Charles Hammond Doddridge, born in Wellsburg, May 5, 1816; died in Chillicothe, Ohio, Oct. 19, 1834.

11—Mary Eliza Doddridge, wife of B. F. Brannan, of Cincinnati, born in Wellsburg, Dec. 20, 1820; died in Cincinnati, April 10, 1857. Their son, Joseph Doddridge Brannan, is Bussey Professor of Law in Harvard University.

12—Matilda Willis Doddridge, born in Wellsburg, Feb. 28, 1827; died in San Francisco, Nov. 20, 1869.

SKETCH OF MAJOR SAMUEL McCOLLOCH.

By Narcissa Doddridge.

Among the earliest settlers of North Western Virginia were the McCollochs, who emigrated from the south branch of the Potomac in 1770, and located on the borders of Short creek, a stream which empties into the Ohio river, nine miles north of Wheeling creek. The family consisted of four brothers, Abraham, George, Samuel and John, and several sisters, one of whom was the wife of Col. Ebenezer Zane, who, with his brothers, Jonathan and Silas, was from the same neighborhood, and about the same period settled at the mouth of Wheeling creek.

The name which graces the head of this article is not unknown to readers of border history, in which some of his daring exploits are recorded. At present, however, we propose noticing only a few particulars, more immediately connected with the final scene of his eventful career, which were communicated to the writer by the widow of his brother, the late Major John M'Colloch, of Ohio county, Virginia, and, in substance, corroborated by Col. M. Moorehead, of Zanesville, and the Hon. T. Scott, of Chillicothe, Ohio.

Between the two younger brothers of the M' Colloch family, Samuel and John, of whom alone we shall speak, there existed a more than fraternal intimacy, arising not only from congeniality of disposition, but from community of interests and pursuits; consequently, they were much together, and their history is in some degree blended. Both were early distinguished for intrepidity and successful prowess in Indian warfare. Possessing in an eminent degree firmness and decision of character, they were wont, in cases of exigency, which in those days of peril were of frequent occurrence, to determine quickly and execute promptly. These qualities, combined with untiring energy and perseverance, in circumventing the various stratagems of the Indians, and indomitable courage in opposing them in open combat, soon placed the brothers in the van of the frontier bands required by the peculiarly exposed condition of the country to be ever on the alert and ready for conflict with the wily enemy, whose frequent irruptions into the infant settlements, for purposes of rapine and murder. kept the inhabitants in a state of continual dread and apprehension.

To many of the savages they were personally known, and objects of fear and intense hate. Numerous artifices were employed to capture them; their enemies anticipating, in such an event, the privilege of satiating their vindictive and fiendish malice by the infliction of a lingering and cruel death. Of this design, on the part of the Indians, the brothers were aware; and in their almost miraculous preservation, in various contests with them, gratefully acknowledged the interposition of an invisible Power in their behalf.

Major Samuel M'Colloch commanded at Fort Van Meter, in 1777, styled the Court House Fort, from the circumstance of the first civil court in North Western Virginia being held in it immediately after the organization and separation of Ohio county from West Augusta. This fort was one of the first erected in this part of Virginia, and stood on the north side of Short creek, about five miles from its confluence with the Ohio river. During many consecutive summers the inhabitants of the adjacent neighborhood sought security from the tomahawk and scalping knife of the merciless aborigines within its palisades; agricultural labor being performed by companies, each member of which, like the Jews of old, when rebuilding the walls of the Holy City after their return from the Babylonish captivity, wrought with one hand while the other grasped a weapon of defense.

On the 30th July, 1782, arrangements were made by the inmates of the fort for the performance of field labor. To the commander and his brother John was assigned the dangerous duty of reconnoitering the paths leading from the river, to ascertain, if possible, whether there were any Indians lurking in the vicinity. Leaving early in the morning in the discharge of their mission, after proceeding some distance the former, impelled perhaps by a sudden premonition of the tragic fate which befell him, returned; and depositing with the wife of his brother John his watch and several other articles, gave directions as to their disposition, in the event of his not returning, and leaving a kindly message for his youthful bride, soon rejoined his wondering companion.

They traversed the path lying along the south bank of the creek till within a short distance of its junction with the Ohio, where they crossed and followed the direction of the river to the Beach bottom, a distance of three miles; when, perceiving no indications of an enemy, they retraced their steps to the mouth of the creek, a short distance above which, they ascended a steep and rugged eminence, well known in the neighborhood by the significant cognomen of *Girty's Point.* The notorious renegade, Simon Girty, having on several occasions, when conducting parties of Indians into the settlement, with difficulty escaped capture by the infuriated whites, by a rapid flight over the craggy and precipitous path.

Congratulating themselves on the absence of immediate danger, the brothers pursued their course in the direction of the fort, on the summit of the elevated ridge rising abruptly from the northern bank of the creek, and had arrived at the termination of a deep ravine which made up from the stream—

John, being somewhat in advance of his brother, and riding round the top of a large tree, which had fallen across the way —when a low, half-suppressed growl, from a well trained hunting-dog which accompanied them, arrested their attention. No time, however, intervened for scrutinizing the cause; a volley of bullets from an invisible foe revealed it. On reaching the path John turned to look for his companion, whose bleeding form, with feelings of unutterable anguish, he beheld falling from his horse, and, ere it reached the earth, a stalwart savage sprang from his covert, tomahawk and scalping-knife in hand. with which to complete the bloody tragedy, and secure a trophy of victory. While the exulting victor was in the act of scalping, the younger brother, with frenzied resolution, suddenly wheeled his horse, and, amid a shower of balls, elevating his rifle, quickly sent the swift messenger of death to the heart of the murderer, whom he had the exquisite gratification of seeing spring into the air, and then fall to rise no more. Having performed this feat he rapidly as possible, his enraged enemies in full pursuit, their balls perforating his hat and hunting-shirt, made his way down the ravine and soon reached the fort in safety; his brother's horse closely following him.

The next morning a party from the fort proceeded to the spot where the sanguinary deed had been perpetrated and found the mutilated remains of their beloved commander. The Indians, influenced no doubt by that species of hero-worship inherent in their nature, causing an unbounded admiration of personal valor, had abstracted the heart of their victim; which, it was afterward learned from one belonging to the party, had been eaten by them; a practice in which they occasionally indulged. Parkman, who was well acquainted with their habits, says: "The Indians, though not habitual cannibals, sometimes eat portions of the bodies of their enemies, superstitiously believing that their own courage and hardihood will be increased thereby."

This fatal rencounter was, doubtless, instrumental in the salvation of the lives of all in the fort; it being subsequently ascertained that the party committing the murderous act consisted of upwards of one hundred warriors *en route* to attack it. After the escape of the surviving brother, aware that notice of their propinquity would be given, and immediate pursuit made, they hastily retreated to their towns west of the Ohio.

The remains of Major Samuel M'Colloch were interred in Fort Van Meter; but not unwept nor unhonored. There were present very many who knew and appreciated the sterling worth of the forest soldier, and by whom the memory of his noble qualities and tragic fate was long cherished; and to this day, in the vicinity where the circumstances transpired, the name and fate of the hero are as familiar as household words.

CAPTURE OF MEMBERS OF THE DODDRIDGE FAMILY BY THE INDIANS.

By NARCISSA DODDRIDGE.

The particulars of the following account of the murder of a member of the family of Philip Doddridge, sen., and the capture of three of his children by a party of Wyandots in 1778, were communicated to the writer by Mrs. Eleanor Brown, late of Wellsburg, Virginia, and Mrs. Ruth Carson, recently deceased in Ross co., Ohio.

Philip Doddridge, sen., emigrated from Maryland in 1770, and settled near the mouth of Dunkard creek, a tributary of the west branch of the Monongahela in Virginia. At the time of this sad occurrence he had a comfortable cabin and a tolerably well improved farm. His household consisted of a wife and four young children, also his wife's father, mother and a nephew, a lad of twelve years.[1] Early one morning in the month of May, 1778, Mr. Doddridge went into one of his fields to work, some distance from his house, his wife also being

[1] The name of this nephew was Augustine Bickerstaff. In the course of his flight from the scene he encountered Lewis Wetzel raking leaves in a field. The savages chased them for seven miles, until they found refuge within the walls of Statler's Fort. The Indians also carried away with them from the mouth of Dunkard two other children, David Pursley, aged seven years, and Susan Potts, aged 14. Nancy Doddridge died some years after her capture and the injury done her by a drunken Indian who had kicked her in the side while on the forced march to Detroit is said to have been largely responsible therefor.

absent; she having taken her infant and gone some miles to the house of a friend, to do some weaving for her family. Her three little girls, between the ages of two and seven years, were left in the care of her parents and the boy above spoken of. While he was amusing the children at the base of a high bank of the creek on which they lived, he espied in the distance a party of Indians approaching the house, which they without seeing him, entered, tomahawked and scalped the aged grandfather, took such articles from the cabin as they fancied, and then set fire to it, leaving the body of the murdered man to be consumed with it.

The nephew well aware that if he remained with his little charge he could not protect them, and would be himself killed or captured, fled to the field in which his uncle was at work, and informed him of what was transpiring at home. They both saw the flames of the burning buildings, and the savages amusing themselves by ripping up the feather beds and throwing their contents high in the open air. Having finished their work at the cabin, the deeply distressed father was compelled to remain where he was and see the Indians bearing off into the forest his three little girls and their grandmother without the power to afford them the slightest relief.

Soon after this catastrophe Philip, with his wife and remaining child, left the neighborhood of the Monongahela, removing to the house of his brother John Doddridge, who had, in 1773, settled in the western part of Washington county, Pa., not far from the present village of West Middletown,[1] in the same county. Philip subsequently purchased from his uncle, Captain Samuel Teter, a farm near his brother's, on which he resided till about the year 1818, when he removed with his family, then consisting of one son, John, and five daughters, to the state of Indiana, himself performing the journey on foot, for although having plenty of this world's goods he was never known to ride on horseback. He was one of the early

[1] See appendix for "Distinguished Men of West Middletown."

friends and supporters of Methodism in the western country, and so exemplary was his life that wherever he was known his influence was felt.

The fate of the grandmother was never ascertained, but many years subsequent to the captivity of their children the parents learned that they had been taken to Detroit, where the oldest girl was sold to a French officer, who finally married her and took her to France. The second one died, and the third, being reared with the children of her tawny captors, became as one of them, married a chief,[1] and although acquainted herself with her parentage, so strong was her attachment to the mode of life in which she had been brought up, that she carefully endeavored to conceal her relationship to her family.

The late Philip Doddridge, Esq.,[2] of Wellsburg, Va.,

[1]This was White Eyes, chief sachem of the Delaware Nation. He was always the friend of the Americans—"Buckskins," he called them,—and in their behalf he thwarted the scheme to unite all the Indian tribes of the west in a league in support of the British cause. His voice was always for peace. He was peculiarly devoted to the American cause, says Hassler's "Old Westmoreland," and even "hoped that a Delaware Indian state might form a fourteenth star in the American union. He was the greatest chieftain ever produced by this remarkable Indian nation." While on his way from Fort Pitt to Tuscarawas, Ohio, accompanied by a force of warriors and militiamen, with the design of further carrying out his purpose to restrain his tribe from engaging in any alliance with the English, he was treacherously put to death; just precisely how is not known, but he is believed to have been shot by a Virginia militiaman.

PHILIP DODDRIDGE.

[2]The Hon. Philip Doddridge, brother of Joseph, was also a man of high character and exceptional attainments. These are adequately depicted in a notable monograph published in 1875 by the late Hon. W. T. Willey, of Morgantown, United States Senator from West Virginia. Mr. Doddridge, who was a lawyer, had served Virginia in her House of Delegates in 1815-16, in 1822-23, in 1828-29, and in the convention which revised her state constitution in 1829-30. In 1823 and 1825 Mr. Doddridge was defeated as a candidate for representative in Congress from the Wheeling district of Virginia but in 1829 he was successful. He died suddenly on Nov. 19, 1832, in Washington City, in the 60th year of his age, while attending the sitting of a committee of the two Houses which was preparing a code of laws for the government of the District of Columbia. Chief Justice Marshall declared that, as a lawyer, Doddridge was second to no one at the bar of the United States Court. It was of Philip Doddridge that Daniel Webster said, while on a visit in Wheeling: "He was the only man I ever feared to meet in debate." When, in 1845, the legislature of Virginia created a new county out of parts of Harrison, Lewis, Tyler and Ritchie counties, it was named Doddridge, in honor of Philip.

Philip Doddridge was born in Bedford county, Pa., May 17, 1773. In the spring of the following year his father, John Doddridge, removed with his family to Washington county, Pa., now Independence township. This section was at that time within the jurisdiction of Virginia, and was presumed of course to be Virginia territory. But the later drawing of Mason & Dixon's line, and definite establishment of the western boundary of Pennsylvania averred that this woman had often been at his house, with other Indians, who came into Western Virginia to sell baskets and other articles. After seeing and conversing with her several times he recognized her resemblance to her family, and one day made some enquiries of her respecting her history, telling her that he was her cousin, and offering to take her to see another of her relations, Rev. Joseph Doddridge. He said she looked displeased, ceased to converse, and never to his knowledge returned to that part of the country.

---

placed John Doddridge's family and property in the latter state, a few miles from the border. Philip Doddridge settled in Wellsburg, Brooke County, Va., in 1796, and that was his home throughout the remainder of his life. His legal practice was quite large, and extended from Virginia into Pennsylvania and Ohio.

A curious episode in his life occurred in 1822, while he was in Washington City as counsel in a case before the Supreme Court. He was seized with catalepsy. The functions of life were apparently wholly suspended. Physicians declared him dead, and preparations were made for coffining. While these were going on Mrs. Doddridge thought she noticed a slight movement of one of his legs, which was raised a little. She pressed it down, and it rose again. Thinking this might not be an altogether involuntary muscular action, she lifted her husband's head high upon a pillow and rubbed his body vigorously with brandy. This gradually brought him back to conscious life. When fully restored Mr. Doddridge said he had been in perfect control of his mental powers all the time, and knew everything that was transpiring. Horror stricken by what was going on around him, and by fear of burial alive, he contrived by a powerful effort to make the slight motions of his limb that had arrested the attention of his wife. In consequence of this narrow escape Mr. Doddridge solemnly charged his friends that, in case death should ever again appear to have come to him, they should be sure indeed before interment that life had really left. So, when he expired in 1832, the President of the United States, the members of the cabinet, heads of departments and friends, assembled to attend the funeral; yet, to meet the wish of the deceased, and satisfy his family and relatives, the large crowd dispersed, to reassemble the next day and assist in burial of the remains in the congressional cemetery.

VAN METER'S FORT.

By NARCISSA DODDRIDGE.

This fort was situated on the south side of Short creek a few miles above its junction with the Ohio river, in Ohio county, Virginia. The land on which it was located belonged to the widow and heirs of Mr. Joseph Van Meter, and was subsequently owned by his eldest son, Morgan Van Meter. It now, 1847, belongs to the heirs of Mr. George Mathews, and adjoins the farm formerly owned and occupied by the late Captain John Bukey, son-in-law to Maj. William M'Mahon.

There are many interesting reminiscences connected with this early fort in the wilderness, some of which have perhaps never been recorded, indicative of the sufferings and bravery of those who lived in its vicinity, and who frequently sought refuge within its rude palisades.

Mr. John Van Meter at one time lived in this fort, and at the period of the occurrence narrated resided on the farm now owned by Alexander Walker, Esq., in the immediate neighborhood of the fort. It was during his occupancy of this farm, in 1789, that a party of Indians visited his peaceful domicile, murdered his wife, daughter, and two small sons, taking the three elder sons prisoners, and burning the house.

Hannah, the daughter who was killed, was washing at a spring a short distance from the house; she had on a sunbonnet and was stooping over the tub, unconscious of danger, when one of the savages stealthily advanced and, supposing her to be an old woman, buried his tomahawk in her head. When the Indians saw her face and perceived that she was young and beautiful they deeply lamented their precipitancy, saying, "She would have made a pretty squaw." This information was subsequently communicated by the notorious Simon Girty, who was one of the party which committed the murders.

The spring at which this tragedy was enacted is still designated as Hannah's Spring.

Whilst these events were transpiring at his home, the husband and father, John Van Meter, was absent at a neighbor's house, Mr. Charles Hedges, breaking flax. He heard the report of the guns, and saw the flames in which his house was enveloped, without power to afford the least relief, well knowing that to go single-handed would but insure his own destruction without benefiting his beloved family.

Abraham, Isaac and John were the names of the three sons carried into captivity. They were taken in one of their father's fields, in which they were at work. The two former ultimately escaped and returned to their friends. John remained with his captors, became attached to their mode of life, and finally married a young squaw. He subsequently visited his father several times, but could never be prevailed on to remain with the whites, preferring that reckless independence, self-reliance and irresponsible freedom enjoyed in forest life, to the vapid and wearisome conventionalities of civilized society.

Several years after the murder of Mr. Van Meter's family, he married the widow of Mr. John Bukey, one of the early emigrants from New Jersey to Western Virginia. Mrs. Bukey had four daughters by her first marriage. Mary, the eldest, became the wife of Major John M'Colloch, of Short Creek, Va. Marcy, the second, married Col. Harman Greathouse, late of Lexington, Kentucky. Elizabeth, the third, from whom the writer has received the particulars of this article, is Mrs. Jacob Roland, of West Liberty, Va. Jemima, the fourth daughter, became the wife of Rev. Dr. Joseph Doddridge, of Wellsburg, Brooke co., Va. She had also three sons, John, Hezekiah and Rudolph. The two former were for some years spies under Capt. Samuel Brady, lived and died in Virginia. Rudolph at an early age emigrated to Kentucky, where many of his descendants still reside.

Mrs. Bukey had but one child by Mr. Van Meter, Sarah, who is now the wife of Robert Patterson, Esq., of Wheeling, Va.

STORY OF CAPT. OLIVER BROWN.

MEMORANDUM MADE BY MR. BROWN HIMSELF AT WELLSBURG, BROOKE COUNTY, W. VA., IN FEBRUARY, 1845.

April 8, 1775, I stood in front of the first cannon fired by the British on the Americans at Lexington.

June 17, of the same year, I was in the engagement at Bunker Hill.

Was with our army on York Island, participated in the battle of Harlem heights, where we beat the British. I commanded a company of thirty men and two field pieces. Lost fifteen of my men killed and wounded.

Next, I was in the battle of the White Plains, where we were defeated.

I was in the battle of Trenton, also in the battle of Princeton; was stationed at Bound brook after that engagement.

Was next stationed at Meed fort.

Was at the battle of Brandywine, where we were engaged throughout the day. At sundown our army drove the red coats into Germantown, where they took refuge in an old stone house. Winter coming on we did not do much.

Next year I was in the battle of Monmouth, where our artillery did much execution.

After this battle I was ordered to Fort Schuyler, where, during the year, we had some skirmishing with the Indians.

I always belonged to the artillery of the Massachusetts line; was capt.-lieut., in the artillery, and served under Gen. Washington four years, by whom I was entrusted with many small adventures, for the execution of which I received his personal thanks.

I was present at the Boston Tea-party, a looker on only.

I pulled down the king's statute in New York, a leaden one, which we made into bullets.

I came to this place, Wellsburg, in 1790, no town here then. The Indian war was not yet ended. I served in the militia ranks. Every one at that early period was obliged to carry arms for self-defense. I believe I am the oldest revolutionary soldier in this state, Virginia.

Capt. Oliver Brown was born in Lexington, Mass., July 25, 1753, and died Feb. 17, 1846, at the home of his son-in-law, Stephen Colwell, near Wellsburg, W. Va., blind but not infirm—the year following the making of the foregoing memorandum.

The statue of George III., referred to by Mr. Brown as "pulled down," was destroyed on the night of July 9, 1776, by a party of 40 men, half of whom were sailors, led by Capt. Brown. It stood on a white marble pedestal 15 feet high, in the center of the bowling green in New York City, having been erected by the obsequious assembly of New York in 1770 to commemorate the anniversary of the birthday of Frederick, second child of the king. Capt. Brown concealed his followers in a dark alley near the statue. At an opportune hour several sailors, having no fears as to punishment for *lese majeste,* climbed up the leaden image of his royal highness and tied ropes around it. When the pull-all-together came these ropes broke. The second attempt, however, was successful. The statue came smashing down over the iron fence that had cost the city $4,000.

"And all the king's horses and all the king's men
Never put it together again—never again."

George Washington issued an order the next day disapproving this adventure of Capt. Brown and his fellows, but his censure was very mild. Capt. Brown, however, always declared later in life that it was the one act of his career of which he was really ashamed. Most of the statue is said to have been taken to Litchfield, Conn., and there run into bullets for the American army, which was putting it to quite a useful purpose. But about 1880, more than a hundred years after this historical demolition, the complete tail of the horse, and parts of the saddle and housings, comprising in all about 200 pounds, were dug up in a marsh near Stamford, Conn., and sold to the New York Historical Society.

In 1790 Capt. Brown, with his wife and children, came west of the mountains and stopped on land on King's Creek, in what is now Hancock county, W. Va., farming there for a short while and then going to the site whereon Wellsburg now stands, where they settled permanently. Patrick Gass's Journal says that in Wellsburg, in 1790, "there was but one building to be seen, and it was a log house on the lower end of the bottom, near midway between the river and the hills."

Here Oliver Brown became in 1800 one of the subscribers to the support of Trinity Church, of which he had become a member, and of which Dr. Doddridge was the rector. Capt. Brown served three years with the militia in the frontier struggles with the Indians. He held a state appointment from Virginia as an inspector of flour, the transportation of which in boats down the Ohio and Mississippi rivers was quite heavy, Wellsburg having become an important point of shipment.

Capt. Brown brought with him from the east his wife Abigail and his Massachusetts-born children—Abigail, John, Sarah, Danforth, Catherine, William and Oliver. Four more children were born in Wellsburg, viz., George, James, Richard and Elizabeth. There are now many descendants in Western Pennsylvania, West Virginia and Ohio, of Oliver Brown and his wife Abigail. One of these is Thomas Stephen Brown, the well-known Pittsburg lawyer—a great grandson.

Worth noting as a curious phase with some of these Brown children is their marriage with ministers of the gospel. Sarah Brown's first husband was Robert Colwell. Four of their daughters chose ministers for life partners. Catherine married Rev. Martin V. Schoonover, a Dutch Reformed minister of Brooklyn; Mary married Rev. Wm. McCombs; Elizabeth married Rev. Robert Fulton; and Harriet married Rev. Samuel McFarren. After the death of Robert Colwell his widow married Rev. Elisha Macurdy, D.D., a noted Presbyterian minister of the early days in Western Pennsylvania, and their daughter, Sarah Macurdy, became the wife of Rev. Samuel Fulton, D.D., pastor of the fourth Presbyterian church of Pittsburg. Sarah Fulton, daughter of Elizabeth Colwell and Robert Fulton, married Rev. Wm. T. Beatty, D.D., first pastor of the Shadyside Presbyterian church, Pittsburg, and their daughter is the famous grand opera singer, Louise Homer—(Mrs. Louise Dilworth Beatty Homer).

Kate McFarren, daughter of Harriet Colwell and Samuel McFarren, became a missionary in South America.

Sarah Brown's granddaughter Mary, daughter of her son Stephen Colwell, became the wife of Rev. Dr. Henry W. Greene, of Princeton Seminary.

Richard Brown, youngest son of Oliver Brown, entered the ministry of the Presbyterian church and preached for many years in Eastern Ohio. His daughter Catherine married Rev. Alexander Swaney, of Cadiz, Ohio.

Oliver Brown's granddaughter, Eliza Vilette Brown, daughter of John Brown and Mrs. Eleanor (Doddridge) Gantt, widow of John Gantt, married Hon. Daniel Polsley, of Point Pleasant, W. Va., judge of the Seventh Judicial Circuit of W. Va., (1862) and member in 1867 of the Fortieth Congress of the United States.

THE TETER AND MANCHESTER FAMILIES.

By William T. Lindsey.

Capt. Samuel Teter, who was one of the conspicuous figures in the early history of Washington county, Pa., where he owned large tracts of land, settled there with the Doddridge's and Wells's in 1773, in what is now Independence township, on the farm of 1,000 acres which he sold in the spring of 1797 to Isaac Manchester. It was named in the warrant "Plantation Plenty," and lies near the present village of West Middletown.

Captain Teter was born in 1737. He took part when a very young man in the ill-fated Braddock expedition in 1755, and in the Forbes expedition in 1758, in which he bore a gallant part, leading one of the assaulting parties at Fort Pitt, in which his little company was almost annihilated.

He was a resident of Bedford county, Pennsylvania, in 1769, and married Mary Doddridge, daughter of Joseph Doddridge and his wife, Mary Biggs. She was an aunt of the Rev. Joseph Doddridge, and also of the famous Indian fighters, the Biggs brothers, of whom Gen. William Biggs of West Liberty, Ohio County, West Virginia, and Surveyor-General Zaccheus Biggs of Ohio, were the most prominent.

Captain Teter left a large family. His descendants have become prominent in professional and business life. All his sons but Samuel served in the war of 1812. George Teter was an ensign in Capt. Samuel Davis' company, Trimble's Mounted regiment, Ohio volunteers and militia. John Teter served as first lieutenant in Capt. Jacob Gilbert's company of infantry, Second (Hindman's) Regiment, Ohio militia, afterwards First (Andrew's) Regiment, and Daniel as a private. Several of Capt. Teter's descendants also served with credit in the Union army during the civil war. Numerous intermarriages have taken place with the most prominent families of Ohio, among them the McArthurs, McDonalds, McLenes and other historic families, individual members of which were Gen. Duncan McArthur, Governor of Ohio, Col. John McDonald, author of "McDonald's Sketches" and Hon. Jeremiah McLene, Secretary of State of Ohio for twenty-three years; and they are also allied to the Allen, Trimble, and Anderson families.

During the years in which Capt. Teter was a resident of Washington county he became the commandant of Fort Doddridge, as related by his nephew, the Rev. Joseph Doddridge. After the sale of his farm to Mr. Manchester he went to Ross county, Ohio, settling on Lower Twin Creek, removing in his old age to the home of one of his sons-in-law, a McDonald, near Marysville, Union county, Ohio, where he died October 8, 1823. His wife survived him until May 3, 1838, attaining the great age of ninety years. Their remains lie buried in the McDonald burial ground near Marysville, where a granite monument has been erected to their memory by some of their descendants.

On "Plantation Plenty" Mr. Manchester lived and wrought until his death in 1851, aged 89 years. His farm descended to his son, the late Col. Asa Manchester, who died in 1896; was born in 1811. Here was raised by Mr. Manchester the fine 15-room brick mansion, now occupied by his granddaughters, which is the most notable of the very few important survivals in this region of the typical architecture and admirable constructive skill of the early days of the republic, being in as entirely good condition now as when built. Fifteen years, from 1800 to 1815, were required in the preparatory and final work. The dwelling was erected on the site and within the lines of the stockade fort prepared by Capt. Teter as a protection against Indian forays. One of the corner stones of this fort is still preserved in the front yard of the mansion.

Isaac Manchester came from Newport, R. I. He was of English descent, maybe English born, and in the arrangement of his Washington county residence and farm buildings he had in mind, apparently, the reproduction of an English manor house and home. The first step in the making of this home was a commodious tool house, in which to manufacture the tools and implements necessary for use by the artisans, farm hands and house help. This tool house still stands on the premises, as serviceable as the day it was put up, and contains all the tools, many of them long since obsolete, with which Mr. Manchester and his mechanics wrought. There are 40 or 50 planes of various shapes and sizes, some three to four feet long, and most of which are unknown to the woodworkers of to-day. Also augers, bits, drawing knives, saws, hammers, hatchets, axes, anvils, adzes, etc., fine tools of every description essential to the elaborate and durable work to be done, for Mr. Manchester intended to build and did build an elegant and artistic dwelling that should last for ages. One hundred years old now, it is as well preserved as the day when the last workman put his finishing stroke upon it. And not a nail used in it anywhere, nor in any of the minor buildings.

It is said by those familiar with the historical aspect of architectural and building construction in this territory, at the beginning of the last century, that Mr. Manchester's artisans must have been brought from east of the mountains to do this special work, as it required a much higher grade of manual skill than was then ordinarily available here. It is doubtful if a duplicate of these premises in unique attractiveness, and impressive stability, combined with rare suggestiveness of "the olden time," exists anywhere else in the United States.

The masonry, brick and wood construction of the mansion and subsidiary buildings was carried forward under the personal supervision of Mr. Manchester. The fine hardwood interior finish, the mouldings, newel posts, banisters, fire fronts, railings, base boards, etc., was executed by mechanics whose peculiar tools for doing the intricate work uncommon here to that period were first made on the ground under the direction of Mr. Manchester. The brick and stone masonry nowhere shows signs of disintegration. The mortar is as smooth and hard as cement. The immense frame work of the great barn, which was finished ten years before the house, is held together with wooden pins. During the finishing of his mansion Mr. Manchester found himself short of a much needed piece of important wood with which to complete a capital of the parlor mantel. Mounting his horse he rode over the mountains to Philadelphia for this wood and brought it home with him in his saddle-bags—a trip of 800 miles.

All the plows ever used on this farm, from the one with which Mr. Manchester first turned up the virgin soil down to the finest modern plow of the present day, are kept in the old tool house. They show every step in the development of the American plow during a century and a quarter. There are also many other discarded implements of husbandry and household work, including wind-mills, flax-mills, cleaning-mills, flails, a cheese press, yokes for oxen young and old, a carriage built after designs of the Napoleonic era, copper kettles, iron skillets, waffle irons with handles several feet long, spinning wheels, tin lanterns for tallow candle illumination, complete outfits for making boots, shoes and harness, a lace-making loom, which could be used now by any one knowing how, a loom for weaving linsey-woolsey cloth, which is a combination of flax-linen and wool, along with many other curious utensils of field, shop and kitchen.

DISTINGUISHED MEN OF WEST MIDDLETOWN.

By William T. Lindsey.

The quaint old-fashioned village of West Middletown was incorporated as a borough as early as 1823. It has been a post-office since 1805. Its roadway was macadamized, its sidewalks flagstoned, and its gutters sandstoned nearly a hundred years ago. John W. Garrett, founder and first president of the B. & O. railroad, and Charles Avery Holmes, the famous Methodist preacher, were born here. Joseph Doddridge lived but three miles distant. Here also lived Col. David Williamson, who led the expedition that slaughtered the peaceful Moravian Indians. Yet —how strange the contrast!—this is also the birthplace of the Campbellite or Christian church, now numbering a million and a half communicants. The building in which the first congregation was organized by the Campbells on Brush Run in 1810 stands to-day in West Middletown, to which it was removed. Alexander Campbell, founder of this great church, was born at Ballymena, County Antrim, Ireland, Sept. 12, 1788, and died March 4, 1866, at Bethany, W. Va., where he had founded Bethany College in 1840. His father, Rev. Thos. Campbell, was a relative and namesake of the celebrated Irish poet. Thomas Campbell came to America in 1807, his son following two years later. Within an hour's drive of West Middletown George Washington owned 3,000 acres of farm land which he sold in 1796 for $12,000. It is now worth half a million or more.

Early in the last century Robert Fulton, the steamboat inventor, bought here a farm which he gave to his parents and sisters as a mark of his affection; and further as a manifestation of pride that on his twenty-first birthday he was able to make them so substantial a gift. Fulton lived in this vicinity for some time, and the hardy yoemanry generally regarded him as a fop, such being the impression made upon them by his refined and courteous manners and unusually genteel apparel. The heavy current of travel flowing westward at that time into Washington county, and through Washington county into the Ohio country, coupled with the building of the National Pike, had greatly enhanced the value of land in the West Middletown section, as also in many other localities, and this fact was the determining influence in Fulton's farm purchase. Many of the Hessian soldiers who had fought for Britain in the war of the Revolution did not return to Europe after the conclusion of peace, and some of them came to this part of Washington county, settling as farmers on a branch of Buffalo Creek, to which they gave the name of "the Dutch fork."

Joseph Ritner, governor of Pennsylvania, had his home near West Middletown. James Clemens, ancestor of Samuel L. Clemens (Mark Twain), settled here many years ago. He lived near Taylor's Fort, now Taylorstown, Washington county, and had twelve children, six boys and six girls. It is said by one of his descendants now living in the west that three of these boys, Jeremiah, William and James, were of the number who took part in the massacre of the Moravian Indians at Gnadenhutten; and that, on their return home, the feeling was so strong against the participants that two of these boys left home. Jeremiah went to Alabama, where, years afterward, his son Jeremiah became a brilliant lawyer, a general of militia, a United States senator, and an author. One of his books was a life of Aaron Burr. James Clemens went to the territory of Missouri, where his descendants are now wealthy and influential. Mark Twain—Samuel Langhorn Clemens—belonged to this branch. William Clemens' son Sherrard became a noted lawyer of Wheeling, W. Va., and represented that district in congress. But any statement that the Clemenses left Washington county because of public disapproval of the Moravian massacre must be taken with allowances. There was probably as much public approval as disapproval; but we shall not attempt to draw any exact line of distinction. The fact that Col. Williamson, who led the expedition, was twice elected sheriff of Washington county after the massacre is of the highest significance as indicating the drift of popular sentiment in the matter of crediting or discrediting him for what he had done. And, of course, the public attitude toward him was extended to his followers, or many of them.

The village of West Middletown was one of the most important stations on the Underground Railroad. Here often came John Brown, the fanatic, the Abolitionist, to buy sheep and trade in wool, and to deepen and strengthen by association with this mysterious line the anti-slavery sentiments for which he later sacrificed his life at Harpers Ferry. A dozen or more frontier forts, ante-dating and succeeding the revolution, were erected at many places in this region to protect settlers from Indian forays; and, post-dating the revolution, here surged in full force in 1791-3 the ominous tide of that Whisky insurrection which almost carried the people into another revolt.

James Simpson, author of many of the footnotes in this book, and a life-long dweller near West Middletown, was born in Washington county, Pa., in 1824, dying December 18, 1902, at his home in Cross Creek township, where he had lived since 1828. He was a successful farmer, with a turn of mind that led him to give his leisure hours to the study and investigation of local and county history, in which he acquired a wide-spread reputation for thoroughness and accuracy. He became an authority on Western Pennsylvania history, accumulating a library of large extent and value. He wrote "Early Sketches of Smith Township" for the Burgettstown Enterprise, and compiled an elaborate and reliable historical record of the old Cross Creek burial ground and the interments therein. His weather reports were sought by all his neighbors and by the local newspapers. He kept a registry of all visitors at his home.

LOGAN, MICHAEL CRESAP AND SIMON GIRTY.

By John S. Ritenour.

LOGAN, THE CAYUGA.

"I appeal to the White Man ungrateful to say,
If he e'er from my cabin went hungry away?
If naked and cold unto Logan he came,
And he gave him no blanket and kindled no flame?"

Three of the most conspicuous characters of the Pittsburgh region during the period covered by Dr. Doddridge's "Notes," from 1763 to 1783, were Logan, the Cayuga savage, Michael Cresap and Simon Girty. Logan is popularly remembered alone for the lofty sentiment and touching pathos of his, "I appeal to any white man," etc.; Girty for his treacheries and cruelties; and Cresap chiefly for the charge made against him that he was responsible for the murder of Logan's kindred at Yellow Creek. It may be of some value to review cursorily, in connection with the republication of these "Notes," such incidents in the lives of these three men as are likely to interest and instruct the reader of this book.

However noble an Indian Logan may have been early in life, he succumbed at last, like many another hapless red man, to the white man's whisky. His savage name, "Tah-gah-jute," means "Short Dress." He got the name of Logan from his father, Shikellamy, as a tribute of paternal esteem for James Logan, secretary of the province of Pennsylvania, and a firm friend of the Indians. Shikellamy was head chieftain of the Cayugas, and a disciple of the Moravian missionaries. He lived at Shamokin, on the Susquehanna river, where Logan, his second son, was born in 1725. Logan died, slain, in 1780; and even in this year, long after the killing of his family, he had accompanied a force of English regulars, Canadians and savages, on an invasion of Kentucky. The crime at Yellow Creek had alienated him forever from the Americans.

Butterfield says Logan was known on the border of Pennsylvania and Virginia because of his friendship for the whites, his engaging qualities and his fine personal appearance. "He was a remarkably tall man, considerably above six feet high," says R. *P.* McClay, "strong and well proportioned, with a brave, open, manly countenance; and, to appearances, not afraid to meet any man."

In 1770 Logan came west of the mountains and made his first home on the Ohio river below the mouth of the Big Beaver. He followed hunting and trapping. He was gradually being alienated then by his dissolute habits from any feeling of friendship for the whites, and history says that in 1772, two years before the killing of his relatives, he was already painted and equipped for war.

In the spring of 1774, on the 30th of April, it is believed, (some say May 3 or 4), Logan's relatives were murdered by whites at their home near the mouth of Yellow Creek, about 30 miles above Wheeling. Just who these relations were is not known, but John J. Jacob's life of Cresap says they numbered three—his mother, younger brother and sister. The latter had there a half-breed son ten years of age who was not slain. Logan's father has even been alleged to have been one of the victims, but this was wholly untrue, for Shikellamy had died at Shamokin as early as 1749. Logan's speech charges Cresap with the crime, but the historians of later days discredit this. Cresap was fifteen miles away at the time. Logan believed, however, that he had directed the deed.

Some time after these murders Logan and eight other savages were on a vengeance raid in Virginia, at the headwaters of the Monongahela, and while on the north fork of Helston Creek they captured two white men, Wm. Robinson and another named Hellew. The prisoners were taken to Waketomic, a Shawanese town on the Muskingum. Here Hellew was adopted into the tribe. Robinson was doomed to the stake, despite the plea of Logan for his life; but before the death fire was lighted Logan with his tomahawk boldly cut the thongs that bound the prisoner and took him away with him to what is now Newcomerstown,

Ohio, where he dictated to Robinson a letter, dated July 21, 1774, directed to Capt. Cresap, asking Cresap why he had killed Logan's family on Yellow Creek? This letter was written with ink made from gunpowder. It was tied to a war club and left in the cabin of a murdered settler to be found by whoever should happen along. Robinson is said to have remained with Logan until the treaty of Fort Pitt, when he returned to his home in Virginia.

The same Fall, at a November meeting on the Scioto between the whites and Indians, at Camp Charlotte, to conclude the treaty which ended Dunmore's war, Logan heard personally from the lips of Col. John Gibson, who was Dunmore's interpreter, that Cap. Cresap himself had told him he was not one of the Yellow Creek party, and had had nothing to do with that crime directly or indirectly. Cresap was far away when the killings were done, and had no prior cognizance that the deed was to be committed.

After the Yellow Creek tragedy Logan at once began reprisals on the scattered white settlers in the Ohio valley and for months fearful barbarities were practised on men, women and children, during which Logan is said to have taken thirty scalps.

The circumstances of the origin of Logan's celebrated speech, or message, are these, in brief: When Lord Dunmore was marching against the Indians in the Scioto valley, in November of 1774, his progress was arrested about six miles from the Indian camp at Chillicothe by the arrival of messengers from there suggesting a suspension of hostilities, with possible negotiation of a peace treaty. Logan took no part in the conference that followed, and was not present. Dunmore was unwilling to conclude so important a transaction without the participation and consent of this influential Indian. He sent Col. John Gibson into the Delaware town to hunt up Logan and ascertain the cause of his aloofness. The two met, and Logan invited Gibson to accompany him to the woods for a talk. Some of the chiefs advised Gibson not do this, as Logan was in an ugly mood, but Gibson paid no heed. His confidence in personal safety with Logan may have been due to the fact that Logan's sister had been his squaw; and it is altogether likely that this woman's half-breed boy who had escaped massacre at Yellow Creek was Gibson's own son.

Logan led Gibson a mile and a half away from the camp, and into a dense coppice, where they sat down together on a log. Here Logan, with passionate vehemence, dramatically related to his listener the story of his woes at the hands of the whites, weeping as he spoke. He used the Delaware tongue. When Gibson returned to Dunmore's camp he told the earl what had occurred, and then himself translated into English on paper the great speech of Logan, to which he had been the sole listener.

When Gov. Dunmore got back to Virginia, after the conclusion of peace, he took this paper with him, or a copy of it, and there it was printed for the first time in the Virginia Gazette, at Williamsburg, on February 4, 1775. About two weeks later, on February 16, 1775, it was republished in New York City. But it was Thomas Jefferson who introduced it to almost world-wide popularity.

Finding in his pocketbook a memorandum of this speech, which he is said to have secured from Dunmore, possibly a complete copy, Jefferson used it in his "Notes on Virginia" to disprove a theory put forth by Buffon and others, to the effect that all animal nature, both human and beast, degenerated in America. Jefferson pointed to Logan's speech as an illustration of Indian character and genius. The "Notes on Virginia" were written in 1781-2, and they included this stigmatization of Michael Cresap, who had been named by Logan as the destroyer of his family.

"A man infamous for the many murders he had committed on those much injured people."

This allegation was modified in a later publication of the "Notes" (1800) but never wholly withdrawn. Luther Martin, son-in-law of Cresap, attorney general of Maryland, a very able man, an active Federalist, and a bitter political opponent of Jefferson, attacked the latter for accepting and endorsing Logan's charge against Cresap. He insisted that Cresap had nothing to do with the crime. And time has sustained him. Cresap had nothing to do with it.

There are two versions of Logan's speech. The one accepted by Jefferson, and by historical writers generally, names Cresap. But Jacob's story of the episode at Camp Charlotte relates that Benjamin Tomlinson, one of Dunmore's officers, heard the speech read three times, once by Gibson and twice by Dunmore, and Col. Tomlinson says that neither the name of Cresap or of anybody else was mentioned in it. Jacob believes that Cresap's name was interpolated either by Dunmore or his malevolent Pittsburg lieutenant, Dr. Connoly, for the purpose of throwing upon Cresap (and thus avoiding their own legitimate burden), responsibility for the frontier irritation which culminated in Dunmore's War; that Dunmore and Connoly thus hoped to divert attention from themselves.

On May 15, 1851, Brantz Mayer delivered at Baltimore the annual address before the Maryland Historical Society. His subject was "Tah-gah-jute, or Logan and Cresap." The purpose was to definitely fix Cresap's innocence of any complicity whatever in the destruction of Logan's family. This address, enlarged and revised, was published in 1867. Mr. Mayer says Jefferson's comments tended to exhibit Cresap in an odious light, despite the fact that Mr. Jefferson had in his possession at the time a letter from George Rogers Clark wholly exculpating Cresap from participation in the slaughter.

On May 15, 1798, Dr. Samuel Brown of Lexington, Ky., had written to George Rogers Clark asking for his recollection touching the authenticity of Logan's speech, and of Cresap's conduct. On June 17, 1798, Clark replied that while Logan had reason to suspect Cresap, because of his conduct several days before the slaughter at Yellow Creek, Cresap was in fact not involved. As to the speech, Clark wrote:

"Logan's speech to Dunmore was generally believed, indeed not doubted, to have been genuine, and a declaration by Logan. Logan is the author of the speech."

On Sept. 4, 1798, Dr. Brown sent Clark's letter to Jefferson. This was two years before Jefferson published his second edition of the "Notes," in which he only modified the aspersion against Cresap.

It was thought for a long time that Jefferson had never got this letter; that it had miscarried; but it was found later among the papers Jefferson had turned over to the government. Mr. Mayer was unable to figure out why a man of Jefferson's position and character had written as he did about Cresap, in view of the accurate information before him. He thinks it may have been one of the phases of the political animosity of the time. In 1800, when Jefferson revised his "Notes," Cresap had been dead 24 years; and Clark's letter had been in Jefferson's possession two years.

One of the earliest publications of Logan's speech omitted Cresap's name. Others embodied it. The two versions brought on a controversy between Thomas Jefferson and his enemies as to the authenticity of the speech, but it decided nothing.

Campbell, in his "Gertrude of Wyoming," paraphrases Logan's speech for one of his heroes, making him say:

> "Nor man, nor child, nor thing of living birth;
> No, not the dog that watched my household hearth
> Escaped that night of blood upon our plains.
> All perished! I alone am left on earth
> To whom nor relatives nor blood remains;
> No, not a kindred drop that runs in human veins."

C. W. Butterfield's "History of the Girty's," (1890) referring to the peace meeting already noted as being held for the making of a treaty to end Dunmore's war, prints the version that Simon Girty was sent to bring Logan to this meeting, and that, while Logan was there on the scene, he refused to be a party to the negotiations. When Girty returned he had a personal talk with Col. John Gibson on the outskirts of the crowd. Gibson then went to his own tent, and shortly afterward returned with a manuscript speech for and in the name of Logan. This was read to the conference. Girty had verbally translated to Gibson what Logan had said to him, and Gibson had put it into English, "which he was well able to do." Girty could neither read nor write. "It is now well established," says Butterfield, "that the version first printed was substantially the words of Logan." This story gives to Girty the credit of being the first translator of Logan's speech, which is altogether improbable.

Col. John Gibson was an uncle of John Bannister Gibson, the great chief justice of the supreme court of Pennsylvania. On April 4, 1800, he made an affidavit before J. Barker, of Pittsburg, certifying to the accuracy of the speech and to Logan's authorship.

Before he published his " Notes " Mr. Doddridge, who had never lost faith in and respect for Logan's character, had written a dramatic piece entitled " Logan, the Last of the Race of Shikellimus, Chief of the Cayuga Nation." Its object was to prove the sincerity of Logan's friendship for the whites.

" I thought," wrote Dr. Doddridge, " his bravery, talents and misfortunes, worthy of a dramatic commemoration. For attempting the task of doing justice to the character of Logan I have no apology to make. The tear of commiseration is due to Logan. Like Wallace, he outlived the independence of his nation. Like Cato, 'he greatly fell with his falling state.' Like Ossian, he was the last of his family, all of whom but himself had fallen by assassinations which, for their atrocious character, are scarcely paralleled in history."

Another literary production by Mr. Doddridge, which appeared in July, 1821, is entitled "The Backwoodsman and the Dandy." It is a quite commonplace dialogue designed to picture the habits and customs of frontier life. Most if not all of this information the author also incorporated in his " Notes."

There are several different stories about the manner of Logan's death. One is that while attending an Indian council in Detroit he got hilariously and viciously drunk and violently struck his wife. She fell insensible to the ground, and believing he had killed her he fled, fearing the blood vengeance of her relatives. While on this flight, alone, and still under the influence of liquor, he encountered in the wilderness a band of Indians with their squaws and children. They did not know of his deed, and he seems to have been in a state of delirium. But he recognized his own cousin, or brother-in-law, Tod-kah-dos. Declaring that the whole party should die, he was dismounting from his horse to begin his work of extermination when Tod-kah-dos shot and killed him, prompted by fear of what Logan might do in his condition. This version is from Dah-gan-on-do, a Seneca, who said he got it himself from Tod-kah-dos. The latter lived until his death in 1844 on the Cold Spring, in the Allegheny Seneca reservation. Logan's wife was a Shawanese woman. They had no children. She recovered from her husband's blow and returned to her own people.

"Howe's Historical Collections of Ohio" credits to Good Hunter, a Mingo chief, the version that Logan was slain while sitting at a camp fire near Detroit with a blanket over his head. An Indian clove his skull with a tomahawk. One phase of the story is that this Indian was a friend of Logan, who had hired him to do the deed, and another is that he was an enemy who seized a favorable opportunity to end the Cayuga's life.

"While intoxicated," says the Encyclopedia Americana (1903), "Logan attacked a party of friendly Indians and was killed by his relative, Tod-kah-dohs, in self-defense."

The story of Logan's death as related by Maj. Chas. Cracraft, of Washington, Pa., to his son William, and repeated by the latter, is that while Logan, under the influence of liquor, was on his way from Detroit to his home on the Scioto, he stopped at the tent of his cousin and asked for food. The squaw told him there was none. He disbelieved her, and beat her with the ramrod of his gun. Then he left. When the woman's husband got home shortly afterward he found her in tears. Ascertaining the reason, he started off on a short cut by which he knew he would intercept Logan. They had some words, and the Indian shot Logan as he was dismounting from his horse. Logan fell dead on touching the ground. This is the story heard by Major Cracraft while himself a prisoner of the British in Detroit.

At this stage of his career Logan had fallen so low that, while in Detroit, and there intoxicated, he was ignominiously kicked out of the commissary house by Capt. Bawbee.* This so deeply offended him that he is said to have declared to a friend he would desert the British, and take up with the Virginians, if he thought the latter would overlook his deeds against them. But he did not live to undertake the consummation of his threat.

"In his intercourse with our race," says Mayer, "Logan lost nothing but the few virtues of a savage, while he gained from civilization very little but its vices. His last years were melancholy indeed. He wandered from tribe to tribe a solitary and lonely man. Dejected by the loss of friends, and the decay of his people, he resorted constantly to the stimulus of strong drink to drown his sorrow."

Where his remains lie nobody knows.

MICHAEL CRESAP.

Michael Cresap, youngest son of Col. Thomas Cresap, was born June 29, 1742, in that part of Alleghany county, Maryland, which formerly belonged to Frederick county. His father, an English immigrant from Yorkshire, courageous, aggressive, capable and enterprising, gave his son a good education. Young Cresap was not successful in the mercantile business east of the mountains, largely because of his easy and generous disposition in allowing injudicious credits, so he came west early in 1774, bringing with him six or seven men to build houses and clear land in the Ohio valley. He made an investment at Redstone Old Fort, now Brownsville. But late in the autumn of the same year Cresap returned to Maryland in poor health. Spending the winter at home, he was back in the spring of 1775 in the Ohio valley with more young men to finish the work he had begun the year before. This time he got as far south as Kentucky, where he is said to have contemplated settling finally. But, being still sick, he determined to go home again to Maryland. Approaching the end of his journey he was met by a friend who told him he had been selected to command one of the two companies of riflemen required of Maryland by resolution of the Continental congress. This responsibility was not in harmony with the purpose that was carrying him home, but he accepted it, nevertheless. He led the first company of Maryland riflemen, some of whom were recruits from Pittsburg, to Boston, where they joined the American army under Gen. Washington. Here he was attacked by fever. Starting home he reached New York city on Oct. 12, but was not able to proceed further, dying there on Oct. 18, aged 33 years. His funeral the next day was "attended by an enormous concourse." A place was found for his body in Trinity church graveyard, on Broadway, where it still rests. But it might, possibly, be difficult to find the marking stone.

John J. Jacob, who wrote a life of Cresap, clerked as a boy for Cresap during his career as a merchant, and in 1781 he married Cresap's widow, with whom he lived for 40 years. He had all of Cresap's books, papers and memoranda; he had known Cresap intimately, his character, nature, purposes, motives and conduct; he was personally familiar with the history of the events of Cresap's life, civil, commercial and military. He insists that Jefferson did Cresap a very great wrong in attributing to him many infamous Indian murders; and, moreover, that no evidence has ever been produced to prove Logan's alleged charge that Cresap was responsible for the murder of his family. "No idea," says Jacob, "was entertained by the Virginia Commissioners who settled the expenses of Dunmore's War, as that he was the murderer of Logan's family, or that he was a man of infamous character as an Indian murderer, or that he was the cause of the war." The commissioners held sessions at Pittsburgh, Redstone Old Fort, and Winchester, which were attended by Jacob, as the representative of Cresap, for the purpose of securing orders for payment of bills for goods sold by Cresap to Dunmore's soldiers. Therefore, when he writes of the sentiments of the commissioners he does so from knowledge gained by close personal association.

Throughout all his home life Michael Cresap had been associated with kindliness toward Indians. His father owned a landed estate of 1400 acres on both sides of the north fork of the Potomac river, in Virginia and Maryland, a few miles above its junction with the south fork. Here, as representative of the Ohio company, which made the first English settlement in Pittsburgh before Braddock's war, Col. Thomas Cresap had engaged Nemacolin, the famous Indian, to mark and lay out a road over the mountains from Cumberland to Pittsburgh. This Nemacolin did, and he did it so well that Gen. Braddock followed it when he marched in 1755 to the attack on Fort Duquesne. While this road was ever afterward known as Braddock's road, its real name should have been Nemacolin's. So great was Nemacolin's affection for Col. Cresap and his family that he left his son George to live with them, and George liked it there so well that he stayed with the Cresaps all his life.

SIMON GIRTY.

There were four of the Girty sons—Thomas, Simon, James and George. Then there was a half brother, John Turner. The first Girty, Simon, Sr., came from Ireland. In this country he married an English girl named Mary Newton. They made their home at Chambers Mills, on the east side of the Susquehanna, above Harrisburg, now Dauphin county, Pa. Here Simon Girty, Jr., the second son, was born in 1741. In 1749 the family removed to Sherman's Creek, in Perry county, along with a number of other settlers, to engage in farming. But the Indians regarded this as an unauthorized encroachment upon their lands, and they protested to the government. Evidently this protest was accounted well-grounded, for the authorities forcibly expelled the settlers and burned the houses they had built.

The Girtys then returned to Chambers Mills, where the father was killed in 1751 in a drunken frolic by an Indian called "The Fish." In 1753 Mrs. Girty married John Turner, who had been a boarder in the family. Turner took them back to the Sherman's Creek valley in 1755, and here all fell into the hands of Indians when the latter captured and destroyed Fort Granville there on the Juniata. All were brought over the mountains to Kittanning. The Indians recognized John Turner as one who had injured their race, so in retaliation they sacrificed him at the stake. Gordon's "History of Pennsylvania" says they tied him to a blackened post, made a great fire, danced around him, heated gun barrels red hot and run them through his body, and after three hours of such torture scalped him alive. Then a savage held up to him a boy who gave him the finishing stroke with a tomahawk. If this is not an exaggerated tale, Turner must have been a man of extraordinary endurance to withstand such treatment so long.

Mrs. Turner and her son John Turner were claimed by the Delawares, who baptised them and carried them off into the wilderness, to Fort Delaware. The other four boys were kept by the Indians for a while at Kittanning. Thomas was recaptured when Lieut. Col. John Armstrong attacked Kittanning in September, 1756. Simon, James and George had been taken west by the routed savages, but all eventually got back with the whites. Thomas had been a captive for only 40 days. Simon was 15 years old when he returned. All three were brought back from the woods when the French had been expelled from the country, and English domination had become assured. Simon had been taken with the Senecas, George with the Delawares and James with the Shawnees. Mrs. Girty and her son John, when delivered up by their captors, made her home in Pittsburgh. It is not known when she died. The Girty boys proved to be a bad lot. This sketch, however, deals chiefly with Simon. He was wholly uneducated, but was a man of talent, and of great influence with the Indians. He made his early home at Fort Pitt, as did his brothers, where he was a laborer, trader, hunter, scout, interpreter, anything, indeed, he could get to do within his capacity.

At the opening of the Revolution Girty joined the militia at Fort Pitt, says one historian. In 1778 he asked for a captain's commission in the Continental service, which was denied him. This is said to have embittered him, and to have been one of the reasons why he joined with Capt. Alexander McKee in deserting to the British.

This desertion took place on the night of Saturday, March 28, 1778, from McKee's house at McKee's Rocks, because McKee and some of his Tory associates were suspected, and with good reason, of instigating the Indians to make war on the colonists, thus aiding the British. "Until within a few weeks of this flight," says Hassler's "Old Westmoreland," "Girty had been a faithful servitor of American interests. In the absence of positive knowledge of any reason for his desertion, he is believed to have been tempted by McKee with promises of preferment in the British service. James Girty, brother of Simon, was then with the Shawnees on the Scioto, having been sent from Fort Pitt by the American authorities on a futile peace embassy. He had been raised among the Shawnees, was a natural savage, and at once joined his brother and the other tories. For 16 years Capt. McKee, Mathew Elliott and the Girtys, were the merciless scourges of the border. They were the instigators and leaders of many Indian raids, continuing their hostility until long after the close of the revolutionary war. They were largely responsible for the general war 1790-94."

In the dispute between Pennsylvania and Virginia as to which had authority over the territory of the Pittsburg region Simon Girty, singularly, sided with Virginia. He was active in behalf of Lord Dunmore in this matter, and also as a scout and interpreter for him when on his way to attack the Shawnees and Mingoes. In the matter of importance of service to Dunmore, and trustworthy discharge of responsible duties, Girty seems to have ranked with those other great lieutenants of the Virginia governor, George Rogers Clarke, Simon Kenton and John Gibson. But in the end he and all his brothers identified themselves with the savages in their bloody border struggles with the white settlers.

Girty's life is so fully described in the frontier literature of recent years that it is needless to reproduce an epitome of it here. (See Butterfield's "History of the Girtys.") After his flight from Pittsburgh in 1778 Girty's course was one of consistent enmity to the Americans, with occasional manifestations of personal friendship. He showed no such feeling, however, to Col. Wm. Crawford, with whom he was well acquainted, and who it is believed he could have saved from burning at the stake on the Tymochtee.

Girty's career south of Lake Erie came to a close with the surrender of Detroit to the Americans in 1796. On March 6, 1798, the British gave him a farm of 164 acres near Fort Malden, in Essex county, Canada, not far from Detroit. Here he lived on his half-pay from the government, on such money as he got for his services as an interpreter, and on the produce of his farm. He had married Catherine Malott, of Detroit, but she had left him in 1797, after the birth of their last child, Prideaux Girty, because of long continued ill-treatment. But when he had lost his eyesight, and was no longer able to take care of himself, she returned to him and nursed him until his death. The renegade had surely secured a good wife. Girty died on this farm Feb. 18, 1818, and was buried there. English soldiers from Fort Malden fired a salute over his grave.

It is hardly worth while to undertake the framing of a personal description of Girty when one historian says "his eyes were black and penetrating" and another speaks of "his gray sunken eyes." Mrs. Girty died in January, 1852. Their children were all thoroughly respectable. John Turner, Girty's half brother, died May 20, 1840, on Squirrel Hill, in the city of Pittsburgh, south of the mouth of Four Mile Run, where he lived on a farm.

The histories relate a good many instances of kindness by Simon Girty, especially to the young. When Christian Fast was captured by the Indians at Lochry's defeat he was about 17 years old. He was adopted by a family of Delawares to take the place of a son who had been killed, and was initiated into the tribe. This was in 1782. Fast was taken to live with the Delawares at Pipestown, on the Tymochtee. But he was discontented and melancholy. In the woods one day, brooding over his captivity, and supposing himself to be alone, he was suddenly accosted by Girty, who inquired of what he was thinking. Fast gave him an evasive answer.

"That is not it," replied Girty. "You are thinking of home. Be a good boy and you shall see your home again."

And Girty made good as to this promise to Fast. He is said to have always been kind to young prisoners.

Says Jonathan Alder: "I knew Simon Girty to purchase at his own expense several boys who were prisoners and take them to the British and have them educated. He was certainly a friend to many prisoners."

Pittsburg, June, 1912.

INDIAN POPULATION OF THE UNITED STATES.

BY E. DANA DURAND, Director of the Census.

Washington, Jan. 22, 1912.

Dear Sirs:—In reply to your letter of January 14, 1912, I give you below a list showing the Indian population at various dates from 1789 to 1910:

Date.	Authority.	Number.
1789	Estimate of the Secretary of War	76,000
1790-1791	Estimate of Gilbert Imlay	60,000
1822	Report of Jedediah Morse on Indian Affairs	*471,417
1825	Report of Secretary of War	†129,366
1829	Report of Secretary of War	312,930
1832	Estimate of Samuel J. Drake	293,933
1834	Report of Secretary of War	312,610
1836	Report of Superintendent of Indian Affairs	253,464
1837	Report of Superintendent of Indian Affairs	302,498
1850	Report of H. R. Schoolcraft	388,229
1853	Report of United States Census, 1850	400,764
1860	Report of United States Census	339,421
1867	Report of Hon. N. G. Taylor (exclusive of citizen Indians)	‡306,925
1870	Report of United States Census	313,712
1880	Report of United States Census and Indian Office	306,543
1890	Report of United States Census	248,253
1900	Report of United States Census	237,196
1910	Report of United States Census	265,683

* This included Texas, not then in the United States.
† Indians of extreme west apparently not included.
‡ The Indian population by this count foots up 306,925, but, by an apparent clerical error, was printed as 306,475.

The figures given are in some instances, as stated, mere estimates by various persons who were supposed to have made a study of the Indians at the different dates. The later returns, from 1870 to 1910, were made from the returns of the United States censuses. I am also inclosing a statement showing the Indian population of the United States in 1910 in the various states and territories.

A preliminary statement giving for continental United States the distribution of the Indian population by states and territories, as shown by the returns of the Thirteenth Decennial Census, taken as of April 15, 1910, was issued December 14, 1911 by Director Durand, of the Bureau of the Census. The statistics were prepared under the supervision of William C. Hunt, chief statistician for population in the Census Bureau, and are subject to later revision.

In 1910 the Indian population of continental United States was 265,683, as compared with 237,196 in 1900, and 248,253 in 1890. According to these figures there was an increase in the Indian population from 1900 to 1910 of 28,487, or 12 per cent. as compared with a decrease from 1890 to 1900 of 11,057, or 4.5 per cent. The decrease in the decade 1890-1900 suggests the possibility that the enumeration in 1900 was not so accurate or complete as in 1890 or in 1910. For the 20-year period from 1890 to 1910 there was an increase of 17,430, or 7 per cent.

The Indian population in 1910 is distributed among the several states and territories, arranged according to geographical divisions, as follows:

New England Division.—Maine, 892; New Hampshire, 34; Vermont, 26; Massachusetts, 688; Rhode Island, 284; Connecticut, 152.

Middle Atlantic division.—New York, 6,046; New Jersey, 168; Pennsylvania, 1,503.

East North Central division.—Ohio, 127; Indiana, 279; Illinois, 188; Michigan, 7,519; Wisconsin, 10,142.

West North Central division.—Minnesota, 9,053; Iowa, 471; Missouri, 313; North Dakota, 6,486; South Dakota, 19,137; Nebraska, 3,502; Kansas, 2,444.

South Atlantic division.—Delaware, 5; Maryland, 55; District of Columbia, 68; Virginia, 539; West Virginia, 36; North Carolina, 7,851; South Carolina, 331; Georgia, 95; Florida, 74.

East South Central division.—Kentucky, 234; Tennessee, 216; Alabama, 909; Mississippi, 1,253.

West South Central division.—Arkansas, 460; Louisiana, 780; Oklahoma, 74,825; Texas, 702.

Mountain division.—Montana, 10,745; Idaho, 3,488; Wyoming, 1,486; Colorado, 1,482; New Mexico, 20,573; Arizona, 29,201; Utah, 3,123; Nevada, 5,240.

Pacific division.—Washington, 10,997; Oregon, 5,090, California, 16,371.

The distribution by geographic divisions of the Indian population of continental United States at the last three decennial censuses was as follows:

Geographic Division.	Indian Population.		
	1910.	1900.	1890.
Continental United States	265,683	237,196	248,253
New England	2,076	1,600	1,445
Middle Atlantic	7,717	6,959	7,209
East North Central	18,255	15,027	16,202
West North Central	41,406	42,339	46,822
South Atlantic	9,054	6,585	2,359
East South Central	2,612	2,590	3,396
West South Central	76,767	65,574	66,042
Mountain	75,338	66,155	72,002
Pacific	32,458	30,367	32,776

A letter from C. F. Hauke, Second Assistant Commissioner of Indian Affairs, dated Washington, February 10, 1912, says:

"The birth rate among the Indians during the fiscal year ending June 30, 1911, was slightly in excess of the death rate. Of 156,631 Indians, being all upon which the office has reliable data, the births during the fiscal year 1911 averaged 36.09 per 1,000 and the deaths 35.55 per 1,000.

"This office has never made a comparative study of the past and present Indian population of the United States and is not, therefore, qualified to state whether there are more Indians in the United States now than ever before in the history of the race."

The Indian population in some states, as shown by the reports of superintendents of the Indian Office of the Department of the Interior, exceeds that shown by the Census Bureau enumeration. Also, the figures of the Indian Office include 23,345 freedmen and 2,582 intermarried whites in the Five Civilized Tribes in Oklahoma, a total of 25,927 persons who, while not of Indian blood, are treated as such, because those in the Cherokee, Creek and Seminole Nations are entitled to share in the lands and funds of these three nations, and those in the Choctaw and Chickasaw Nations are entitled to share in the lands of those two Nations.

The 1912 figures of the Indian Office, compiled from reports of Indian School Superintendents, supplemented by information from advance report of 1910 census for localities in which no Indian Office representative is located, show a grand total of Indian population of the United States, exclusive of Alaska, of 322,715

Five Civilized Tribes, including freedmen and intermarried whites		101,287
By blood	75,360	
By intermarriage	2,582	
Freedmen	23,445	
Exclusive of Five Civilized Tribes		221,428

THE FRONTIER FORTS OF WASHINGTON COUNTY.

The frontier forts, blockhouses and stockades, as they were variously called, situated within the borders of Washington county, and dating from 1770-73, were about 37 in number. Most of these were in the western part of the county, in the sections drained by Raccoon Creek, Cross Creek, Buffalo Creek and their tributaries, all emptying into the Ohio river.

In the Raccoon Creek region were Dillow's blockhouse, named for Mathew Dillow, in Hanover township, on Fort Dillow run; Beelor's fort, named for Capt. Samuel Beelor, near the village of Candor, in Robinson township; McDonald station or fort, at the present town of McDonald; Burgett's blockhouse, built by Sebastian Burgett, where Burgettstown now stands; Vance's fort, named for Joseph Vance, one mile north of Cross Creek village, in Smith township, on the headwaters of a branch emptying into Raccoon Creek; Hoagland's blockhouse, named for Henry Hoagland, on the north branch of Raccoon Creek, in Smith township, near Leech's old mill; Cherry's fort, on the Cherry farm, in Mt. Pleasant township; William Reynold's blockhouse, one and a half miles southwest from Cross Creek village, in Cross Creek township, and Wilson's blockhouse, on the Wilson farm, in Mt. Pleasant township.

On Cross Creek were Alexander Wells's fort, near the junction of the north and south forks, in Cross Creek township; Col. James Marshal's blockhouse, in Cross Creek township, which was never attacked so far as known, and Downey's fort.

On the north fork of Buffalo Creek, in Independence township, were Doddridge's fort, three miles west of West Middletown, two miles east of Independence Town, and three-quarters of a mile southwest of Teter's fort; also Teter's fort itself. Doddridge's fort took the place of Teter's fort, which had become indefensible. The latter had been built by Capt. Samuel Teter, and enclosed about one-eighth of an acre. It was one of the first forts in that locality.

On the south or Dutch fork of Buffalo Creek were Rice's fort, 12 miles from the Ohio river, Miller's blockhouse, on the farm of Clinton Miller, in Donegal township, Wilson's fort, 12 miles from the Ohio river, and Wolfe's fort, named for Jacob Wolfe. The latter was situated five miles west of Washington.

Then further to the south, near the western line of the county, were Roney's blockhouse, large and strong, built by Hercules and James Roney, in Finley township; with Campbell's blockhouse, still further south, in Finley township, on the north fork of Wheeling Creek, one and one half miles from Good Intent. Ryerson's fort, in what is now Greene county, was on the south fork of Wheeling Creek.

Off directly toward the east, some miles from Campbell's blockhouse, according to the Pennsylvania state map, was Lindley's fort, on the north branch of Ten Mile Creek, near the present village of Prosperity. This was one of the strongest forts in the western country.

Still other forts were Allen's fort, named for John Allen, near the line between Smith and Robinson townships, and used before Fort Beelor was completed; James Dinsmore's fort in Canton township; Beeman's blockhouse, on Beeman's run, which empties into the north fork of Wheeling Creek; Abraham Enslow's blockhouse, in East Findley township, on Wheeling Creek; Forman's fort, on Chartiers Creek, opposite Canonsburg, according to the historical map of the state; Bayon's blockhouse in Cross Creek township; Taylor's fort, near Taylorstown, on Buffalo Creek; Norris fort, on the land of William Norris, in Chartiers township; Lamb's fort, four miles from Rice's fort, likely on the farm of Luther Davis, in Hopewell township; a fort in West Bethlehem township, at the village of Zollarsville, on the north branch of Ten Mile Creek, 16 miles from Washington; forts Milliken and McFarland, built respectively by James Milliken and Abel McFarland on their farms in Amwell township, near the border of Greene county; and Woodruff's blockhouse, on land owned in 1870 by Nehemiah Woodruff.

Hon. Boyd Crumrine, of Washington, Pa., writing to the publishers of this book about the so-called old fort at the village of Zollarsville, or "Jobtown," referred to above, says:

"I have been familiar with it from boyhood, and have studied it in all its aspects. It was undoubtedly a protective fortification, built upon the high point of level land between the junction of Ten Mile Creek and another smaller stream coming into it at Ullery's Mills; real earthworks, and nothing like the blockhouses which our pioneers constructed. Nor was it, in my judgment, built by the Indians of the days of our settlements. They never built earthworks. But it must be the remains of the work of the mound builders of a race preceding the Indians. Besides all, there was no need for it by our pioneers. Its locality is just between the Quaker and the German settlements in that section, and the Indians were always at peace with both the Germans and Quakers. I do not know of an instance of an Indian raid down the valley of Ten Mile Creek, eastward from the locality of Prosperity, or through East Bethlehem or West Bethlehem townships. Of course there was many a raid through the southern part of Greene county."

In Fayette county, Pa., so far as the historical records disclose, but three white persons were slain by Indians during frontier days. Fayette, like some sections of Washington county, was practically immune from savage forays.

Dr. Alfred Creigh's history says Becket's fort was near the Monongahela river, but there is no definite data available as to its existence or location. The only fort in Washington county known positively to be near the Monongahela river was Cox's fort or station, built by Gabriel Cox, on Peters Creek, in Peters township, one mile from Gastonville and 14 miles from Pittsburg. There is doubt, however, as to its exact site.

AN ELEGY ON HIS FAMILY VAULT.

By JOSEPH DODDRIDGE.

Where Alleghany's towering, pine clad peaks
  Rise high in air and sparkle in the sun,
At whose broad base the gushing torrent breaks,
  And dashes through the vale with curling foam,

My father came while yet our world was young,
  Son of the trackless forest, large and wild,
Of manners stern, of understanding strong,
  As nature rude but yet in feeling mild.

Then our Columbia, rising from the woods,
  Obeyed the mandates of a foreign king,
And then the monarch as a father stood,
  Nor made us feel his dread ambition sting.

For him no splendid mansion reared its head,
  And spread its furniture of gaudy forms,
His was the humble cot of forest wood,
  Made by his hands, a shelter from the storms.

No costly dress, the work of foreign hands,
  Nor silks from Indian or Italian realms,
His clothing plain, the produce of his lands,
  Nor shaped with modern skill, nor set with gems.

Simple his fare, obtained from fields and woods,
  His drink the crystal fountain's wholesome streams,
No fettered slave for him e'er shed his blood,
  To swell in pomp ambition's idle dreams.

Look back, ye gaudy sons of pride and show,
  To your forefather's humble, lowly state—
How much they suffered, much they toiled for you,
  To leave their happier offspring rich and great.

With meek Aurora's earliest dawn he rose,
  And to the spacious, trackless woods repaired,
When Boreas blew in autumn's whirling snows,
  To hunt the prowling wolf or timid deer.

And when stern winter bowl'd thro' leafless woods,
  And filled the air with bitter, biting frost,
He hunted to his den the grisly bear;
  Nor without danger faced the frightful beast.

The shaggy native cattle of the west,
  The bounding elk, with branching antlers large,
The growling panther, with his frowning crest,
  Were victims to his well aim'd, deadly charge.

In hunting frock and Indian sandals trim,
O'er lengthening wastes with nimble steps he ran,
Nor was Apollo's dart more sure in aim,
Than in his skillful hand the deadly gun.

To masters, schools and colleges unknown,
The forest was his academic grove,
Self taught; the lettered page was all his own,
And his the pen with nicest art to move.

Think not ye lettered men with all your claims,
Ye rich in all the spoils of fields and floods,
That solid sense, and virtue's fairest gems,
Dwell not with huntsmen in their native woods.

When chang'd the woodsman, for hard culture's toil,
To fell the forest, and to clear the field,
And cover o'er with waving grain the soil,
He was the husband, father and the friend.

His was an ample store of ardent mind,
Rich in liberal and creative arts,
To trace the landscape with correct design,
And ply in many ways the tradesman's parts:

With feeling heart sincere and ever kind,
He was the friend and father of the poor,
His was the wish for good to all mankind,
And pity often taxed his little store.

His length'd years of sickness, toil and pain,
When cherish'd by religion's heavenly call,
Strong was his faith in the Redeemer's name,
He sunk in death and died beloved of all.

My father and my friend, it was thy aim
To make thy children rich in mental store.
To thy expanded mind the highest gain;
And may they honor well thy tender care.

My mother, sweetest, loveliest of her race,
Fair as the ruby blushes of the morn,
Adorn'd with every captivating grace—
Her piety sincere and heavenly born.

With hope elate she saw her little throng,
Ruddy as morn, and fresh as zephyr's breeze,
Chanting with voice acute their little song,
Or sporting thro' the shade of forest trees.

By fatal accident, in all her charms
Snatch'd from her babes, by death's untimely dart,
Resigned me to my second mother's arms,
Who well fulfilled a tender mother's part.

Say, then, shall the rough woodland pioneers
Of Mississippi's wide extended vale,
Claim no just tribute of our love or tears,
And their names vanish with the passing gale?

With veteran arms the forest they subdued,
With veteran hearts subdued the savage foe;
Our country, purchased by their valiant blood,
Claims for them all that gratitude can do.

Their arduous labors gave us wealth and ease,
Fair freedom followed from their double strife,
Their well aim'd measures gave us lasting peace,
And all the social blessedness of life.

Then let their offspring, mindful of their claims,
Cherish their honor in the lyric band—
O save from dark oblivion's gloomy reign,
The brave, the worthy fathers of our land

My dear Eliza[1] (Oh! fond hope beguil'd)
Sweet as the rose bud steeped in morning dew,
Tho' withered now, I claim my lovely child;
Nor have I bid thee yet a long adieu.

Sweet little tenants of this dark domain,
Yours was but a momentary breath,
You ope'd your eyes on life, disliked the scene,
Resign'd your claim, and shut them up in death.

Soft be your rest, ye tenants of my tomb!
Exempt from toil and bitter biting care;
Sacred your dust until the general doom
Gives the reward of heavenly bliss to share.

[1] The author's daughter, aged fifteen. (D)

INDEX

Spotted something that isn't quite right?

Let us know and we'll fix it for future reprints.
And as a thank you for your diligence, we'll
send you a free Sothis book of your choice.

publisher@sothis.press

This page intentionally left blank

Except of course for that line above. And this one.
And whilst we have your attention, perhaps you'd
like to follow us on Instagram @sothis.press. Go on.

Made in the USA
Columbia, SC
19 June 2025

59564919R00195